The SOE on Enemy Soil

CHURCHILL'S ELITE FORCE

By R.A. Fallick

THE SOE ON ENEMY SOIL
CHURCHILL'S ELITE FORCE

Copyright © 2003 by McCleery & Sons Publishing
All rights reserved.
No part of this book may be reproduced or transmitted in any form or by any means electronic or mechanical, without permission from the publisher.

Author - R.A. Fallick
Publisher - McCleery & Sons Publishing

International Standard Book Number: 1-931916-17-9
Printed in the United States of America

Prologue

Many books have been written relating the exploits of men and women who operated in enemy-occupied countries during the Second World War. The few I have read appear to be from the pens of ex-officers with evident access to files and records. It occurred to me that perhaps a Royal Engineer sergeant's story—written from memory, without the aid of records, and almost devoid of names of places or characters—might be of interest.

Most stories give accurate dates and place names. I very much regret that, on many occasions, I did not know where I was, and even if I had known the name of a place it was probably in code. It doesn't matter. It is the impression on the mind that constitutes the memory.

Unlike thousands of folk who have since, recalled their thoughts and movements at 11:00 a.m., September 3, 1939, I did not hear the broadcast that announced we were at war. What was I doing? I was filling sandbags. No, not with sand, but with soil, chalk, earth, gravel—anything that would stack and form a wall.

I was a twenty-year-old sapper in the Royal Engineers, having joined that famous corps at nineteen, nine months before the start of Second World War. The initial training period was tough and was due to last nine months, but by the middle of August 1939 the pace slackened and older men began to talk in terms of war. Some who had served over twenty years began to fear they would not be released; others, like me, tried to hold on to the image of what life would be like later on: "After twenty-one years you'll be out with a pension and still be a young man." Or, "You'll only be forty when you have done your time." And so on.

By September, several hundred of us had been moved from

Chatham to Shorncliffe, and were living under canvas—an Army term denoting that we slept in tents: "Bell, Eight men, For the use of." Since tents afforded little protection, there was an urgent need to dig trenches, and to this end I became one of a team digging slit trenches: straight sides with the earth thrown forward to face the enemy, designed to accommodate two men.

At about ten past eleven that day I heard the war was on, and there was no doubt in my mind that the report was correct, for at about the same time the air-raid warning sounded. With fear in my heart, I dashed to the nearest trench, only to find it was already occupied by *four* men. At the next trench, which I figured owed me something because I had dug it, a padre, complete with a Bible and a copy of "Three Men in a Boat," pulled me in. When I saluted and called him "Sir," he assured me there was no need under the circumstances. He asked my age, looked at the empty sky, and addressed me as "My son." The other occupant, a sapper, sat low in a corner with his hands clasped over his steel helmet. For the padre, he was "Poor fellow."

When the cookhouse call came after the All Clear, everything was different. Instead of using the big dining tent, we were told not to congregate in large numbers. Armed with our rifles, respirators, enameled plates, and eating irons, we formed a thin line for our first war-time Sunday lunch. From the field kitchens, the cooks produced a stew, plum duff, a mug of tea, and—just in case Hitler buggered about again—a piece of cake for tea.

After that I caught the eye of a corporal, who asked me to help him perform a Very Important Task. So I filled some more bloody sand bags!

Thus ended my first day of war. (A day when some poor chaps—not many, thank goodness—all of a sudden went lame). But as I nestled between my blankets, I took comfort in the fantasy of my elders that it would all be over by Christmas.

I will skip the adventures leading up to the ending at Dunkirk, except to say that, many years later, I was at the twenty-first birthday party of a man who was also using the event to announce his engagement. One of the 39/45 fame brigade was there, holding forth about how, when he was a pilot in the Royal Air Force (RAF), he had always dropped his bombs down the funnels of the enemy ships. His young audience was spellbound.

After a few more drinks, mostly Wincarnis, he went from strength to strength, until his wife could stand it no longer. She stood up, told her husband to shut up, then announced to everyone that he had not been well after the very cold winter of 1939: "He had to rub his chest with Vicks for nearly six years."

The party went a bit flat after that, and people started collecting hats and coats. I helped gather up a few glasses and took them to the kitchen. I thanked my hosts for a very pleasant evening and the birthday boy apologized for his uncle's outburst, adding the question, "Did you have a party on your twenty-first?"

I replied that I did indeed. There were several thousand of us, just a few friends I knew well, the remainder just people on nodding terms. We even bathed that day and there were fireworks, too. Then we all, or mostly all, went home in boats and had lots of ham sandwiches and coffee. Like all big affairs of this kind, quite a lot were sick.

The bride-to-be asked, "When is your birthday?"

"The first of June," I said.

A voice behind me said, "There you are, another one telling bloody lies! Who ever heard of fireworks in June?"

It was old Funnel-Bomber's wife!

When the girl looked at me in disgust, I thought of those left behind, who would not like for me to let it go at that. To clarify thing, I told them that I left the beach at Dunkirk on my twenty-first birthday, although at the time I did not know the date.

For that, I got a drink. And a kiss.

"Who gave you orders to leave France and desert the scene of battle?" asked the RSM.

You could have heard a pin drop, except my brains were making a noise. I looked round at the captain. He shrugged his shoulders.

CHAPTER ONE

After Dunkirk, my company was reformed in North Wales. As a reward for a certain job in France, I had become an Acting Unpaid Lance Corporal, a rank I nearly lost in a reduced-in-rank review.[1]

For the review, I had to go to a barracks in Yorkshire and report to the guardroom. Shortly after I arrived at the barracks, to my surprise, our company's second in command, a captain who had just been awarded the Military Cross (I will later explain how that came about) appeared. I thought he was back in North Wales, where he had signed my railway warrant the previous day. But here he was, bright as his new medal ribbon, chatting away as we made our way toward the imposing headquarters of this unit.

"Excuse me, Sir," I asked. "Why are you here?"

"You'll see soon enough, Corporal," he replied.

I didn't like the sound of that last bit, but by then we were inside the building and in the presence of a very large Regimental sergeant major (RSM). I stood before the desk, feeling like the accused on a charge for some misdemeanor.

"Who gave you orders to leave France and desert the scene of battle?" asked the RSM.

You could have heard a pin drop, except my brains were making a noise. I looked round at the captain. He shrugged his shoul-

---

[1] Characteristically, Fallick played down the incident: "A Lieutenant RE found himself in a situation, having fallen with one foot trapped under the surface root of a tree. Nearby was a stick-bomb with burning fuse. Seeing his difficulty, I threw the device where the blast did no harm. Quite a simple action, but lucky for him someone was near at the time." Later, when he filed the requisite paperwork, Fallick was criticized because he had misspelled two words in his report of the incident.

ders.

"You may sit down if you wish," said the Commanding Officer, a colonel. "What have you to say?"

"I don't know his name, sir, but he was a German officer."

You could have heard just the pinhead drop after that. But the RSM soon put a stop to all these awkward silences. In a loud voice he said, "Explain yourself, lad! And stand up!"

The CO looked pretty straight and said he hoped I could give a satisfactory explanation regarding that remark, so I gave a brief account of the events leading up to the fact that with all transport either burned or bogged in the deep mud, we walking wounded made our way slowly toward the coast. Enemy aircraft were busy unloading bombs and strafing anything on the ground. After attacking, the planes would return to their bases to rearm flying very low. The pilots would have the canopies open and would show their teeth as they hedgehopped over us. We no longer took cover; there were so many, and being tired and hungry, we just kept walking. The pall of smoke in the sky was our target, and we all agreed it was like a mirage; it seemed never to get any closer.

Suddenly, we heard the sound of a motor. It was a combination motor bike, with a German officer on the seat and a companion in the sidecar. The machine stopped, and the officer, looking most frightening in his black leathers and goggles, approached us with his revolver drawn. Speaking in perfect English, with no trace of German accent, he asked, "Where are you from?"

No one spoke for a moment.

"You," he said, pointing his gun at me, "Where are you from?"

"I don't know the name of the place, but it was about six miles away," I said, pointing to the direction we had come.

He laughed, returned his revolver to its holster, and said something in German to his colleague. I noted his mate was not amused; in fact, he swung a vicious-looking machine gun around and covered us. I also noticed he let the safety catch off.

The German officer came up close to us and said quietly, "You English are finished; you will never rise again; you will not even see your green fields or your families. We will destroy all the

men and children; we will, in the near future, rape all English females capable of childbirth, and start a race that will conquer the
world within the next twenty years."

At this point, the RSM lost his patience. He gave me a prod
with his stick and shouted, "Answer the question, lad."

The CO held up a restraining hand and said, "Carry on, Corporal, and please be seated."

I sat and continued. "He then smiled and explained he wanted to know what part of England I came from. I replied that all I
would say was my rank, name, and number, which made him laugh
again."

"It's no use being like that now; it's finished. There is no
British Army anymore, so where do you, or did you, live?"

"I live not far from a place called Chichester."

The other lads groaned at this, but the German said, "Oh!
That is Bishop Bell's area—near Tangmere."

I nearly fainted at this and for other reasons.

"I know the area very well; I was educated at Bournemouth
and spent many a happy hour in and around Portsmouth until early
'39," he said, then added, "Go on, beat it; head for the smoke that is
burning the guts out of the British Army. You have my consent to try
your luck against the finest fighting force in the world. You are not
worth taking prisoners and I have killed more than my share of your
so-called soldiers led by the old school-tie brigade. Go on, before my
trigger-happy friend loses his patience. He, unlike me, has never seen
the English before."

With that, he started up his bike and went off.

"I was three days at the beach, near Bray Dunes, and spent a
lot of time with pontoons getting the wounded out to the boats. No
one ever said we were to leave France; there was no one to say anything. We just made our own way, like sheep. *But the German officer
said go to the beach, and we did.*"

The colonel lowered his eyes for a moment, then looked at
me and with a smile said, "I'm sorry about this, Corporal. You may
go."

We both stood up and I saluted. He put on his cap, returned

my salute, and shook my hand. "Perhaps one day we will meet again," he said. "Good luck! Look after yourself."

The RSM followed me out and slammed the door, a bit too hard, as it bounced open a few inches.

"Wait there lad," said the RSM.

I did, and as I waited, I heard the colonel say, "Now, captain, what possessed you to bring a young NCO here and humiliate him, or did you get an unexpected lesson on how to give a concise and descriptive account of what the men in the field suffer?"

I heard no more, but in a moment, the RSM reappeared and beckoned me to his office. Much to my surprise, he gave me a mug of tea!

CHAPTER TWO

After a taking a course on bomb disposal and being posted to a unit, I gained another stripe. Business with the bombs was brisk, so much so that I did not have time to get the two stripes on my great-coat. I was due for ten days leave and was asked to report to the Officer-in-Charge's (OC) office to collect my railway warrant. When I went in, the OC of my section handed me my pass and warrant and said, "Go to the Quartermaster on your way out and draw yourself another stripe; you have been made Lance sergeant."

He was one of the few officers I had met who was what I called "a real nice bloke," a round peg in a round hole. He had a way of getting things done and he never forgot to say, "Well done," if it was good. At the same time, he could be the other way, but I do not recall ever having had the rough edge of his tongue. He liked a sense of humor, and I know I often gave him cause to grin. It was so on this occasion, as I thanked him for putting me up for promotion so soon after getting to Corporal.

He said he had been hammering away for months, but Records were being awkward, so he got the War Office to lean its weight on it.

I said thank you again and added, "Do you think you could ease up a bit, as I have two stripes on my battledress tunic, one stripe on my greatcoat, and now you say I am to collect yet another. I shall use all my leave sewing bloody stripes!"

He laughed. "I'll see what I can do for you while you are away!"

Little did he know what was to happen ten days later.

I had my leave and returned via London on my way to near

Birmingham. It was a very slow journey, as the Germans were over-head, causing the train to wait until it was safe to proceed. At the station we were told that owing to enemy action, we would be taken directly to Coventry, where Military Police and TRO would sort out who went where. As we arrived very slowly in Coventry Station, we were told to stay where we were. There were terrific explosions all around us, rocking the carriage violently. Adorned now with my correct rank, I ventured out on to the platform to see what was going on and was suddenly grabbed by a major, who said, "Quick, the telephone exchange!"

I leapt back into the carriage, grabbed my kit, and ran after the major. The air was thick with smoke; every few seconds there was the scream of bombs and the frightening crump of explosions.

In the streets the rubble, glass, and general destruction was like a bad nightmare. I never saw the major again, but I did see the contents of shops—groceries, watches, clothing, footwear, everything one would expect to see in shop windows of a High Street—being trampled underfoot and squashed by the wheels of the ambulances, fire engines, and other services.

I was supposed to be on my way to my unit and would be reported AWOL, so I decided to find an officer and get him to note my presence. At last I saw one. He was trying to bandage his right wrist. I did it for him, and he thanked me, calling me "sergeant." It was the first time I had been called that.

I explained I was away from my unit and asked him to note I was reporting for duty. He told me that if I went down to the end of the road to the bank I would find my unit there.

"What a bit of luck," I was thinking, when suddenly I heard someone shout, "Look out, Sarge. Get down!" Before I could see who had called, I was blown against a wall by the blast of something; I never did know what. Memories are a bit vague, but I recall sitting in the passenger seat of a WVS mobile canteen, nursing a nice cup of tea, and being told to take two or three Aspro. A kind lady popped her head through from her serving area from time to time, asking, "How are you now, dear?"

I heard her clear enough, but could not make out the silence.

No more bombs, just a lot of motor engines revving, and lots of shouted conversations. It was getting light and jagged outlines of brickwork were just beginning to show. People were appearing, wandering along over the rubble.

I noticed I still had my kit with me. I looked in my haversack. Shaving tackle, towel and some food my mother had packed for the journey, the sets of Corporal's stripes.

I left the van and joined the people, now very many, heading for the center of the smoldering, steaming city. I asked a man how I could get to the bank. With tears in his eyes and a broad Midland accent, he directed by pointing and naming two streets. Then, realizing there were no longer streets, he covered his face with his hands and sobbed.

I found the bank and the company sergeant major. "Where the bloody hell have you been?" he yelled.

"On leave," I said.

"I know that, but look at your uniform; you look like a rag bag."

I looked down at myself. I had a torn blouse, my trousers were greasy and bloodstained, and one gaiter was missing.

My Section Officer appeared from inside the bank, took one look at my new rank, and said, "Good. I want you to help the ARP. Get some chaps together and go to the depository."

I found four men and led them down to where I assumed the depository was. The vaults were thick with smoky dust, but intact. I recognized the boxes of explosives and other stores necessary for demolition work. We waited for ten minutes, then I sent a chap to tell our officer we were ready. The chap returned with officer, bad tempered this time.

"Does this look like a place to store furniture," he shouted. "I want you over at the furniture depository, *now!*"

The furniture depository was a large building with a basement that had an air raid shelter. Water from the fire hoses had flooded the basement, and when fallen masonry blocked the exit many people had been drowned. Removing the bodies was the task I found I had charge of in my new capacity.

It was a gruesome experience, a nightmare. It was so unreal. I recall my thoughts at that time—I had just turned 21—it seemed fair enough to be fighting and even withdrawing from France. But this—this was in England. How could we fight an enemy that had now gone home? Not one of the bodies we were pulling out, people who had been alive the previous day, had ever harmed a German. What deadly weapons these men, women and children had surrounding them: walking sticks, hats, handbags, tinned food, ration books, clothing coupons, and many more buoyant articles. I pulled out nearly a hundred and could stand it no longer. I was violently sick. I walked away, signaled my lads to follow, and returned to the bank. As I did, I reasoned I could normally see the funny side of most things, but this one had me beaten.

Shortly after the Coventry raid, the Hun started on Birmingham, this time with bombs having time delays, diabolical fuses designed to detonate the explosive after the bomb had landed. The trial and error drill for dealing with these cost a lot of lives, but slowly a technique was evolved which, at least, gave some chance of rendering the thing safe enough to move.

It was during these defusing jobs that my sense of humor slowly returned.

After some three weeks of dealing with bomb fuses, seven of us were sent for a rest in Cheshire, well away, they said, from a target area. We were encouraged to have our fair share of beer, which we did, and the day after arriving in our new billets we were told to report to a local army HQ and let the medical officer give us a general check. That way, it was assumed, a further examination at the end of our "holiday" would confirm our fitness for normal duty.

We all suffered with the shakes, unsteady hands being of no use for fuse work, and after the MO had tested reflexes, eyesight, and blood pressure, he sat at his desk and wrote the report. Suddenly, he asked, "Do you drink much?" Without thinking, I answered, "Not really, I spill most of it!"

We both laughed at this, and I am certain that that outlet of laughing did me more good than anything. I felt better at once and my hands were steady within minutes.

While we were resting, the enemy switched their attack to Liverpool, and we were given two hours notice to get to the dock area. Seven unexploded bombs had been reported during the night. The broad accent of the sconcer trying to tell me where two of them landed meant nothing to me, and, to be fair, he couldn't understand my southern accent, either. So he pointed and guess where he indicated? In the mud! Now when a bomb hits the ground and does not explode, it buries itself, according to the angle of descent and the type of soil it encounters, so it "jinks" until it stops. It generates a fair amount of heat as it thrusts into the earth, and then, even after having stopped, moves itself. There is evidence of its point of entry, *but not in mud*.

When it lands in mud, you cannot walk to it or row a boat to it. When the tide comes in, it is almost impossible to deal with the problem.

Firing a charge often brought success, with the tamping effect of the mud and water magnifying the explosion.

CHAPTER THREE

A move to a village in Somerset came next. I was sent to a large country house that had been loaned to a famous Guards Company to teach basic explosives to the officers and men. I was to be "on their strength" for rations and bedding for ten days. I arrived on a Sunday afternoon and was made welcome in the sergeant's Mess. Next morning, I was told to fall in with HQ Section. This short parade was taken by the RSM and preceded breakfast. The Company formed up on the gravel drive outside the big house and I was told to take my place on the left of the front rank, which I did.

We waited for some time and then the house clock chimed a quaint note. From the imposing entrance behind, I heard the footsteps of one person, then the scrunch of gravel, then silence as the RSM marched onto the grass. He seemed to go quite a long way before he halted and turned about. He thrust his cane under his arm and visibly filled his lungs. He stared, let go his breath and almost cautiously moved forward. Several steps more and I could feel he was looking at *me*. We had not, as yet, met.

Suddenly the air was filled with his voice. The birds left the surrounding trees, and nearly all of Shepton Mallet must have heard: "Who's that silly little man on the left?"

Later, in the Mess, we had a few beers and I enjoyed his company. I liked to get him talking about what it was like to be stationed in London, particularly about the incidents on mounting guard at Buckingham Palace.

I heard his voice again before I set the "test" at the end of my period.

Two officer cadets, on probation awaiting confirmation of

their commissions had, unbeknownst to me, seized on a remark of mine to the effect that water increased the effectiveness of explosives and I had mentioned that when the Navy used depth charges, the shock would stun any fish that were near. These two cadets somehow obtained some primers and detonators and planned to have a go with some trout in the stream adjoining the big house. Unfortunately, as they were about to fire the bait, the RMS came into view. In their haste to rid themselves of the evidence, they ran and threw the smoldering safety fuse with detonator and gun cotton primer into the ornamental pool situated in the center of the lawn. The two explosions were only seconds apart. The first one sent up a large spout of water and the second uprooted the fountain, which was in the form of a young woman holding a bouquet. She fell flat on her face only a few feet away from a wet RSM!

It was only a few weeks after that little incident that I saluted two young Guards officers; they smiled and acknowledged my respect. I was pleased to see they had not been unduly punished.

A few more weeks and I was posted to the very same Training Battalion in which I had done my training as a recruit, but this time I found myself on the staff of the Chief Instructor.

It was there I met men who were to become great friends, two in particular, both corporals from having done a stint at Gibraltar. Great men these two. They joined with me for many months, a most happy and rewarding period both with regard to instruction and to keeping a certain landlord solvent.

The routine was that I was attached to a training party and would lecture in a classroom on whatever subject the program indicated. Then outside to the training area for the practical work. The corporals would instruct their sections and I would have overall charge of the lot. There was, of course, the chief, a major, and his assistant, a captain. It all worked very well, in spite of being in the line of fire regarding the flight path of enemy planes on their way to London.

One of my friends, like me, survived the War, but one of this friendly trio was to die in very tragic circumstances in India. *"Bill, you are not forgotten!"*

And *Dudley* to you, a noble third of us, thank you for your continued friendship.

Before we were split up on various postings to separate units, we three musketeers were occasionally joined by Eddie, another NCO. I though he was an old man, as he was excused marching, but then I thought, "That's reasonable." After all, he was 32!

Sometimes our duties prevented us from being together and on one occasion I went into the town on my own to our favorite pub. The landlord and his wife were most friendly, even to the extent of having us join their family one Christmas Day for dinner.

On this occasion, as I neared the pub without my friends, I saluted two officers on the other side of the street, then entered for the favorite refreshment, a pint of "Old." I think the landlord relied on us lads for his living; at any rate, we seemed to have some kind of telepathic arrangement— when we were 50 yards away, a pint was pulled! This time it was different. As I put my hand in my pocket, one of the officers said, "I'll pay for that and two more."

They were an odd pair. Both were full Lieutenants in my own Corps, but one was a bit shaggy and not very military in his manner, while the other was bright and alert. It was the bright one spoke and paid for the beer. I raised my glass, saying, "Thank you, gentlemen."

Young "shaggy" looked at me like he had never seen a sergeant close up before, and what was more, didn't much care for what he saw. So we sat down, all caps off.

The bright one said, "You don't remember me, do you?"

I looked hard and replied, "No sir."

"You can cut out the 'Sir' in here. Does Nobby Clarke ring a bell?"

I thought hard and explained that the only Nobby Clarke I knew was a corporal when I was a recruit. I recall he was an ex-boy from Chepstow who chased us from morning to night.

"Yes, well I'm going to chase you again. I want to see some pips on your shoulder. Do you remember the night scheme when I told you I wanted every knot to be perfect because the Chief Instructor was going to check every fastening the next day—in daylight—and that, if you let me down, I'd have you on jankers for a week?"

I laughed as I recalled the incident and reminded him that I did not get the jankers. He agreed and bought more beer, six or seven pints by now and double-banked at that, owing to the landlord's treating us from time to time. When "Time" was called, the family asked the three of us upstairs for supper. And we went!

I noticed "Shaggy" had trouble with the stairs. Think there were more steps at the top, he did a kind of goose-step along the landing. I loved it. I had never seen an officer in his cups before, and I liked it even more when, ignoring the landlady's invitation to "go on in and make yourself at home," he insisted on trying to get into the small airing cupboard! I was all right, having been there before and a friend of the family anyway.

"I don't wish you to mix it, but you are welcome to a drop of Scotch," offered the landlord.

"Yes, that's right," said his wife, "enjoy yourselves while you can. Poor boys, my daughters are nurses at the Military Hospital and often tell us of the injuries they deal with."

We had more drinks with a very tasty meal, albeit Spam in some form, during which Nobby said, "Well, what about this commission then. Can I say you will see major Hood tomorrow?"

By then I had had my fair share of booze, but was in control of myself, and I replied that I didn't know a major Hood, and what was more, I didn't wish to be an officer, since, from my experience, all they did was to ask silly questions when I was busy, then say, "Carry on, sergeant!"

At this, for the first time I heard "Shaggy's" voice. He laughed and fell off his chair! He was still grinning when Nobby and I carried him back to barracks. We left him in the guardroom.

Later, I was ordered to report to HQ Company office and see the OC, a new man, replacing his predecessor, who was now posted to the War Office. I knew the CSM (company sergeant major), was duly announced, and in I went.

The major rose and shook hands. A kindly type, he wore 1914-18 war ribbons and gave the impression of having seen a fair bit of the rough in his time.

"Sit down, m'boy, and have a smoke." He offered a Richmond Gem cigarette and lit it for me. Always wary when higher ranks treated me like this, I was prepared for anything, and wondered how he would broach whatever was the reason for this téte-á-téte. But he caught me off guard with his opener.

"I'm new here as you know, and you are the first NCO I have had the pleasure of meeting. How do you get on with the girls?"

Well, I was prepared for anything, but this—it really shook me—but I replied that I was not much of a Romeo and had noticed no long queues of females clamoring for my services.

His next question was just as bad.

He asked if I could tell him the name brand of the matches he had used to light our cigarettes? I replied that he had used a lighter, not matches. This appeared to please him; then he asked if I would like a cup of tea? I said I would and he called out to the CSM and ordered two teas. These were brought in by the CSM's clerk, an Auxiliary Territorial Service (ATS) girl. She was a pretty girl and I had seen her about when doing my rounds as orderly sergeant.
I said "Thank you" and gave her a smile.

She put my mug down heavily and gave me a frosty look.

The major noticed this and remarked that he could see I was right about the females, adding that perhaps a different uniform might improve matters, and had I ever considered applying for a commission?

Ah! so this was the reason for the interview. Now I had a direct line of thought. Matches and girls, indeed! What next?

Well, next was a question from me: "Would you be Major Hood and do you know Lt. Clarke?"

It was his turn to be surprised. "Yes, I am. How on earth did you know that? But I do not know a Lt. Clarke. Now, come on sergeant, how did you know my name?"

I explained a little about the meeting in the pub and that I had put two and two together. I also added that perhaps he had once interviewed a NCO named Clarke, who had subsequently passed through OCTU. To which he muttered he "had seen so many . . . "

"Would you take a commission if you had the chance?" he asked. "Quite easy, about £40 for the kit, a four-week training, and then, as an ex-NCO, you would be full Lieutenant. How about it? Go away and think about it; come and see me tomorrow, but do not discuss it with anyone."

I thought about it and decided I was not officer material. Anyway, I fancied the rank of warrant officer (WO) instructor. That way, I would do the same job as I did as Sgt. Instructor, but get a higher rate of pay and keep my friends. Also, I had only the Third Class Army Education certificate, the war having stopped any further examinations. So I turned it down.

A fellow sergeant, who took the plunge, got his pips and was posted. When he wrote, he had an address in America and said he was having the time of his life. He didn't say what he was doing, no doubt because of security, but he did say he wore a flash on his shoulder with the words "British Army"—what he did I never did know, but it occurred to me that in future, if a senior officer suggested that I should take advantage of an offer, I would do well to take his advice. After all, being interviewed was a feather in the cap.

So ended my one and only chance to become a General. Ah, well, I had it confirmed I need not worry about being snared by Dockyard Lil or NAAFI Annie. But I did know the difference between a box of matches and a cigarette lighter!

Little did I know what was in store for me within the following three weeks. Clever things these majors, for the one that had seen me disappeared after a few days. He was from the War House and had taken his impression of me with him. In writing.

Nothing of the interview was mentioned in the Mess, and the sergeant who was to be commissioned gave not hint of his decision. When he left, it was assumed he was on "leave." All of which demonstrated the good security in the unit.

CHAPTER FOUR

The Kent countryside was looking good one April morning when, after giving a lecture on safety precautions when firing real explosives, I sent a man to the nearby detention camp to warn the staff live firing would be taking place that day.

I should explain that this area had a firing range since 1914. But between the wars someone had sneaked a slice of War Office property and built a detention camp. On "firing days" warning signs were clearly posted on a large notice board, and the firing officer hoisted a large red flag, warning local householders that at 11:00 a.m. and 3 p.m. precisely, immediately after three blasts of a whistle, they could expect their windows to rattle. Even the birds flew off when that whistle sounded. However, before any charges were laid, the detention camp had to be warned of the impending blasts. When they got this message, someone, no doubt at "the double," would have to lower all the lavatory seats, otherwise it seemed, the said seats would clatter down and crack the pans.

Shortly after getting things organized for the firing, I counted the rifles and found I had an extra rifle. Surely nobody had two rifles. Where had the extra one come from?

I had the roll called and found a stranger in the ranks. It turned out he was in the Home Guard, lived nearby, and didn't think I would mind him being there. And Mum says, "Would we all like a nice cup of tea before we went home?"

I thanked him for showing his keenness, and while walking him to the gate, explained that we would not dream of his mother making forty-odd cups of tea, but thank her all the same. As he crossed the road to his home, I re-closed the gate. No sooner had I done so, than a L/Cpl. on a bicycle appeared, red-faced and blowing hard. I was to return to barracks at once.

This was awkward, for someone had to be in charge of the firing, if you see what I mean. Not only that, but having marched the three miles to the range, how was I to get back as fast as the message indicated?

I need not have worried, for along came an army officer's vehicle. Rather fast, I thought, the vehicle crossed the road, and without slowing, rammed the gate, and stopped in a cloud of steam.

The L/Cpl. who, by that time had regained his normal color and got his lungs working properly, was now very pale. I regret to recall, I was laughing!

You see, the driver, who was now inspecting the bent metal, was a second lieutenant that nobody wanted. The only reason he was in the Army was because his uncle was Brigadier Sir Something, Something Else.

He and I had "crossed swords" a few weeks earlier during some drill on the square. The RSM had been told to make sure the junior officers were able to execute drill movements correctly for ceremonial parades, and I was landed with this task. I often did this; in fact, we all took our turn and very enjoyable it was. They were a wonderful bunch of chaps and put up a fair show. My personal regret was that, unlike the men who wore boots with steel studs, the officers' footwear did not make that lovely crashing note when marching and halting. But I felt compensated for this for the sheer sense of power obtained by having command of thirty officers under my thumb! No, not really. It was very rewarding to be told afterwards that individuals had at last managed to change step or change into slow-time, etc. Nevertheless, to get them marching toward a brick wall and delay the order to "about turn" right at the last minute, often produced some relieved expressions.

It was on this occasion that the "gate-crasher" objected to my calling him out as "marker," to enable the remainder of the class to "fall-in." I explained quietly that it was quite easy, all he had to do on the command "marker" was to march forward seven paces, halt, and stand at attention.

He said he felt shy being out there alone, and, anyway, the colonel might be watching.

I replied that not only was the colonel watching, but the Adjutant and the RSM were there, also.

What I did not say was that the remainder of the class were very amused. The colonel, evidently, was *not*, for he came over and asked me if all was under control. I had no option but to explain that I was merely trying to get the officer concerned to overcome his lack of confidence. I had chosen him as marker and he would perform even if we stayed there all night, Sir.

The colonel called the reluctant hero to one side and had a few words. When the colonel finished speaking, the officer turned away to rejoin the class. The CO stood quite still, but biting his lip.

I called the group to attention, put on my officious voice, and said we had just witnessed a very basic lack of respect. Pointing to the offender, I told him to march back the CO, salute, apologize, and salute again. He did this and returned to the class, muttering that he was going to report me to Uncle.

So now we were together again, with an audience, for apart from the L/Cpl., there were several civilians. They had never seen an Army vehicle driven hard into a metal gate before.

As the steam subsided, the officer reached in and rescued his cane. I had climbed through the fence and was about to see what could be done to part the very intimate relationship of the metals, when the Lieutenant said, "You have not, as yet, saluted me, sergeant." I then did so and explained that I had done so previously, but no doubt I was obscured by the steam. He accepted that.

He then said, "What do you think?" Which must rank next to the other stock phrase, "Carry on, sergeant."

We had a problem. Who was going to take charge of the training, how was I going to get back to barracks, what would we do with the vehicle, and how would we repair the gate?

The L/Cpl. suggested I borrow his bike, "Cos you are wanted urgent, Sarge."

So I made a decision; well, someone had to. There were over twenty spectators by now.

"Corporal," I said, "Go next door and inform the sentry at the detention camp that firing is cancelled for today, then go to Cpl. Smith at the firing pit and tell him the same. Ask him to march the men over here ready to go back to barracks, then get on your cycle and find the sergeant and tell him I am driving in a front-damaged vehicle without water in the radiator."

"What about me?" says the officer. To which I replied, "That's all right sir, you can get back with me in the truck."

"I don't mean that—what about me being in charge?"

"You lost charge when you forgot to brake," I muttered, mostly to myself.

The fan blades were embedded in the radiator core, but we managed to get the bonnet up far enough for me take off the fan belt. Then the buckled wing was belted clear of one wheel and I started the engine and got into reverse gear. It worked. I turned the vehicle around, gave instructions for the repair of the fence and the locking up of the explosives, got "His Nibs" in the truck, and headed for barracks.

When I arrived, I saluted the CO and I apologized for my untidy appearance and delay in getting back, adding that no doubt the transport officer would be quite entertaining at dinner that evening.

The CO then said, "This is Mr. Bannister from London."

I made to salute, but he waved it away and offered his hand. I looked at mine, still oily from the motor incident. He ignored the dirt and shook warmly, inviting me to sit and explaining we were waiting for the Chief Instructor.

The two men chatted away, which gave me the chance to observe the stranger in civilian clothes. What was he and why was he here? It was obvious from their conversation that the two men had not met before. They did the weather bit, especially for the time of the year, then agreed that it could sometimes be a bit dodgy, training so close to the nearby dockyard, and what a worry it was to have nearly a thousand men confined to one barrack block, and so on. What they did not say was why I was present. I was under the impression the CO's office was most private, except to other officers and the RSM.

And that is exactly what happened next. The RSM announced the Chief Instructor (CI) who entered, saluted, and handed the colonel a file of papers. The colonel opened the file, looked briefly at the front page, and offered it to Mr. Bannister.

Mr. Bannister was much more thorough. He read the lot. I looked at the CI and he winked at me! I thought that things were looking up at last. Three weeks ago, I had the girls and the matches with a major from London, now I had a wink from a colonel. I also thought that soon it would be my turn to have a read of foolscap, for it must have been good, as the visitor had started reading from the beginning again. When he finally finished, he handed the documents back to the CO, and turned to look straight at me:

He said, "I am very impressed with your record and must warn you that very shortly you will be given a railway warrant to a place in Surrey. You will travel to London with me tomorrow, where you will be interviewed. Your warrant to Surrey will signify your special posting from this unit. We four in this room must remain the only people having knowledge of this, so you must understand that for the rest of today and this evening you will be expected to behave as normal, which may be difficult regarding your friends. You will also have to pack your kit, all of it, make up your bed and get yourself to the station by 2400 hours; our train is the first one to Victoria after midnight."

He stood up and shook hands with the CI, making it clear it was a form of dismissal. As the major made for the door, he turned to me and said, "Come and see me before you go." I nodded.

The CO said that Mr. Bannister would be welcome in the Officers' Mess for dinner, etc., until it was time to leave. Mr. Bannister turned down the invitation, explaining he would make his way to the town and find a place well away from the barracks. He then spoke to me again, this time in a friendlier tone, more as an equal.

"Sorry to spring this on you so suddenly and I'm sorry for the mystery that surrounds you, but if you can get out of here tonight without any bother, you should. If you do it right, you should be officially absent tomorrow. Your friends will be asking each other questions until tomorrow afternoon. The colonel will have an explanation that will explain your absence. All right?"

What could I say? Other than getting out of barracks, it seemed easy enough, but what about the sentry at the gate? Even the dumbest recruit would query a sergeant leaving after dark with full pack and kit bag. I couldn't say I was on leave, for I had no pass and what was I to say to anyone I met who knew me? They all knew me, one way or another. Such were my thoughts at this time. Then, suddenly, I had a brainwave.

I turned to the CO.

"May I make a suggestion, sir? I realize you do not yet know the details of the smash-up this morning at the firing range. It caused me to cancel the practical work in addition to being called here. You will learn that I brought the damaged vehicle back to save the recovery lads turning out, especially as the driver was 'you-know-who,' so what about me having your permission to be driven back to the range to make sure all was secure. I could take all my kit with me out of sight in the truck and leave it at a house in the town, and if Mr. Bannister were to come with me, my presence would get us out of the gate easier in daylight. We need not go anywhere near the range; in fact, we will go to a pub where the family are friends of mine. Give me an hour to see the CI and pack my kit and we are away."

The two men exchanged glances, grinned at each other and sat down again.

The CO told me to go and see the chief instructor and clear up any odd ends of training, etc., and then have a go with my idea. When I was ready, I could collect Mr. Bannister from this office. And on the way out, would I ask the RSM to organize two cups of tea.

I left them with a much wider scope of conversation and made my way down to the CI's office. He said he was sorry I was going and regretted that there was no hope in the foreseeable future of my getting W.O. rank, and as I had turned down the chance of a commission (to which he added he thought I was a bloody fool, as he was an ex-NCO, and look where he was), it seemed that I fitted the requirements asked for by a war office memo, hence the tweed-suited gent from London.

He said he had given me a good report and he knew the colonel endorsed it, together with the RSM, so all he could say was that it was a mystery as to which unit I was to join and he hoped I would write and let him know where I was and what I was doing. Little did either of us know that my next address would be just a number: ___ Horse Guards Parade. And that all correspondence was forbidden.

So we shook hands and I made tracks for my room. It was a funny feeling to pack things which that morning were not important. Now they were, and so was the time. If I looked sharp, I could get out before my bunkmate returned from his training session for the day. I hated not having the chance to say good-bye, and wondered about the sergeant's Mess Dance on Friday. I was the emcee and in charge of the general running of the function. I had made out the invitation cards. I knew it would all go on just the same, but what a way to leave my friends.

Our transport stopped outside my favorite pub, the one with the friendly landlord, at nearly opening time. Mr. Bannister helped me stack my kit outside the saloon bar and the truck drove back to barracks, out of sight.

The pub door opened and the landlord laughed when he saw me, saying I was often the last to leave, but seldom the first to arrive!

We went in and I could see the landlord was a little puzzled about my companion, so I introduced him as my Uncle Herbert. I kept a good straight face when I said, "Do you still like your lemonade, Uncle?" With an equally straight face, he said he only had lemonade "when your aunt is around, but now we are on our own, I'll have a pint!"

I visited the gents' and thought tonight might be my last visit here. I did not enjoy being in the bar knowing that I could not explain why I would not return, and when, at last, "Uncle" and I said goodnight and the landlady said, "See you tomorrow," well, you can imagine how I felt.

At the station, there were the usual late travelers, mostly sailors and a few civilians. The train was not in, so I decided to rid myself of the few pints of beer. I was ready for the automatic flush to splash my boots, but it didn't attempt it. This was something new as, for as long as I had been old enough to use public toilets, they always flushed when I was committed.

The train appeared at last, belching smoke and steam from all its private parts. There was very little light on the platform, just a fierce red glow as the fireman opened the firebox to add more coal. Between us, we heaved my kit into a carriage up the front of the train, then we waited on the platform near the engine. Too near, because suddenly the monster did what the toilet should have done. It sprayed me with a jet of steam, saturated my boots, and then deafened me as it blew off excess pressure. Then it whistled!

The journey to Victoria was the usual slow-stop-slow type of progress. Blackout material covered the windows to avoid lights indicating the railway line, although the enemy made a good job of finding their way to London even with this precaution. Even so, whenever the firebox was opened for more coal, an aircraft above could get a good idea of the route.

There were just the two of us in the carriage and I suppose I looked pensive. Mr. Bannister asked me if I were feeling bothered about the interview and the impending trip to a place in Surrey?

I was glad to talk and said that I was not so much worried about the future, but a bit alarmed by the haste of the move. He explained that it was all a question of security, and when I knew the type of work I would be expected to perform, I would understand the reason for the caution. He then asked me about the vehicle incident. earlier and I told him about the same way I related it previously. Much to my surprise, he was very amused by my account, although I must admit to laying it on a bit.

We did quite a few miles at quite a fast speed and the rhythm of the chuffer made me doze. We were stationary when I awoke and my companion said we were about ten minutes away.

On the platform, I was told to wait with my kit. Mr. Bannister headed for the RTO office, returning shortly with a bottle of beer and a L/Cpl. Military Police (a red-cap). After the beer, we wandered over towards the cross-channel platform, and for one horrible moment I thought we may be going to France. Soon, however, a taxi arrived.

Mr. Bannister opened the door and said, "In you get, old son."

I sat down with my kit around me. The Red-cap sat beside me, but Mr. Bannister remained outside the cab. He shook hands through the window and said, "Good luck to you; just stay your natural self, and, ·sergeant, your introduction of me as your uncle confirmed my opinion of you. Well done! Don't be surprised if one day you meet a Very Important Person."

He made a motion to the driver and we headed out of the station. When I looked back, he was still standing, watching the cab out of sight.

CHAPTER FIVE

It was my first stay in war-time London. I had been through many times, but had never seen the sand bags built so high and deep outside the frontage of important buildings. I had no idea where we were. I asked the Red-cap, a man of few words, where we were going? "Near Baker Street, " he said.

Our destination was a building that had once been a hotel. I say once, as now it was a sorry-looking wreck: no roof, just a few large tarpaulins to keep out most of the rain, but the windows seemed intact. Inside the rooms that once were no doubt nicely furnished, a motley selection of people appeared to have taken over. I detected French accents and many more I did not recognize. A man in a blue uniform, rather like a policeman with a helmet, told me I could find a bed for the night "with the Dutch section."

I was shown to a bed in a large room. There were about twenty beds in this room, some with sleeping bodies, some with men lying flat on their backs smoking. I dumped my kit beside my bed, unlaced my boots, and reflected that, when I tied those laces, I had no inkling of the strange events the day would bring. And they were not over yet, for just then the sirens sounded. In the distance came the sound of anti-aircraft guns. Someone said to me, "Helmeting on. Come downstairs."

The former basement kitchens served as an air-raid shelter, and with no windows above ground level, there were plenty of lights, and the gold old WVS with the tea. I found a quiet corner and studied the scene. Most of the people wore a type of denim rig, some with tunics, some not. Two or three men had very elaborate uniforms with shiny buttons and what was more, some of the people were females.

I heard snatches of conversation about ops., groups, drops, Jedburgh, Arisaig and much more. Talk about being in the Dutch group; this was all double-dutch to me. I lined up for another mug of tea and asked the WVS lady what all these people were. She said she thought they were some kind of refugees. I didn't know for sure what they were, but they certainly were not that. Within an hour it was dawn, and by that time, I had found out. I was in the company of a most select international group of very brave human beings: men and women dedicated to work in enemy-occupied countries.

Later, after a wash and shave, I was escorted to another hotel, a famous one that had been taken over as part of the War Office. In what was once the foyer, I was asked to wait. It was still a foyer, but the receptionist was a very smart uniformed security officer, who appeared to be protected by an elaborate metal grill that also protected the large staircase. Many men, mostly in city clothes, rolled umbrellas, and bowler hats, entered, collected a salute and a small card, disappeared upstairs when the gates were opened.

I was beginning to think I had been forgotten, when a man suddenly appeared, gave me a green card about the size of a luggage label, and asked me to follow him. We walked along corridors past dozens of doors, some marked with strange looking abbreviations such as OP/SEC/N and the like. My guide was silent until we had reached the height of 500 feet, where he pointed and said simply, "Along on the right, Room 98; go in and wait."

The room was sparsely furnished, just an army table with two forms either side, the window obscured with a blackout screen— not at all up to London hotel standard. A plain 60 watt lamp lighted the room. I waited.

When the door opened, I was surprised to see a young officer appear. He was in the Army uniform of the Green Howards, wore a black eye patch, and walked with a limp, aided by a stick. He looked no more than 22 years old.

He invited me to sit opposite him at the table, opened his briefcase, and withdrew a pen and a single sheet of plain foolscap. In spite of his disabilities, his cheerful manner never changed. I've never since seen a man smile so much.

He asked my name, noted my uniform, rank and corps, then put down his pen, smiled some more, and asked, "Do you have any idea the type of work you may be expected to do for the duration of the war?"

I replied that, having spent the last few hours with the "Dutch section," I put two and two together and assumed it was some kind of cloak and dagger stuff. "But with all due respect," I said, "if this is a sample of the headquarters, and if you are any form of advertisement, then I only hope the Navy are in control." He laughed, even though I meant that to be funny!

When he had resumed his official interviewer manner, he warned me that I might be expected to serve in any part of the world, to which I replied that as I was A-1, I was under the impression that I could be sent anywhere, anyway.

He went all serious and said that while this may have been so until the report from a Mr. Bannister had been studied, I was, to all intents and purposes, no longer in the Army as such—except, of course, regarding pay. That would remain the same. There would be no promotion, no awards, no mentions, and little praise. And the phrase, "anywhere in the world," in this case meant quite simply "behind the lines" or in enemy occupied territory.

"Of course, as a sergeant you would not be treated very well if caught, so you may, if you survive the very strict character investigation and do well with your training, be granted the honorary rank of captain. That should qualify you for better treatment by the enemy if caught. But remember—you may be tortured to give information regarding your knowledge of agents and any French Resistance workers.

"We think you are a good risk. You are a skilled artisan in electrical and mechanical work, you have a natural ability to eat 'humble pie,' and for your age you appear to be able to disregard authority if you think it unfair. You also possess a quality that could mean trouble for you through a natural assessment of fair play. Let me warn you. There is no room for anything fair in this organization, and if you feel the Army as you know it—one that fights in companies and regiments—has gone mad, let me assure you *they* will continue to act in the traditional manner. *You* will not be in the news, for you do not officially exist.

"Well, what do you say?"

I said it was a frightening outlook, but I would have a go at the training. To which he warned that, if having acquired knowledge I failed to make the grade, I might find myself spending a period of time in Scotland, possibly for the duration. But then he smiled again and all was well.

We both stood. He took a paper from his case and gave it to me, saying, "There is your warrant to Camberley. The RTO will tell you where to go."

He shook my hand, and as I saluted, added, "I'm so sorry, I should have invited you to smoke. I no longer can with only one lung."

He indicated my way back to the ground floor, but made his way farther inwards. I watched him with his stick. I could not see his face, but I knew his countenance was not one that smiled.

CHAPTER SIX

At a place in Camberley, I reported to a major. He objected to all form of foot-stamping and saluting and said that David would show me my room. David took me to an upstairs room furnished with a camp bed, a bookcase, and a table and chair. A barred window offered a view of lawns and garden. He told me he would bring me some coffee, then left the room and bolted the door from the outside.

When the coffee arrived, it was like peacetime. Real good stuff; so were the ham sandwiches. The man, David, wore soldier's trousers and shirt with civilian shoes, and I asked him what the hell was going on and what about the toilet. He said I would not be here long, and if I needed anything, just knock on the door. Then he left.

After the coffee, I needed to let it out, so I knocked. He led me to the toilet, saying he would be just outside the door! And that was locked.

The meals were first class and with every one I asked how much longer was I to be cooped up in here? And always, he said it would not be long and not to worry. I read the story of the Test Matches England vs. Australia until I thought I would get sunburned. Then one evening David brought in another camp bed, saying that I was not to be alarmed if I woke up in the morning with a friend. I was told not to wake him, as he might be short of sleep.

Well, he was there and not short of sleep. When I awoke, I saw a man sitting on the edge of his bed, wiping a dagger-type knife. There was a radio playing music. Then the news: "This is London; here is the news read by Stuart Hioberd. "Last night Admiral [name omitted] was assassinated. It is not yet known by whom. The German High Command claims . . ."

My new friend switched off the wireless and continued wiping his knife. Suddenly, he said, "Lovely weapon this; I'd like a set of darts as good," and with that he flings it towards the door without taking any apparent aim. It went in about three quarters of an inch. He retrieved it and sat on my bed.

"The bastard went down like a stuck pig," he said.

I put two and two together and swallowed hard, thinking that I was in a rum outfit. First I am cooped up in a locked room, then I am joined by a man with a knife who listens to a news item, switches off, and then he sits on my bed and says, "The bastard went down like a stuck pig,"

I swallowed a couple of more times and asked him if he could give any idea why I was a semi-prisoner, and what was the idea behind the interviews, etc., to which he smiled and replied, "You will be told soon enough, don't worry. There is a code of conduct that prevents me from telling you anything. I do not know who you are, but I will admit I am the person that put the knife in the Admiral and you could learn something from my attitude."

"That's all very well, but will I be expected to stick knives in people?"

"Well, no, I doubt it. I don't suppose I would have got the job if I were not in the trade in Civvie Street."

"You mean you are a murderer?" I asked.

He laughed fit to bust. When he recovered, he said, "I am a butcher in Aldershot."

Many days after, my steward brought the breakfast one morning and quietly tipped me off that later I would be able to go below and see the boss. Sure enough, the bolt clanked, and he told me to go downstairs and see the guv'ner.

I went in and let rip my pent-up feelings. The man behind the desk was a major and continued to write something as I spoke. Eventually, I dried up, and when I was silent, he looked up at me and quietly said, "Can you do as you are told?"

I replied that I bloody well could.

"Well done," he said. "Take this envelope to the Staff College and then come straight back here to me."

I walked through the town, across the main road, and approached the Staff College via a small wood-decked bridge that spanned a running stream. On the bridge a soldier leaned on the rustic rail. As I neared him, he turned and spoke.

"Morning, Sarge, going into the College?"

I said I was going to the Medical Officer (MO) to deliver an envelope. The soldier pointed to a large red cross painted on the wall of the building, and I made my way around the square to the M.I. room, noting that on my left were the famous steps up which the adjutant rode his horse at the end of certain parades.

Inside the building, I found the waiting room and took my place with other soldiers. When an orderly appeared to call the next victim to the doctor, I offered him my envelope, saying that I had been asked to deliver it to the MO He took the thick package and shortly returned, asking me to follow. I found myself in the presence of, yes, another major!

He explained that by rights he should give me several jabs, but as I was going home on ten days embarkation leave, it did not seem sensible to make me suffer, so would I promise that I would get it done on the boat?

I suppose I looked a bit confused, so he added, "Of course, you may only be going over the Channel—never can make out what your lot is up to. Still, I suppose you do. Anyway, good luck, whatever happens." And he shook hands warmly.

At the door, I saluted him. He smiled and said he thought it would be a good idea if I got out of that habit and gave me my documents to take back.

On the way out, I had to go past the stream, and much to my surprise, the soldier was still there. I looked at the clear running water and asked if he had any work to do.

He said he lived in Motherwell and it was too far to go home in a short leave, so he kept local and what about a coffee? We walked towards the route back to my "cell," which meant going back through the town. When we got to Woolworth's, he wheeled in and held open the door for me to follow. He led the way towards the restaurant and ordered two coffees. I said I would pay, as I was a sergeant.

We drank up and made our way out into the street and to-wards my turning into my little "prison." At the driveway, he said that was as far as he went, said, "Cherrio, Sarge, and thanks," then went back to town.

I knocked at the door marked private, went in, handed over the documents, and waited for the major to speak. When he did, he said, "You, sergeant, cannot do as you are told."

I started to explain that I had been to the College, but he held up his hand and said, "I told you to come straight back here to me from the College, but you have been into Woolworth's and had a cup of coffee. Not only that, you were in the company of another person who was allowed to see where you lived."

I stammered out that I had only just left, and he interrupted again to explain that, in the organization I was now in, obeying orders was more important than those in the conventional army.

"Don't forget that," he said. "Meanwhile, go back to your room. I will send up your warrant that will get you home tonight to sleep in your own bed for a few days."

Within an hour I was on my way home, knowing nothing about what the future might hold.

I warned my parents that I was due to go abroad, possibly out East, as I was due for the jabs. They asked if I had been issued with tropical kit and I said, "No." The conclusion from that was that I was not going very far, if anywhere. In fact, I went back to Baker Street and started a long series of training stunts that amazed me.

CHAPTER SEVEN

During the next phase of my training, I was allowed to skip the explosives bit and spent my spare time in a local milk bar; that is, I received no explosives training, but found myself visiting experimental groups and reporting on my opinion. Some of the things done with plastic explosive were certainly not as laid down "in the book," and I found I had a distinct advantage with my regular training plus field and bomb experience.

It was after giving a verbal report that I was told exactly what SOE was all about.[2] Just as well as I didn't know it existed! But the enemy knew, which made things difficult.

On the day I visited my first experimental workshop, I was told to wear the uniform of a captain, with a plain short coat to hide the rank. This honorary rank, it was explained, was to give the authority to gain access to various places, and if I was captured would or should provide better treatment than could be expected as a NCO. And although the visit was a part of my training, the results would be noted.

So, with a head bursting with do's and don'ts, I made my way to an address in north London where I was assured I would be expected. This particular little group was experimenting with booby-trap devices and was headed by a T/A major, a civilian, and a L/Cpl. These three, plus some administration staff, worked together in

[2] Editor's Note: The Special Operations Executive (SOE) was a highly-secretive organization created by Winston Churchill in the summer of 1940 to co-ordinate resistance activities in German-occupied Europe. F section, with headquarters at 64 Baker Street in London, dealt with occupied France for sabotage and the organization, training, arming, and support of Resisters. SOE was highly secretive, with little communication between individual sections. It was disbanded in 1946; surviving files are still classified.

peacetime. The major was the boss of a farm that made measuring instruments. That much I knew as I found the entrance to the small building. The door was marked "Ladies Cloakroom," and I was greeted by the L/Cpl. I had been told about. He was about five foot nothing, very elderly, and had lots of medal ribbons but very few teeth. In his hand he held a mug of hot liquid. He blocked the doorway and said I couldn't come in because, "We are expecting a top brass bod. Thinks he's going to teach us about bangers, and I can tell you that we don't want any nosey sods round 'ere, 'cos me and the major are working on a secret weapon." He was interrupted by the appearance of his boss, who said, "Come in, m'boy." And I entered the Ladies.

It was very hot inside, like a greenhouse with no vents open, and I removed my top coat. The L/Cpl. saw my pips. He opened his mouth, stood at attention, and with his mug still in his right hand, saluted.

The major was an eccentric old chap and started chatting away about his firm he had before the war and how he formed a company of territorials with about twenty of his employees. His hobby was chicken farming, but they had to go.

While he was talking, I noted the contents of his laboratory and steered the chat more in line with my visit. It seemed that plastic explosive was the problem. He was trying to make this putty-like material resemble horse excreta. There was a terrible looking concoction in an old wash boiler (hence the heat) and the straw was evident as was sawdust, dyes, and evil-looking stuff in jars. I noted he had several pressure switches which, when set, would detonate the manure if squashed by a motor vehicle.

Before leaving the lab, I was able to sample some of the corporal's refreshment. I asked if it was tea?

He said, "Well sir, it's in the mug usually used for tea, but it will taste more like coffee and Oxo."

I drank most of it, and only the man in civilian clothes noticed my grimace. He gave me a wink and looked at his watch. As I left, I thanked the major for his hospitality and quietly asked if there were many such groups or sections such as his. He replied that there were too many, some not even responsible to anyone at all.

"Who are you under?" I asked.

"Oh! The Minister, of course," he replied.

I had walked only a few yards when I was joined by the civilian. He said hello and did I fancy a drink?

I must admit that I put up my guard a bit, as I did not know for sure who he was. He could be planning to trick me in some way, I felt, remembering the visit to Woolworth's and the coffee. But I need not have worried, as he was with SOE, and what was more, a sergeant like myself in the same corps.

Over our drink, we discovered that our army numbers were quite close. He said he could not be operational, as he had ear trouble due to being too close to a charge. But during those three pints of beer, I learned more about SOE than I knew before, plus many things that were planned for the future, including a subversive force that was to be even more exclusive than the SOE itself, with each member being presented to the Prime Minister. "If you are called to No. 10, you will know you're in."

I subsequently met the PM on three occasions, none of them at No. 10; so, although I did not know it at the time, I was in.

My drinking partner left to go back to "his nibs," and wished me good luck with some envy. I never knew his name, but I was and still am very grateful for his friendly advice.

I later witnessed the live firing tests of the major's experiments and reported my opinion to my boss. He seemed to regard my findings quite highly and said that one day he would allow me to go to France to play with these and other devices. I explained that he was quite welcome to my opinion and that a visit to enemy-occupied France was not necessary as a reward. Needless to say, I went, but not before many weeks of learning how to shadow a person or shake off a follower, how to pick a pocket—taught by good conduct "dips"— not to remove a wallet but to insert an item in a person's pocket without his knowing. Such things as incendiary devices. A sure item to warm up a party!

Sitting on my stool in the milk-bar one day, I was slapped on the back by a soldier who greeted me with a cheerful "Hello, Sarge," which was very astute of him, since I was wearing civvies at the time. He was right, of course. We knew one another from earlier days. But he was in the army proper and I was in the— what was I in and what was I? I wasn't a spy or an agent. I made a mental note to find out what I was. In the meantime, my colleague had placed his bottom firmly on the stool next to mine and was more than ready for me to tell him where I was stationed and so on. In the light of many forceful lectures on security within SOE, I had to assume this chap buying chocolate-flavored milk shakes was also "in the firm" and was trying to trick me into saying something out of turn. There was only one thing I could think of, so I said he must be mistaken and left my place at the bar.

I was gratified for him to accept that he possibly knew "my brother," who was in his lot.

I returned to my base, which was in the basement of a library. At a table sat three men and one girl, all French. They had been warned to stand by later that day to be dropped into France to back up some organizer short of personnel. I joined them and found they spoke quite fair English. I tried to get the butterflies out of their tummies by telling them a pack of lies about how I had been nine times and there was nothing to it. It didn't cut any ice, but at least I noticed they were calmer.

I went to my room, switched on my old Philco, heard the news, and got a bit of "Itma." I say a bit because I was visited by the boss, who said he was glad I was in, as the major at the lab I visited recently had had an accident. Not a bad one, but nevertheless, he was out of action for the moment. He asked me to go there, find out exactly what had caused the accident, and give him a written report.

"You have four hours," he said. "Excellent training for you and a help for me."

I made the investigation and wrote my report. This is roughly the content of that finding:

> The personnel of the establishment
> concerned was in the charge of a T/A offic-
> er named major _____, who was assisted
> by a long-serving NCO, Lance Corporal
> _____. These are the only two characters

involved with the circumstances resulting in the injury to the private parts of the officer. It seems that tidiness was not up to normal military standard, no doubt owing to the nature of the work. However, from time to time the old NCO would have a good clear up, a sweep round and even clean the windows. This would appear to have been the case on the day of the incident.

While the cleanup was taking place, the major was engaged in trying to assemble a tricky device that was to be a booby-trap. In his eye he wore a jewelers' glass, and with steady hands, had just reached the crucial part of the assembly when the old soldier slammed his foot down, stood at attention and shouted, "Ready for inspection, SIR."

This startled the major to the extent that his hands crossed, the contraption collapsed and fired a small amount of sulphur in his lap, causing the injury to his private parts.

Signed _____   Date _____

I handed the above report to a nice-looking FANY (First Aid Nursing Yeomanry) and told her to read it over to me to make sure it sounded all right. She started off well enough, but sensed it was a bit like the First of April, then laughed a little, then a lot, and at the end was almost hysterical!

"It can't be that funny, can it?" I said.

Later that day I was sent for. At my knock, I was bade to enter. The boss was in the company of four men, all strangers to me, each of whom gave me a steady stare as I stood just inside the office.

The boss picked up a document and offered me, asking me to examine it. I quickly saw it was my report and thought I had gone too far with my humor, especially when all the faces were so stern looking. I said I had written the report and handed it back. The men's gazes went from one to the other and suddenly, as though by signal, they all laughed! Much to my surprise—and delight—I was clapped on the back and generally applauded. What was more, a bottle and glasses were produced. I took a sip and remarked that it was a drop of good stuff. The boss said, "It should be. It is the same as is enjoyed by the PM."

He also warned that, should I ever find myself in the company of the Great Man, to be sure not to do any funny stories. He hated them. He added that he would send my report to him, just to cheer him up a bit and let him see the morale was good.

One of the men asked what, in fact, was the real cause of the major's incapacity, if my report as such was a bit of a spoof. Confident now that I was well and truly accepted and with talk of Prime Ministers—well, I couldn't resist another version. So, fortified with my brandy, I said seriously that the real truth was funnier than my account, so I had intended giving the true explanation verbally, anyway.

"You see, gentlemen," I went on, "the major was in the lavatory, in the sitting position, attending to nature, when he dropped his lighted cigarette between his legs and it lodged in the forest and sort of fused itself to the bushes."

It was like the first night of a comedy in that office. Even I laughed at my own humor. I dare say those men were under a lot of pressure. After all, they ran the most complicated force of fighters in the world, so the light relief was welcome. At the end, however, it was quite seriously pointed out that there was little scope for funnies. Time enough for that after the war. So why not the truth?

I said the major had merely sat down on a drawing pin, had been given an anti-tetanus jab and would be back to work tomorrow. I added that, anyway, they all knew that because the SOE member worked with the major and was present when it occurred. I thanked they anyway for the training exercise.

The boss shook hands in dismissal, saying he hoped I was not after his job. Which I though was a nice compliment.

CHAPTER EIGHT

I came to appreciate later the thorough attention to detail during the training. What I did not realize at the time was the enormous amount of training given to others less fortunate than me. I had a much easier time than others. Let me explain.

The force was made up of men and women of many nationalities, each potential member having been selected as because he or she was of a certain calibre and possessed a specialist knowledge of some sort. Individuals who couldn't ride a bike, row a boat, gut a fish, use explosives, kill, use a compass, drop by parachute, or control their countenance would be selected because of their skill as a linguist in European languages, or because they had a first class record in one of the services and had shown themselves to have a sense of self-discipline.

In order for his particular talent to be used, he might have to experience hard training to develop the skills needed to survive long enough to perform his task in enemy occupied countries. And, at the risk of being boring, let me add another example. A man I knew was a fisherman by profession. He not only skipped the training for self survival, rowing and navigation, but he was able to teach others these arts. Of course, these are practical activities and he would not be called upon to use a language. This is why, compared with some, I had an easy time. I was country born, so knew a duck from a dandelion, had a good knowledge of electrical and mechanical work, and had been in a Corps that was proficient in all field activities. I was a training battalion instructor and a senior NCO with battle experience.

I was also very frightened! No one shook more than me when

the bombs or shells screamed down. No one felt more sick when that wailing siren sounded the air-raid warning. If there had been awards made for the frightened, then I would have a chest full. And I would have collected another medal soon after making the report regarding the major and his seat on a drawing pin.

I was sent out into the blacked-out city of London and told to go to an address and contact a certain man, give him a message, and receive a reply. He would then make his way back to base, and I was to follow him.

If I could.

I found him, delivered the message, and within minutes lost track of him. As far as I was concerned, he had vanished into either thin air or a deep hole. And that is when I would have earned my scared medal.

There was a bright moon, but large clouds reduced the light exactly when I needed to look at the street layout. I could see a barrage balloon unit to my right and was making for this great silver monster swaying in the light breeze.

I took a short cut and walked close beside a large advertising hoarding, thinking I would ask the balloon crew if they had seen a man dodge that way. My idea was to get back to the safety of my quarters, whether I found my man or not, since the searchlights were concentrating and that meant they had a bomber lit up. It also meant that the ack-ack guns would be firing, which in turn might make the pilot decide to get the hell out of it and dive for cover, an idea I shared with him.

Without warning, however, there was a vivid orange light, an enormous explosion, and a force 10 gale. Thank you, hoarding! You saved my life, for you protected me from the very thing I was making for—not a barrage balloon—*a land mine.*

What a hole! But guess who made up the crowd to see if anyone was hurt. My man.

Two people had slight cuts from glass and the remainder, including "old Watson," walked away. He made no attempt to look back and, no doubt shaken by the blast of the mine, had given up all effort to dodge me. I closed up to within a few yards and matched my footsteps with his and soon recognized the area. A good job he knew the way! Once inside the building and in the light, it was a bit dodgy going down the stone steps out. As soon as the door was in sight I ran ahead and opened it to let him through.

He was livid! I got a big ticking-off and the threat to have me posted to the Highlands for the duration of the war. My boss gave me a wink and asked me to wait outside. Later he said I had been lucky with the shadowing and avoiding injury, adding—that is what it all amounted to in the end—just luck.

I was given 48 hours off and told to have a break for a while, so I had a few beers!

I learned later that the man I shadowed and so luckily caught was quite a top man in something and did his best to try to get me posted back to my unit, mainly because I caught him. He did not seem able to appreciate that it was the explosion that canceled the 'exercise; as I said at the beginning, he lost me in the first few yards. I was thinking of the details covering the last few hours while having my beer. What with the blast and his harsh words ringing in my ears I did not enjoy my drink that evening. I even wondered just how much more you could give of yourself, when your best was not good enough.

I had none of the recognized training, other than the parachute drops, the shadowing, and pocket-picking. I did not have to learn Morse since there was a radio operator in the team, one of the very brave FANYs. But I did use the S-phone, I recall.

Interest in the story may now be flagging, but bear in mind that your mental picture will be different to that of any other, and it is not easy to express the stresses that existed in the mind of a 23-year-old, and many incidents have been omitted. Looking back, I find that, as in life in general, it is the small things that stick in the mind. In my case, I can recall vividly the periods of training, but cannot remember the details of the action. I think the humane side of things were important in those days and it is a pity that we have to wait so long after the incidents before we are able to tell our stories. After all, everyone who lived through those times could write a book, but because truth is stranger than fiction, it would not even get published, which to my mind is a serious thing, since it means that when the men and women, now in their fifties in early 1976, are gone there will be no one left to set a standard. No code of behavior, no sense of values, no memories. Many times I have been told in one way or another, "Forget the past—think of the future!"

Well, all right! Let's think of the future. But do you know anyone in your circle of friends, or your relations, or your neighbors, who has successfully gained experience from tomorrow? Or next year?

Experience, therefore, must come from the past. Surely. But perhaps that is why the England we fought for so desperately is in the state it is in today. That is why we learn that the government and the unions are getting together to solve the problem of vast unemployment and to stop those green things that are loosely called £1's worth a little more. Bloody fools! You wait till later on in my story and see what I thought years ago compared to what I think today. It appears to be the same game but with a different set of rules.

I am sorry to lead off like that, but I had 48 hours off, so why not you? Precisely my principal, you see!

While still based in London, I was briefed with some other chaps, including some Royal Marine officers, for an assignment that involved going to the north coast of France to collect beach samples. What we collected would be examined by experts to gain information regarding the best place to land an invading army.

Two teams of ten men practiced on an English beach when the nights were suitable. Tapes and pegs were used to plot the route from the water's edge with samples taken at intervals, each man being about five yards apart, with Marines to give covering fire, if necessary. At the end, tapes and pegs were collected and all very quietly climbed aboard inflatable dinghies and so to Naval craft and home. Five times we did this for real and between us collected nearly three hundredweight of French coast. Of course, these missions were conducted in silence since German guards patrolled their coastal defenses. I cannot vouch for the following incident—I was assured it was true—concerning a similar task force which apparently did its job on New Year's Eve. Imagine then a young Jock officer flat on his stomach doing his job, busy leading his men taping and pegging, then having his concentration shattered by a hand on his shoulder and a Highland voice saying, "Happy Hogmanay, Sir."

CHAPTER NINE

While stationed at Baker Street, I had taken a liking to frothy coffee and spent a lot of off-duty moments consuming this drink. My milk bar was just off Baker Street, down a side road. Since I was there so much, it was decided to hold a mock interrogation as a security exercise.

Three officers and a civilian in turn questioned me as to where I sat—was it always in the same place, etc. Well, I did not admit to always facing the door, and I did not mention knowing a quick way out at the back. (I still, to this day, face the door. I am doing so as I type this!)

As I had nothing to hide and the environment was not as frightening as it would be if the Gestapo were in action, I found it easy to stick to my story that I merely went to the place to have some light refreshment. I came out with good marks, but it was suggested that I find out who had "shopped me." I was told it was a male with whom I had worked, and I was given a week to name him.

It was no doubt a good exercise to try to find out who the "informer" was, but I had to flit from one class to another; the only spare time I had was when I was excused from subjects such as explosives. Even then, I was often pressed into service as instructor, so there was little chance of getting a lead.

As the deadline approached, I was asked if I had any idea who it was and what had been so far my method of inquiry. I had to admit defeat and did not really know where to start. To be honest, I did not bother very much, but evidently these tasks were not intended to be taken lightly, and on the last day, I was told to "get a wiggle on" (some years since you heard that expression?).

Quite by accident and with enormous luck, I found out and named him. "Good lad," was my reward, but it didn't end there.

How did I find out? I explained that I spent some time with a group of five men and a girl wireless operator who were waiting for a signal to go to an airfield bound for France. They all had the jitters. Only the girl had been before, and she did her best to exude confidence. I tried to help by explaining my little problem, and much to my surprise, the girl said it had to be the man who failed to get himself lost on the shadowing test. I was not very impressed with this theory, but as time was short decided to claim that he was the informer and add that I engaged the help of a female who mentioned the grudge aspect.

I received a further "Good lad" and that was that.

This may not be very interesting reading, but it was part of the training. Later it will be seen how important these small details were. Bear in mind that once that plane took off or that boat sailed, those dreaded words, "You're on your own," became a stark reality. So far, the incidents have concerned the training. Later comes the action.

I remember one lecture given to about thirty of us by a smartly dressed man, who based remarks on his own personal experiences behind and with the enemy.

He had apparently once found himself in a large house, and in order to hide had finished up behind a long curtain within feet of enemy officers having dinner. He said his biggest worry was the noise his heart was making as it did its job. He wished none of us ever to experience such a torture.

He also told of posing as a German maintenance man in a small castle where the second in command was a homosexual. This officer had taken a fancy to him and would insist on holding his arm and wrist while doing the rounds every other night. The officer mentioned that he thought the pulse rate was high and was suspicious. Our man got out of that one by saying that the close contact made him feel excited. The silly Jerry was satisfied with just that, as he was on a fantasy trip.

At the end of the talk, we were taken to Regent's Park, and

sitting in a semicircle on the grass in full view of passersby but with discreet speech, we learned more of this man's exploits. He asked questions, including how could one remain more in control, as in the case of hiding behind a curtain. Suppose he sneezed, or even fainted. I spoke up and said that when standing still for long periods, I was told (remember Nobby Clark?) that to raise the heels slightly would keep the circulation going and prevent fainting. He apparently had not heard of that little trick, and judging by the number of troops that do fall during ceremonies, I assume they do not know either.

At the end of his chat, he emphasized the importance of being observant. Everything was of importance: people, their habits, especially their mannerisms, routes to and places, landmarks—in fact, all the things taken for granted were important. He gave us a break for ten minutes. We walked around and stretched our legs. We were in civilian clothes and of obvious military age, which prompted many strange looks from passersby, some of whom no doubt had relations in the forces.

He told us to gather round and questioned us with regard to how much we knew of one another, then walked away a few paces.

Turning and facing us, he asked, "Who could stand still for two hours, and I mean still."

No one spoke or moved.

I caught his eye, or he caught mine. In any event, he called me over. We sat on the grass, and he said quietly that he would give me an hour to install myself in Madame Toussaud's waxworks, dressed in steel helmet, battle dress, and with rifle. I would be expected there by the staff and I was to try to stand still without being detected by civilian visitors. In the meantime, he would stress to the remainder of the class the importance of observation and later would take them to the waxworks. By rights, he claimed at least one of them should recognize me or detect I was not wax.

When I arrived at the exhibition, sure enough, I was expected. A uniformed staff member explained that the services—a sailor in traditional dress, a soldier in battle dress, and a pilot with flying kit—were depicted in the foyer. The soldier, however, had been removed and I was to take his place. He suggested I "spend a penny" and expressed a hope that I had not recently eaten onion or radish.

I took my place between the two other services, the attendant adjusted my dress, and there I was on my own. I soon developed a shallow breathing technique, and blinking was all right if no one was looking. The visitors stood in a respectful attitude and I wished my two colleagues had been alive to witness this. It was quite moving.

I did fine until the class trooped in unexpectedly. Then I nearly blew it. Whereas the civilians came in ones and twos, here came about thirty, all at once.

"Form a queue," someone said, and the semicircle they formed meant that many had to shuffle past me within inches. I felt the eyes of one bore through me until he dropped something and I was saved. The instructor was last in, and he ignored me like the true professional that he was. My body temperature had increased and the sun had moved further, so that I could see the reflection of all three of us servicemen. I could feel the perspiration on my face and my chin-strap was making my face sore. Swallowing was difficult without making a noise, and I suddenly had the horrible thought that, should a bomb drop nearby, I would have to protect my eyes from that glass.

I heard someone asking the time and from the reply worked it out that I had to last about twenty more minutes. I wondered what the reaction would be from anyone present when I was told to relax.

One lady from Yorkshire put her face close to mine and said to her companion, "Ee! Gladys, they're reet real; see th' mucky face!"

As though that were not enough, a lady with a small dog on a lead entered and went to the pay box. I heard a man explain that no animals were allowed in the exhibition. Unimpressed with the rules, she reappeared and hooked the log lead over my rifle. I nearly went incontinent, but managed to control myself.

I hoped the class leader saw my new friend; in fact, I hoped he would manifest himself very soon, since the dog had made its way to the rear of my legs and I had to resist the pull on the lead. I decided that, if necessary, I would freeze my right arm and let the rifle drop. I had pins and needles anyway. Surely the time was up. But, no, I had to suffer one more incident. The dog cocked its leg on my nicely blancoed gaiters.

Suddenly the leader appeared, laughed at the dog lead, and relieved me of the rifle.

"Well done," he said. "Hop it now back to your quarters and change into civvies and wait for me in the library."

To walk was hell. My hips were a solid mass of ache, my legs did not go where I wanted them to go, and one thought was in my mind. A hot bath was all I needed, followed by a stiff drink. I ignored the wartime rule of five inches of hot water and helped myself to much more, on the grounds that I had while standing in the exhibit I had come across several people who apparently economized with water to the extent of not having a bath very often.

The stiff drink came from the class leader and he let me in on a secret. He explained that these stunts were designed not so much to determine if a person could obey an order but also to study the person's reaction. After a few more tests, I learned I was ideal for a job, and the leader felt I should now know the hiding place of the brandy, which was behind some books on the fourth shelf up of an enormous bookcase. Little did David Copperfield know how many times he was removed!

But the best reward came from the class the next day, when several grouped around me and asked, "Where did you have to go when he sent you off from the park yesterday?"

Later, two of us were sent to report to a security officer, a lieutenant colonel with what appeared to be the manner of a kindly uncle. It always amazed me to find that men holding positions like his were what I call "very nice," whereas some with less exalted responsibilities and rank were more often than not very officious and "not very nice."

The officer invited us to take a seat, slid a packet of cigarettes in our direction, and pushed a button on his side of the desk. The door behind him opened, and a very attractive girl entered. She wore the kind of clothes that I admired—white short-sleeved blouse, very dark skirt, light stockings—and a pleasant smile. No doubt standard kit for offices in those days, but I did not frequent such places, so it was for me quite a treat.

"Three cups please, Sue," the officer said. "Then fingerprints, photos, and all the rest of it. I am sending them to Wales, away from the bombs for a while. Warn Simpson and the others."

We had our tea and then were fingerprinted and photographed. The colonel dismissed Sue and asked not to be disturbed unless it was "red." He then opened a steel cabinet, pulled out a drawer, and invited us to join him. He explained that the drawer contained the facts about and whereabouts of every British agent, and he wished to impress upon us the fact that one false move or slip of the tongue could endanger the lives of those men and women, to say nothing of the French Resistance and others working for the common cause. He pointed out that the files in the drawer were red in color. He then opened another drawer, which contained nearly as many files. The covers were black.

He outlined the plan for the two of us in Wales and explained that the training had a twofold advantage. First, it would give us some experience away from the staff in London, with the added use of a coded system for reporting. Second, if our work was successful, we could do a service to the security arrangements of whichever organization we worked with.

He asked if there were any questions. I said I was quite clear with regard to the assignment, but was it wise to be so open with the contents of the filing cabinet?

He smiled and in turn, looked us both straight in the eye, and asked how else could he show his trust in us. And how did we know that there could be duplicate files elsewhere in the country; indeed, how did we know but what they were not fakes?

He went on further to stress that he and those under and above him had to place enormous trust in those that worked in the field, and since their work was carried out against all the principles of comfort—irregular meals accompanied by constant worry and fear—the first requirement was to establish a bond between all operators, including many who would never actually meet in person, indeed might only be known to one another by a code name. Such were the complex relationships implanted on our young minds by that officer that day in London. The colonel was very good at his job and his integrity rubbed off very effectively.

CHAPTER TEN

So, what was the job in Wales? I can neither say nor spell the name of the place. But I can say that on a clear day, it was easy to see Mt. Snowden; in fact, it was so clear and near-looking one day my pal accidentally called it Everest!

He was a nice bloke, like me a sergeant, but in another specialist unit. He was known to me as Len.

Len and I were charged with two tasks. The first one was to keep an eye on a certain small railway station where it was suspected that some gentlemen alighted from the train, made their way into the country, and operated a device that enabled the enemy to receive wireless messages out at sea. We were to take turns at keeping tabs on everyone, and if we suspected anything, report as instructed. We would be billeted with an elderly couple nearby and both the couple and the station master had been told to give us any assistance required without question. We were given a fortnight to do the job, wished good luck, and here we were.

In the hope that the reader gets a smile out of this serious assignment, I will go into it with some detail.

Len said he would take the first watch at the station, so I made my way to the billet. "Nearby" in London was not "nearby" in Wales. It was nearly a mile. All I had to do, said the station master, was follow a well-worn path along the grass.

On arrival, I met Mrs. Jones, who asked where the other one was. I explained we were taking turns and he would arrive tomorrow.

It was a Saturday, and Mr. Jones was not at work; in fact, he proudly showed me his new wireless and promised I could listen that night. There it stood on a side table, complete with R.T. battery—a slim, flat grid-bias battery plus the two-volt accumulator, all very necessary power units to make the thing work. A swan-neck loud-speaker completed the indoor equipment. The outdoor equipment consisted of a long aerial and an earth tube with a wire leading into the room and connecting to the receiver. (My hobby was making such receivers and I was interested.)

After a meal, Mrs. Jones asked if I would be kind enough to go to the station, meet her niece, and perhaps carry her bag when she arrived on the train. I said I would, and thought it would give me a chance to see how Len was making out. Mrs. Jones explained that her niece was a nurse and stayed with them every other Saturday. I asked how I would know her, to which Mr. Jones replied, "You'll know her all right, boyo!" He demonstrated his confidence by forming his hands on his chest.

I walked the footpath back to the station and found Len had installed himself in the small waiting room. He said he had not seen a train, but there was one due soon. I asked if he had eaten and he said that the station master had some sausages for them both. When the train arrived they were having a fry-up just inside the firebox of the engine.

I need not have worried about the identification of the nurse. She was in uniform; in addition, she was also very aloof. I made myself known to her and offered to carry her bag. She ignored me and set off at a cracking pace to the house. I need not have bothered meeting her train, and returning to the Jones' place, took my time behind her, thinking back to the time of the interview with major Hood.

We were going to listen to "In Town Tonight." There were only ten minutes to go when I got back, and Mr. Jones was itching to switch on the wireless.

Mrs. Jones, however, entered the room, walking backwards and towing a long, galvanized bath, which she positioned in front of the fire. When she came back, she was carrying two pails of hot water, which she dumped in the bath. I offered to help and added two more.

On my return with the final load, I was greeted with a surprise. The nurse had removed her uniform and was about to get stripped for a bath. This had not been on the training agenda, so I admit to being a trifle baffled. I had not assumed that the water was going to be used in this way.

When the young lady removed her bra, and it became obvious this was not a male nurse, I announced I thought I would have an early night and left my chair, making for the door.

A series of whistles and shrieks came from the loudspeaker as Mr. Jones manipulated the twin tuning condensers, then got it—loud and fairly clear. He saw me standing by the door and I repeated I was off to bed.

"But what about my wireless?"

I was about to open the door when he and I looked at the maiden sitting in the tub. He looked at me with some understanding and said, "No, no, boyo. Sit down—she won't splash you!"

The bedroom was very large. It had to be in order to accommodate two double beds, a gigantic wardrobe with a matching chest of drawers, and odd chairs. I climbed aboard and sank into a deep pit of feathered mattress. I slept the good sleep.

After breakfast, I made my way slowly along the track that led to the station. I worked out that it was silly to have this twenty-four hour on and twenty-four hour off system. It meant that the one on duty was bored stiff and the one that was off had even less to do. It was worse for Len, since he had not been exposed to the bombs and raids as I had, so did not appreciate the rest aspect of the job—and a fortnight was a long time. So I made up an alternate plan and put it to Len. He agreed and added something that had not occurred to me: in the event of there being someone to deal with, it would be much easier with two of us.

So we consulted the station master and wrote down the times of the trains. It worked out that roughly there were four a day, six at weekends with passengers, and all sorts of odd ones during the night, which were goods trains. With a list of times to study, we settled down to working out how best we could watch for our unknown enemies. That done, there was nothing to do for the next two hours.

We filled the time by taking a stroll along into the village.

The post office was also a general shop, or had been in peace-time. The stocks were a little low by now, but ala the late Rob Milton, the postmaster was also the fire chief, a special constable, the taxi service, the owner of the one and only petrol pump, and for all I knew, the local midwife as well. He was a real Welshman, though. Couldn't understand a word from him. But he was very pleasant, I felt.

We returned to the station and had a look at the next train that puffed and chuffed away without any incident, except a very animated conversation between the station master and the guard. I gathered that either the Germans had blown up the moon or flat racing had been restored.

The next steam visitor was only an hour away, according to our time table, and I thought I would confirm this with "his nibs" and guess what? The silly old fool said that the times he had given us were the times the trains *should* arrive, but now they came at any old time! He explained that there was a war on.

I suggested to Len that he should get his kit up to the house, get himself installed, and have a wash and shave—if there was any hot water left! When I told him about the nurse in the bath, he went off the platform towards the house with a brisk, determined step.

I settled down with his book, *No Orchids for Miss Blandish*, by Peter Cheney.

I read as far as page seven and the door opened, with a very agitated station master, saying something like, "I'm sorry, bach, but your friend seems to be cock-legged. Look you."

Indeed, my friend was certainly cock-legged, for poor old Len was white of face and walking in a most peculiar fashion. With some difficulty and in obvious pain, he sat down on one of the waiting room seats.

"Why," he demanded, "didn't you tell me about that bloody goat?"

The station master looked at me for a reply.

"What bloody goat?" I responded.

Now the station master eagerly turned to Len for an explanation.

"The one that butted me from behind. The one that is tethered to a steel wire running from the house to the station."

I looked at the rail man, who said, "Oooh! *That* goat."

I was in some doubt as to whether or not I should report that we had a casualty, so suggested that we both go back to the house.

Sure enough, there was the goat, tethered to a wire stretched tight along the grass about seven feet from the footpath.

Well—I didn't know. My part of the adventure was with nurses. Not goats.

I hated jobs like this, that consumed a lot of time but had no visible result. I still do. There seems to be little point in them. So I said, "Sod the trains, let's get some sleep," and started up the stairs. When Len followed painfully, I thought of the nurse. It seemed natural to me to ask Mrs. Jones if her niece would have a look at my friend's back, seeing as she was a nurse.

"Oh, no! I don't approve of that," Mrs. Jones said. "Having a young man and my niece in a bedroom together, see."

"But I will be there as well," I replied.

"Exactly!" she replied, adding, "'Tis Sunday, you see."

Well, I rubbed Len's back as best I could, then undressed and flopped into my large nest. We chatted in between Len's attempts to get comfortable. When at last he found a position that was non-aching, I put out the light. Immediately, as if by some magic, there was a loud creaking sound. It went on for a long time, then ceased with a thud, and everything was silent.

"What the hell was that?" asked Len.

"Don't know, but it didn't happen last night. And that strange glow on the wall above your head wasn't there, either."

There was a rustling sound from the direction of the other bed. Then I heard the click of the bolt of Len's rifle. I got out and put on the light. There was the answer. The wardrobe door had swung open and hit a bookcase, which had a full length mirror reflecting the light from the moon through the curtains.

It was the weight distribution that made the floor move enough to open the door. A cigarette packet put it right!

We slept well, but not before having a good laugh at the experience, and not before Len telling me of a similar episode on his
wedding night.

It seemed he and his bride stayed at a small hotel and had not
been in bed very long before they heard a terrific clatter through the
wall.

His new bride screamed and hung on, and when he found his
bedside light, Len saw the time was nearly midnight. He could see
nothing in the room that could have made such a noise and settled
down again, until a banging, whirring, clanking noise had them both
out of bed. It was then that they discovered the noise was the mech-
anism of a large advertising clock situated in a cupboard in the room.

Sleep came shortly after that, and in the morning, we made
our way along the track to the station. This time the goat was on his
way back to the house. When he spied us, he gathered speed, straining his tether, and leaning over like a speedway rider. As he sizzled
by, Len had a few words with his rear view.

When we arrived at the station, we went into the waiting room
and studied the time table for what it was worth. The station master
came in with a very tall man dressed in a tweed suit. The rail man
was hopping from one foot to the other and speaking very quickly.
What with the speed of his overworked tongue plus his Welsh accent, I had no idea of what he was saying. The tweed man held up his
hand and indicated that he wished to be alone with us.

When the door had closed, the tall man said quietly that he
had arrived by train and in a disused quarry had set up a wireless
device that would transfer the engine noise from British aircraft flying overhead. The receiver was in a craft out at sea. He added that it
was easy to do this, because there were no security guards on duty.

We tried to speak at the same time in our defense, explaining
that at no time did any passengers get off without one or both of
being on duty.

"But I did not arrive with my equipment on a passenger train;
I hid in a *goods truck*."

Len and I looked at one another. He had his mouth open. I
don't know how I looked, but I felt a fool. I always felt stupid at

some of the training methods. It was not easy for me to pretend. I stopped doing that when I was twenty and saw lots of dead and wounded people lying around.

"Well?" asked the tweed.

"Don't know," offered Len.

I said there was a train coming and went on to the platform. Well—there *was* a train coming!

Mr. Tweed called me back, suggested we sit down, and quietly explain to him exactly the routine we had adopted and everything that had happened since we started.

Len got in first with his encounter with the goat. He related the experience with the wardrobe door, the visit to the post office, and how he had helped fry some bangers on the footplate of an engine. Then he dried up and looked at me for confirmation. I agreed with all this, and asked a question.

"Which SOE department are you from?"

He gave a wry grin and said, "I am from the section that will not be very impressed with your conduct when I make my report. But I hope to collect a fiver. You see, they told me I couldn't get anywhere near you lads without being challenged. I said I could, so the bet was made." He added, "You do realize, don't you, that all this is intended to prime you for the real thing. You won't find a kind uncle type like me appear suddenly in a little French town and help you out. When you are out there, you are on your own.

"Anyway, I've done my part; the rest is up to the colonel. In the meantime, I will take over your room at the house; you two can return to London. But remember, it would do you no good if I am easy with my report." And looking at Len, added, "We are not fighting goats!"

So we trio returned to the house. Much to my surprise, I saw Mrs. Jones' smile of welcome to "Tweed." I also noticed he ducked neatly under door frames, as though familiar with them. And what was more, having stood aside to let him go upstairs, I realized he knew which room we were using.

I excused myself and went down to the outdoor toilet. I had no inclination to use it, just sat on the well-scrubbed seat and lit a cigarette. I thought that this combination would help me think. Well, it did, but it was of no help. I didn't know what to think about, except that we had made a muck of the whole affair. I could hear the man at Camberley say, "You cannot do as you are told," and all that with the coffee in Woolworth's.

When I joined the others, I found they had a bottle of home-made wine on the table. Mrs. Jones poured me a glass and said it was Mr. Watson's favorite.

I said, "Cheers. And who is Mr. Watson."

The Welsh lady's hand flew to her mouth, as if to take back the words.

"It's all right, Mrs. Jones," said Tweed and, turning to Len and I, added. "I am Watson, an old friend here."

Mrs. Jones left us alone after a while, and Mr. Watson said he would not "put us in the picture" regarding all this cops and robbers stuff. It seemed that there really was someone at work about twice a month with a transmitter, and although no damage had been done, we, the British, had to find out who was responsible for sending the messages. All we knew was that they were on the same frequency as the lifeboat, which was one of the few to have a radio link, and it was an astute operator who had made the initial report.

The police had failed to find anything, so the security boys were saddled with the job and he, Mr. Watson, had been here five times before without getting a lead. Then the colonel had the idea to send lads under training, like us, to try our luck with only limited knowledge of the true facts. Then he or another would appear and pretend he was the "Baddie."

On all previous occasions, the two trainees did the twenty-four hour watch as instructed. We were the first to disobey, so he would finish out the fortnight himself.

So now we knew. There was no doubt about it; they meant what they said. Talk about "One upward jump and remain."

Len and I packed our kit in silence, took a last look round the room—noting the flat cigarette packet under the wardrobe—and went downstairs. We went into the kitchen to say good-bye to Mrs. Jones, who offered, "Such nice boys they always send."

On the way out, I noticed the long bath—the bath! "Once a fortnight." No, it couldn't be. Or could it?

Mr. Watson came with us to the station. Len asked him how he got on with the goat.

"Oh! fine," he said, "Great chap."

Len muttered to himself.

Mr. Watson walked over to the steel wire and lifted it up about six inches. It thumped back in place. Within a few seconds the animal appeared from the direction of the station, thundering along towards us. Len shouted to Mr. Watson to get out of the way of the bloody thing, but Mr. Watson stood his ground, one foot either side of the wire. The goat slowed down and Len nearly had a fit when the man from London *stroked it*!

On the platform, we stood together as the train steamed in. We let the station master chop bits out of our tickets, but as the doors slammed, I took the plunge, hoping the train moved as soon as I had finished speaking.

I asked Mr. Watson if he had met the niece, and if so, did he realize she visited every other week. I suggested he try to carry her case. If she allowed this, he should have a look inside. If she refused, he should ask why?

Back in London, Len and I parted company. I did not see him again, but heard he was out in the Far East. No doubt he thought that goat would never find him out there.

I, to put it mildly, was read the riot act and was virtually confined to my quarters. Now I longed to be back in a normal unit, training the troops in ordinary army skills—even if we did use blocks of wood to represent explosives in the early training period—with the good old sergeants' Mess and the store man of HQ Company, who was to become a famous comedian and sadly die in his prime, the late Arthur Haynes.

Some time later, when I was summoned to the inner office, and Sue again made the tea, I found an unexpected welcome from those present. They were all smiles as they all shook hands with me.

"They've gone raving, bloody bonkers," I thought. And then came the question.

"What put you on to the niece?"

"What niece?" I asked.

"The one in Wales."

They were still smiling, so in I went with both feet.

"Well, it was simple, really," I explained. "As soon as I had the facts from Mr. Watson, it all made sense. You see, the girl arrived every other Saturday, or twice a month, as it was put officially, so when I offered to help carry her case and she refused I thought it odd. But when she stripped in front of me, I knew it was not a Welsh habit. After all, she had not just come up from the pit, so it had to be her or tied up with her."

I left the office feeling ten feet tall—especially when they said old Watson would not get his fiver after all.

CHAPTER ELEVEN

If by now you are wondering when the story is going to start, I suggest you skip the next few pages. You see, there would be nothing to tell if there had not been any of this unusual training. And since, for various reasons, I have left out more than I have related, you would not have the adventure until the very end. Also, if you miss this section, you will not know what happened after Mr. Watson lost his fiver!

You will note the station security job employed two of us. Well, the next one was a solo effort and strangely enough, in Wales once more, although not in goat country. This time it was in a town and my instructions were simple.

I had to enter a specific building, remove an object or documents that would obviously be missed. I would then report the details of the incident to my superior, who would notify the department concerned that their security had been very slack. The "stolen" property would be returned, with the warning that the operator could have left a bomb.

This was more like it, I thought. Especially as I was oriented properly, and knew that the reason for the job was twofold. One, it tended to keep the victims on their toes regarding their security and two, it gave trainees like me the opportunity to learn the art of "conning" one's way into the seat of operation.

My job was to remove documents, but in case I found that impossible, I was supposed to take a "bomb" (an explosive device with time delay) and place it where it would do most damage. My target was a town hall that administered local government with wartime necessities.

The "bomb" was an empty two-pound toffee tin I concealed on my arm under my overcoat. I was in civilian clothes and I walked up and down outside the sandbagged entrance to the big building, sizing up the place and wondering where a quick exit might be. Much to my surprise, I was not nervous, and I grew up a little when I realized I liked to be in charge of the situation, instead of being way down the chain of action.

With an open mind, I went up the steps and through the swinging doors, through the black-out screen, and found myself in a large room rather like the hall of a large bank. There were sections marked off along a huge counter, with notices indicating various services or advice, such as food or clothing coupons, etc. The walls were covered with posters advising the public how best to deal with incendiary bombs, potato blight, and so on. Others invited people to "Join the AAP," or informed them that "Fire-watchers" were wanted. One that caught my eye said, "Join the Home Guard." That was it! I decided to get my bomb under the chair of the officer in charge of the local Home Guard if I could.

I swallowed hard and went up to the counter to a young woman of about twenty-three or so.

"Who do I see about joining the Home Guard?" I asked.

"Well, I doubt if there is anyone on duty now, but if you like, you can go downstairs and see." She pointed to a door marked "Private."

This was too good and easy, I thought, as I went down the stone steps. The walls still had the appearance of a recent paint-up, with one notice in large letters, "Mayor's Robing Room."

What a gift met my eyes when I saw another sign: "Home Guard HQ" But the door was locked.

A voice called down, "Was there anyone in?"

I remounted the stairs, explained that the door was locked, and together we went back into the entrance hall.

The young woman said that if I left my name and address, she would see that the major was told, and would I like a cup of tea?

I said no to the name bit and yes to the tea.

She led me along corridors with notices on departmental doors.

Traffic was brisk, with girls and elderly men going through one door into another. Most of them had pieces of paper in their hands. We went through a door marked "Surveyor," and I was astonished to find myself in a very large room with eighteen to twenty desks, with a man seated behind each desk. The room was stuffy, the curtains were drawn, and the fires were full on.

No war in here, I thought. Not like at home.

"This is Mr. Hornoy," said my guide. "He is a HG sergeant and will help you. Do you take sugar?"

I said, "Yes, please, if there was any, but never mind if not." There was plenty of sugar.

Mr. Hornoy wanted my name and address, my occupation, and wondered why I was not in the Forces.

I had to get rid of the tin soon. The room was hot, and it was awkward maneuvering a cup of tea with the coat on my arm. Why were they not suspicious?

I evaded the question about my not being in the services and had two thoughts running through my mind at the same time. I wanted the name, or at least the address, of the Home Guard commander, so I asked the girl if she would join me for a drink that evening, thinking she might be tell me what I needed to know. She said she would see me when she left the office.

I said that surely the correct place to discuss HG affairs was in the Company Office. Mr. Hornoy thought that was a great idea and led the way down again to the office. He opened the door with his key and proudly bade me enter.

I was in. Looking around, I saw the walls were covered with maps of the local garrison. Colored pins indicated something or other, and a sand table depicted the physical features of the area.

Mr. Hornoy sat, found a document, and began writing. I felt my heart beat faster but I knew it was too soon to try to leave my bomb.

I thought fast. I took my own pen from my pocket, approached the chair, and deliberately dropped the pen.

"Blast it!" I said, bent down, and taking advantage of the shadow and the cover of the coat, slid the tin under the chair. I picked up the pen and folded my coat over the chair back.

I had cramp in my fingers and forearm from holding the "bomb" for so long. I waggled to get the blood flowing again, and the excitement I felt was a great help to get my heart pumping away. I did it! So far, so good. Now, if the bomb was real, I would be wise to get out. With dignity, of course.

My Hornoy was now ready with his document. "Sign here," he said, "and I will get you enrolled on next parade, which will be on Sunday."

"Ah! well," I sighed. "You remember I dropped my pen a few minutes ago? Well, when I bent down to pick it up, my back went out again. It is a troublesome complaint I have with my back. That's really the reason I am not fit enough to be in the Forces. Can't do PT (physical training) or drill with a back like mine. I though it was all right until I bent down to pick up that pen, but it seems to have started again."

Mr. Hornoy came over all sergeant-like.

"You've wasted my time, and my break period is over. Try joining the ARF and be a fire-watcher."

I apologized and together we returned to the main hall, where he escorted me out of the main doors. I walked as "painfully" as I could and said "Good-bye."

I waited across the road for the staff to appear on their way home, hoping to catch the girl I had seen earlier.

I felt pleased with myself, but feared that somehow, some way, someone would find my "bomb" and probably say, "That's a handy tin, I wonder who left that under a chair. Will have to get someone to pay more attention when they have a sweep round."

What was I afraid of?

Little did I know that I was about to be taught a sharp lesson in the art of being a saboteur.

I saw the girl, she smiled a welcome, slipped her arm through mine, and said she would take me to her home for tea. I even met her parents. What I really wanted was the name of the H.G. commander, or his phone number. All this was wasting time, as I was anxious to let my chief know of my success.

She said she normally played the piano at a local "hop," and we could have a drink on the way to the dance. This we did, and I casually asked the name of the HG boss. I noticed she evaded the question, so I thought I would try again later.

At the dance, I had a waltz with her, then excused myself to phone my chief. He was pleased and said never mind about ascertaining the address; I had done well on my first effort.

I felt pretty chuffed at this. I was off the hook. And I looked forward to the companionship of the girl. They were jiving when I rejoined the few dancers. I asked her to go on the floor. After a few moments, she slapped my face hard. I asked for an explanation, and she said, "There is something odd about you, and anyway, the way you have just danced proved there is nothing the matter with your back—you should be in the Forces."

What a lesson.

I had completely forgotten about my back.

There were many security stunts like this one going on, some with near disastrous results. One chap was savaged by a dog, another was wounded by bayonet, still another was tied hand and foot and left in a guardroom cell at a RAF camp. As I mentioned before, this training was twofold. It tested the security of the unit concerned and provided experience for the operator.

One of my colleagues was able to get through a wire fence, past Alsatian guard dogs, con his way through the staff, and then leave behind a two-pound cocoa tin marked "bomb"—under the chair of the Wind Commander!

Those of us doing these jobs rarely were present to see the air turn blue! Such was the case with a certain large department of the Ministry of Food. Of course, on the whole they did first class work, but on one occasion they did have a weak spot.

It was to such a place I was sent with the task of putting the department telephone system out of action. The switching system was located in a large room with three positions for the operators under the overall charge a supervisor. My cover story was that I was on sick leave from the Army and was keen to get groups together for evening lectures on how to deal with incidents such as bomb or fire damage after an enemy raid.

The subterfuge was a shame, really, as the people were, on the whole, very nice and kind. They invited me to their homes, and on one occasion I found myself at a whist-drive, which was not my "cup of tea" and not much help to my partner. I trumped her ace.

My task, then, was to put the exchange out of order, without doing any real damage and without getting caught. It was easy, really, once I had the confidence of the staff.

Outside the exchange room was the records office. This was staffed by semi-retired civil servants, many of whom had obviously been clerical all their lives. I was asked to wait in this office until the telephone supervisor was free to see me. I used my time to practice the observation rules I had learned in training. I had memorized the route from the entrance to this room and noted that, in reverse, it was my best way out in the event of a quick exit being necessary. All this assuming I might be challenged by an "enemy."

I noticed one man had a continual supply of tea brought to him by a girl of about sixteen. It seemed that tea was not rationed here, as it was at home. I suppose it was only natural, after all, this was the Ministry of Food.

Another man had a huge pile of documents in his "IN" tray and very little in the "OUT" tray. I mentioned this by way of conversation "just to be friendly," and he explained that he was an old hand at the game. By keeping to this system, he was entitled to an assistant for not being able to cope—when his No. 1 paid a call.

Finally, I was asked to follow a young lady who take me to the supervisor. As I neared the exchange, the old blood moved a little faster. The supervisor was a middle-aged lady—all tweeds and shooting stick type. She said she had heard of me through my lectures in the local hall and what did I want, and be quick, as this was an important building and of great importance to the war effort,.

With tongue in cheek, I said that, as so many of the staff had been so kind during my leave listening to my little talks, and as I was due back on normal duties the next day, I felt I should give her the benefit of my experience regarding the exchange and access the drill to be observed in the event of a near hit by bombing, and so on.

She snorted a bit, and I sensed I would have to tell a much stronger story. I added that she should ask for an axe, a saw, and a large sheet of flexible asbestos.

"What on earth for?" she exclaimed.

"In the event of invasion, I suggest you use the saw to cut the phone cables, the axe to hack your way out if the door sticks, and the asbestos sheet to smoother the fire!"

"My God," she said, going very pale.

"You should sit down," I said, opening the exchange door for her. She staggered to a small desk and rummaged in her handbag. *I was in.*

Having assured the telephone operators that all was well, I went behind the switchboards, where it was my turn to exclaim "Good God!"

The tweedy lady joined me at the back of the switchboard, and looked at it as though she had not seen it before.

"Look at all this beeswax on these cables!" I said.

"Well, what about it?"

"Don't you see the fire risk," I explained. "Look, let me make a phone call to someone and I'll get it sprayed with anti-fire."

"All right, use my phone."

"No, I'll use this one, provided for the use of the test engineers."

I switched the lever to "exchange" and phoned my chief. I was hot and sticky, not only from fear of being caught, but because there was an enormous coal fire burning in the room.

My boss answered, "Yes?"

I replied that these switchboards would be destroyed within the next 15 minutes and I should make myself scarce.

"Where are you now?"

"Leaning against the switchboards, with my bomb, ready to plant."

"Blimey! All right, get out into the street before I send a signal to the Security Office. Ring again from a phone box when you are clear, but say goody-bye to all and keep calm on the way out."

I had made myself known to many of the staff during my

attempt to con my way into the exchange and I felt sorry for them, after the roasting they were due to get for allowing a stranger into the exchange. Until then, they probably thought, "Such a nice boy."

Thinking back that evening on the day's events, I found it a frightening situation when I realized that I, as a very inexperienced trainee, could wheedle my way into an important administration such as a ministry building and a home guard company headquarters. After all, if I could do it, surely the enemy would also find it easy, especially an enemy like the German officer I had the chat with just before reaching Dunkirk. He was good enough to have been a Member of Parliament.

It was not a pleasant thought to realize the country was so vulnerable.

So far, so good, but not all these stunts were without injury. People did get hurt.

Silent weapons, knives, strangle holds, breaking limbs and many other diabolical methods of damaging the human frame had to be perfected. At five feet, nine inches, and weighing around ten stone, ten pounds, I found myself a nice average in most respects. Very fit and full of fun, confident in my own abilities, having seen at close hand death and destruction at a very impressionable age and, although not by any means academic, very practical with the countryman's logic that often confused superiors with university training. And, although I was often in trouble, I still found many were prepared to take my word as good enough.

So with confidence I joined others to learn the art of how to maim or kill without a weapon.

The instructor was a man of about thirty, of Eastern origin, who was even more fit. At the end of his course came his finale. How to kill by a handshake.

He explained, that in his country, greetings and farewells were exchanged by placing the hands together and bowing, the bow being lower as the rank increased, but in European countries the custom was to shake hands, irrespective of social standing.

"On condition," he said, "you promise you will never attempt to practice the following exercise, I will show how you can kill with a shake of the hand that will leave no bruises or mess, and a medical examination will confirm a spinal disorder. This is the one exercise you will not practice with anyone other than an enemy."

Shortly afterwards, someone had a birthday and bottles were opened. The new-found knowledge of the killer shake was in the minds of most present as it was intriguing, since we had not seen the result of the move, other than with a skeleton.

After the beer was gone, someone found some whiskey, which later led to fisticuffs between two chaps. A well-meaning older man insisted they shake hands and be friends. They eyed each other, and I sensed trouble. Their eyes were glassy with drink and there was a hint of hatred. I nudged my pal, we went forward to keep them apart, and this was interpreted as a signal for a free-for-all. Soon there were cut lips, bleeding knuckles.

When it was over, we all cleared up, and after a lecture on behavior, I was invited to shake hands with one of the fighters. My grip was normal; his wasn't. It lasted only a second, but my neck ached for days—*I think he tried.*

Trying to get these events into some logical sequence is not easy, although it should not detract from the general interest of this account regarding the training of an operator. As I've said, some were hurt, or killed. Such was the case when an instructor approached an explosive device to find out why it had not fired. Against all basic precautions, he tampered with the thing instead of blowing it up in situ, with the result that he took the full blast plus the shrapnel effect and wound up in many pieces.

He left a widow and I was asked to make this new state of affairs known to her. As can be imagined, it was not a job I relished. To make it worse, she was at a dance and appeared to be happy and enjoying herself when at last I found her. I noticed she was wearing a black dress. But how to broach the subject? I had a drink at the bar and watched her. She was laughing and chatting with friends, and I thought at first that I would let her carry on and tell her after the dance ended. But as time dragged, and she became even happier with an occasional drink of what looked like sherry, I thought it would be best to call her to one side and get it over with. That decision demanded another drink for me. More time passed, then I thought I would get one of her friends to bring her to a quiet corner, and with a bit of support I could say my sad piece.

That seemed to be the best idea, so I had another drink, made my choice from the ladies, and asked her if she could spare me a moment in the lobby. The reply was that she certainly could not.

I explained it was important and urgent. She said I would do better, perhaps, with someone younger, more of my own age, and anyway everyone there was happily married.

That did it. I jumped at the chance to say that one of you is no longer happily married; in fact, she—indicating the person concerned—is now a widow, and I would appreciate your help in telling the sad news.

She was shocked and burst out crying, so I assumed she knew the late instructor. It turned out he was her brother.

Trust me to choose the wrong one.

On three other occasions, I had this sad assignment and it ranks with the most distressing memories of the war years. The sight of a policeman or a serviceman at the door must have been a dreadful moment for the person in the house. I learned a lot from this first experience and was a bit more professional the other three times. I have to admit though, the first one was a bit like being thrown in at the deep end.

As a contrast, almost immediately after this I found myself attending a féte.

There were the usual people there and the theme was home-grown produce. Many women had learned how to pickle, and some men soon found the taste of dandelion wine very much to their liking.

The festivities were interrupted when the local siren sounded an air raid warning. Everyone moved from the grounds and assembled inside the village hall, which I thought was silly in case of a direct hit.

The vicar seemed to be in charge. He stood on the small stage and said something but nobody heard a word; they were all talking at once. The vicar gave up in the end, went behind a curtain, and reappeared with a megaphone. Thus amplified, he announced that, if everyone would kindly be seated, there would be a panel of local celebrities on the stage, ready to answer questions regarding life in wartime. He indicated several people, who mounted the stage, and seated themselves at a long table. One empty seat remained. Guess who was asked to fill it.

Well, when I had taken my place and looked to my left and right, I found that, apart the vicar, who introduce me to the others, there was a JP, three local councilors, two WI members, and a lady who seemed to disapprove of the others. She was all tweeds and shooting stick, and I couldn't help thinking she probably had a goodly supply of sugar and other rationed items at home.

The minister started the ball rolling by thanking all for being present, adding that they were all proud to have a soldier sergeant in their midst, and then invited questions.

The questions started.

One elderly gentleman asked if it were possible for Mrs. Dalrymple (tweedy) to keep her conversations a little shorter on their joint party line.

Tweedy snorted a bit and, with a very sharp tongue, said she would talk on the phone as long as she liked, to which the old man replied that it was his number that they shared, which brought forth the observation that, judging by the few conversations she had overheard, it was only about a few pounds invested by the local bank, and judging by the bored tone of the bank manager, none of it was worth listening to.

That got the old man on his feet and, with stick waving, he threatened to have her cut off.

At this point, the vicar intervened and restored order, suggesting a question from a younger member of the audience.

A girl of about fourteen asked if it was true that when twins are born they share the same age?

Old sour tongue got in first, saying, "Of course they do, silly girl, next question?"

The girl looked embarrassed at the sharp answer and sat down.

The audience murmured to themselves and no one asked a

question.

I think it was the J.P. that then said, "Now, come on, sergeant, how about you adding your voice to this little gathering?"

I stood, and much to my surprise, they clapped!

"I would like to give the young lady a more accurate answer to her baby question," I said.

"What on earth do you know about that kind of thing?" from the sour one.

The audience booed this remark, and I detected the panel's animosity toward this lady.

"Look, Madame," I said, "This girl asked a feasible question, and as a female, you could have given her the information she needs."

I addressed the girl, "Look, Luv, only one baby can be born at any one time. If there are two or more, they enter the world one at a time, one after the other. As to which is the eldest, well, the first one is and the last one the youngest. Therefore, in the case of a multi-birth that occurs near midnight, it is possible for them to have birthdays on different days, before and after midnight alters the date, see?"

"Thank you," she said, and the people clapped and cheered as though they had just learned it was peace again.

I knew it was the uniform mostly, plus putting old tweedy in the shade. But she leapt to her feet and shouted, "Sergeant, I intend reporting you to your commanding officer, and I'll remind you that there is absolutely *nothing* that you can do that I cannot."

The audience, by this time, resembled the crowd at Wimbledon, looking first one way, then the other.

She paused for breath, but before she could say any more, I said, "When you have made your report, may I suggest you try doing something I can do that you would find impossible?"

Flushed now, she snapped, "And what, pray, would that be?"

"With respect to the vicar here, I challenge you to piddle out of a railway carriage window!"

The reverend gentleman led the applause.

CHAPTER TWELVE

After this, it was back to the boss and seated with a cup of Sue's tea, I was asked how I felt about doing a live jump, at night. I replied that I didn't think much of the Ringway system at Manchester. I did the daylight ones with no bother, but when the night drops were cancelled for some reason, I had to ascend in the basket of a balloon in the morning with dark glasses on and then jump. The contraption swayed from side to side, it creaked, there was no noise except the wind, and apart from an instructor, I was alone. I ventured that, as a hobby, I didn't think the idea would catch on!

He nodded at this, and said that the report from Ringway was perfectly satisfactory as, indeed, was my ability to stammer convincingly, and would I like another cup of tea?

I replied that if Sue had the job of bringing it in, then I would have a cup every fifteen minutes for the duration of the war.

The tea she brought, complete with smile, was to be my last for a long three weeks.

"I think you are ready for an op," the bass said.

I went hot and cold.

"There are many who could do the job I have in mind for you—they can speak the languages and are experienced. They are also known in the area concerned, so a new person will have to go. I am sure you can do it. Whether or not you return—is another matter."

Suddenly Sue and her tea were not important.

I was kitted with French clothes—everything, including underwear. It was inspected every day, not for neatness like a uniform, but for evidence that it had been worn in England. Nothing was left to chance. I had a new name and was made to act out the stammering idiot I would be if I were caught and questioned.

When "they" were satisfied, I was taken to an airfield and introduced to some pilots who further introduced me to those wonderful little aircraft known as Lysanders. I mentioned that I didn't fancy jumping out of one of these and was told there was no jumping. "If you leave one of these, it is because the pilot has turned it upside down and you have fallen out."

Lots of tales have been told about these aircraft and the uses they were put to and it may seem boring to hear it all again. But remember, there have been millions of football matches. No two alike exactly, but each player has his own account of the play, and his memories. So with me.

At the briefing, the pilot appeared to be most uninterested and paid little attention to the officer with the maps. He was of tubby build, with the fashionable growth of hair on his top lip. Apart from that, he exuded great confidence. There was no doubt he had heard it all before. Unlike me. I had all the training bits going on inside me.

Old "whiskers" looked at a document, turned to me, and said, "Let's go."

The briefing officer said, "Good luck," a FANY said, "This way," and we went.

The pilot slid open the door and invited me to get aboard. I found myself seated facing the tail and I jumped a bit when the intercom asked if I were army. I said I was, and he said, "Good show. Here, sit on this."

He passed back a thick book and explained it was a London Telephone Directory, A to K, much warmer than L to Z. He also handed me a hip flask at the same time, asking if I was cold.

I replied that I didn't know which were the cold shivers and which were the scared shivers. He said the contents of the flask would deal with both kinds, adding, "Sip it at first, but have the lot in small doses. You have one hour and seventeen minutes before you land and by then your breath should have cleared the mist from the glass enough for me to see the ground."

I laughed. He *was* joking, wasn't he?

We bumped along the ground and when my stomach sudden-
ly felt heavy, I knew we were up. I had the feeling that I had forgotten the reason for the flight and found it difficult to appreciate that
this was the easy bit. The hard part was to come.

"Know where you are?"

I jumped at the sudden voice.

"No idea."

"Just over the coast now and heading out to sea."

There was a strong smell of petrol and burnt oil and I began
to regret being in such a confined space. I also realized I had not
moved my legs since sitting on my A to K. I moved a bit and thought
I preferred the old Dakota aircraft with more space, a bench, and
other chaps for company—even though it meant a jump by parachute. I didn't know which was worse and was not too happy with
the knowledge that I was in a position to find out!

I had another drop of "medicine" and began to think more
clearly. I formed the opinion that some people were born so much
alcohol below par. I worked it out that I could give of my best after
several whiskies and made a mental note to experiment after this
flying greenhouse job was over.

"Have you seen the furnace of a factory?" I did not jump this
time.

"No, have you lost one?" This was bloody good stuff in this
flask. The intercom chuckled. "Look down to your right. There—see
it?"

I saw an oval circle of orange light and described what I had
seen.

"Good man, that is a fine landmark—won't be long now—
hope the RAF boys are all at home tonight—can do without any
bloody searchlights."

Minutes passed, and I finally got the shivers sorted out once
and for all. They were one hundred percent scared shakes, no doubt
about it. I could feel the trickles of perspiration running down my
back. I thought it was crazy of somebody to send me on a stunt like
this. Surely there were experienced people available. My thoughts
were cut short by, "Don't talk to me." At the same time the engine

cut.

I looked round at the pilot and saw him looking first one side and then the other. The plane rocked, the nose lifted slightly, and we bumped the ground softly and stopped almost immediately.

To get out was a performance, as my body was hot but my legs were cold and stiff.

"Over there." The pilot held my arm and pointed toward a small, flashing light.

We shook hands, and he said, "Good luck, son; see you again soon. And son—look after yourself."

As I started to make for the light I had been told to follow, it went out. I continued to walk in the direction I thought it was, but it was very dark. What a start, I thought to myself. We have the Navy, the Army, and the Air Force. New Zealand, Canada, Australia, and goodness knows how many more make up the Allies, yet they have to send *me* out here to occupied territory to say "Wild Duck" to a bloody torch that doesn't light.

Behind me the Lysander engine started, and almost at once changed tone with the climb. At the same time, something touched my arm and a voice said, "Apple."

"Wild Duck," I responded, but not in my own voice.

Another hand took my free arm and between two invisible figures, I stumbled along over grass, then through leaves, and finally along a hard surface. As I grew accustomed to the darkness, I judged my companions to be about my own height. We were a silent trio that entered a farmyard. I knew *that* by the smell.

Inside the farmhouse kitchen were the items one would expect to see: many pairs of old boots, brooms, cartons that once contained animal foodstuff; in fact, a typical farm kitchen. And at a table, to complete the scene, sat the farmer's wife, a portly lady who twisted her fingers together with an obvious show of nerves. That much I noticed as my escort led me through the kitchen to a parlor. I cannot recall the type of lighting in these two rooms, but I do know it was very dim.

One of the two men said in quite good English, "Sit, please; your friends will come soon." His colleague left us alone.

The time dragged, and I began to think back over the last few hours. What a lot had happened in a short space of time. I remembered the mug of tea at the aerodrome, old "Whiskers" and his brandy flask, and so on—it all came back. So, too, did thoughts of my parents and my home.

That did it. I felt a lump in my throat and could have cried. I fought it hard and felt a sick sensation in the stomach. It would have been a relief to have blubbered, but I did not want to let myself go in front of the silent figure seated opposite. Who was he? What part of the business was he going to perform?

It was cold in that room, and my shirt was clammy and uncomfortable from my having sweated on the plane. In fact, I found my entire clothing coarse and somehow foreign. Which, of course, it was. It was French and very much used; fumigated, they had said, and frequently checked to make sure it betrayed no link with England. No English tobacco dust in the pockets, no bus tickets, etc. Indeed, French tobacco dust existed and, of all things, a few shucks of onions and odd pieces of raffia could be found, if someone looked. You see, I had work papers, all currently dated to show I was a stammering onion-seller recently kicked out of the Calais area.

But the real reason I was here was to damage a part of a factory and I was supposed to work with others who would make themselves known to me.

So far, however, all I had was a silent Frenchman, who seemed to be content to study his boots.

The temperature in the room was dropping; it was just after midnight, and it was a very frosty November.

I stood and stretched. I wanted a smoke and a drink. I decided I was too inexperienced for this kind of job. But after all, why be so sad; I would be back in England the day after tomorrow, they said. That would be Saturday, and I would have plenty of drinks and smokes. I imagined being debriefed and dismissed and reckoned the feeling would be much the same as that of having safely landed after a parachute jump.

I went back to my chair, produced my part packet of French cigarettes, and offered one to my companion. He waved his arms a bit and muttered something about "fumer," which left me in some doubt as to whether he did not smoke or I should not, so I didn't. But then, as if by magic, all my needs were fulfilled in a matter of minutes, for suddenly there were voices through the door. Then into the room came a man who, in lovely English, said, "Come on through; bring any kit you have and meet us all."

The kitchen was brighter now and much warmer. I was invited to sit at the table and this gave me a chance to study the other occupants of the room.

"Let me introduce you," said one.

"This is the owner of the house, Pierre, and his wife, whom we call Madame. They have a daughter, Marie, who will, I hope, appear shortly with some refreshment. Over in the corner, busy with her pad and pencil is our wireless operator, Laura."

At the sound of her name the girl looked up and smiled, and by the time I had shaken hands with them she had closed her book and came forward to join us at the table. She shook hands with me, using both of hers, and squeezed her welcome without a word being necessary. The last person I faced was the man who had kept me company in the parlor. He did not appear to have a name, but had very black teeth.

The one who had made the introductions explained that he was Peter and that we all were in an area commanded by a man known as Ajax. Pierre and his family were very pro-British and risked their lives daily to help with the hiding of supplies, acting as go-between and providing shelter. His young daughter, Marie, had only recently grasped the significance of her parents' peril, but could be trusted within reason.

"I want you to know that you can speak freely in front of anyone in this room, including Marie," said Peter.

He looked at me and raised his eyebrows for some confirmation of understanding. I nodded and mentioned that I was hungry. Again, as if on cue, the food arrived, borne in by Marie, a cuddly seventeen-year-old. I caught her eye and she served me first. She returned with more food and wine, placing two bottles in the center of the table and one bottle beside my plate. I saw the look between her and Laura. It was Marie that blushed.

When she finally sat at the table with her own meal, I noticed she had changed her dress and her hair had been recently brushed. She left her seat on one occasion to refill my glass, to which I murmured, "Merci."

"No speaking French!" This from Peter. "Sorry, old chap, but you have to take out of your mouth each word and check it before you say anything on this job."

Suddenly, Pierre slapped his hand on the table. The noise startled me.

"Why does he not speak? How are we to know him in the dark?"

I made to remedy this by saying that my cover was—but Peter held up his hand.

"We know your cover, who you are, and that you can stammer your way out of trouble, but I see Pierre's point, so what about a drop more wine and tell us about your training? That is, when the table is cleared."

Pierre spoke quietly to his wife, and she and Marie took away the empty plates and coffee cups. Old "black-teeth" was dismissed and left by the back door. I noticed the icy blast of cold air as he closed the door.

So, there we four were: Pierre, Peter, Laura, and me, and they wanted an extract of my training experiences.

Why, I wondered? Surely they had their own memories. I decided on a humorous tale, had more wine, said to myself, "Which tale to tell?" I then went through many of the experiences related in previous chapters, which they appeared to consider either very funny or sad. All very flat, really, since they had their own fund of stories.

I was halfway through telling them about a parrot that had been born into a circus family when Laura suddenly held up her hand and silenced me. She went to her wireless and sat with her back to me. She appeared to be listening intently to a message through her headphones.

Pierre left the room, and again I felt the cold blast of frosty air enter the kitchen, or whatever they called the room we occupied. Peter quietly asked me if I knew what to do if ever I listened to the BBC? I replied that it was imperative to move the tuner off of the BBC wavelength and on to a French station. I added that I had been told of this in training and that many had been caught in the early days when the Gestapo switched on and heard an English program. He nodded and seemed pleased with my answer.

I then asked him if he would tell me something that baffled me. He said he would try; what was it? I did not find it easy to phrase my thoughts, but eventually asked how it was possible to operate in enemy-occupied country without being caught. After all, imagine it being reversed; would the Germans find it possible to do this in England?

He was quiet for some time before he answered, and even then found it difficult to muster his thoughts. When he did, he said he supposed it was not a fair comparison, since the fact that England was an island and if the Germans were in control it would mean the end of the war and a British defeat. Then he sparked up and did a bit of table-thumping, adding that this is precisely why we were here and I should not forget that, although we might feel alone, there were many people back at home who were with us in spirit and most anxious regarding our welfare.

I could only think that sitting in this French farmhouse was a very long way away from home, but at least I had some idea of the magnitude of the fight, and grew up a little bit more.

Suddenly, Laura switched off the radio, looked at Peter, and said, "Friday."

Marie cleared the table and returned to the kitchen.

Peter and Laura gazed at the door for a long time. I noticed Laura was drumming the arm of her chair with her fingers. Peter followed my train of thought. His look caught her eye, looked down at her hand, and her fingers relaxed.

Four knocks on the back door startled me. When I made to answer, Peter restrained me and held up a warning hand.

Four more knocks and my companions quickly rose, peeled back the sticky covering of the table, and withdrew what turned out to be a sketch. They motioned me to join them and briefed me with details of the factory and adjacent roads. After some twenty minutes, I was telling them my part of the operation. Again and again, I had to say my piece.

When they were satisfied I knew my part, Peter rolled up the plan and left the room. I heard him go upstairs. Laura and I smoothed out the table covering, sat down, and looked at one another. Suddenly she laid her hand on mine and looked almost lovingly at me. She was quite lovely, about my own age, twenty-four I guessed. Hair nearly shoulder-length, brown eyes, very white teeth, and clear complexion.

"Scared?"

•I nodded and sandwiched her hand in mine; it seemed to give me some kind of comfort.

"Do you trust us?" she asked.

"Yes, of course, but I put no faith in that gendarme bloke," I replied.

"Don't worry, he has been cleared; in fact, he has worked for us before. You must remember, none of us can operate without the cooperation of the French."

I nodded. "Are you Peter's woman?"

She laughed and withdrew her hand.

"Good lord, no. My man is a pilot. As a matter of fact, there are very few romances in the firm."

After a silence, she asked me again to tell her about my training. I dare say she thought it was a good ploy on her part to help me relax. I produced a bottle of wine that Marie had slipped me earlier and filled two glasses. Laura said it was not wise to drink after being briefed, in case we were suddenly called for action. I said to hell with that, we could see a lot of bottles out before Friday.

"I tell you what," I said, "I maintain I have a fair old sense of humor and I'll tell you about the French girl, already trained as a wireless operator, but not too good with the English lingo. You know, don't instead of do not, and "up the wall" for being frustrated, and so on. Well, I was killing time in London waiting to come out here, and I was told to help this Domonique with her everyday English.

"I had a bit of bother one day, having seen some Russian sailors. Don, as I called her, asked what the letters were around their caps—you can imagine, all XYZ. I explained that the letters were Russian and that the material was called a tallyband and that British sailors had RMS in English letters. I thought I had explained it very well, but she looked puzzled until, suddenly, her face lit up and she said, 'Ah, oui! Of course, we have French letters on ours!' "

Tears rolled down Laura's the cheeks as she laughed at this. I think the wine helped, too.

Peter reappeared from upstairs. He expressed his disapproval of our mirth, explaining that the Germans had the habit of wandering around at night.

Pierre entered through the back door.

"It's Friday," said Peter to Pierre's unspoken question.

"Bon!" He smiled at me encouragingly, and produced a bottle. I looked questioningly at Laura, and she responded, "Oh! well, it is cold outside, and Pierre has been on the lookout during the briefing."

Peter said it sounded as though we were rehearsing for a concert party, instead of a serious mission.

I spent the few days until Friday touring around the village, still dressed as an onion seller, my strings of onions almost covering the front wheel of my bike.

On Thursday, I was shown where to go if anything went wrong. I asked Peter if he could explain how it was possible to plan a raid and also plan for a failure, since no one was to know just what was likely to go wrong?

"Don't be so bloody awkward!" he snapped.

CHAPTER THIRTEEN

Friday came. The time to go was minutes away, and I hoped I could remember my tasks in the planned sequence. After all, the only people I had met were Peter, Laura, Pierre, and Pierre's wife and his daughter, Marie. I had been told that there were twenty Resistance members in the team to give us protection, but did they know me? Had they seen me on my onion rounds?

I had to stop thinking. Peter was staring at his watch, and suddenly he slapped my back, said, "Good luck. Let's go!"

It was fairly dark; our feet cracked the frost, and I remembered to walk with a slight stoop and out of step with my companions. No military habits now—except the self-discipline . . .

We were a silent trio as we walked along the road toward the factory. I wondered what it would be like to walk back. How could we ever get away with it? It was surely impossible.

All too soon, we were within the area. There was the wire fence. Then, without warning, Peter launched into a torrent of French, to which Pierre joined. Then they started fighting and shouting. They ignored my cries of dismay, and my stomach turned over when lights came on, dogs barked, and chains rattled.

Bayonets appeared and we were forced to enter the factory courtyard. All was confusion. Dozens of people emerged from the building, shouting in French or German. Peter and Pierre had their hands raised, while I had my cycle handlebars wrenched first one way, then the other. My onions went crazy.

Suddenly shots were fired. At once the shouting ceased; men ran off in different directions. I heard the voice of the gendarme nearby. He motioned me inside the building. I looked back and saw my two friends following, hands still raised. We were in.

More shots, a siren sounded, and then "Now!" from Peter.

I detached the string of explosive, ran into the workshop, and quickly identified the metal tube I had seen in the sketch.

The "onions," plus the time delays, went into that tube very quickly. I bent the metal delay to start the acid action and ran back to my prearranged position at the entrance, but there was no sign of Peter or Pierre.

My heart was thumping as I dashed into the darkest area, trying to search the gloom for my friends. Suddenly, there was an explosion behind me, followed by two more, and then, as if by magic, Peter and Pierre appeared out of the darkness, each squeezing an arm in recognition. There was a burst of machine gun fire, bullets whining very close. Instinct made me drop flat, but my colleagues pulled me up and dragged me along between them. We crossed the road, turned right down the lane I knew so well as the turnaround point of my walks.

"What about my bike?" I panted.

"Any explosive left on it?"

"No," I gasped, "I used all I had prepared."

"Then —k the bike."

I thought later those were the hottest six pounds of onions ever produced in France. But now there were transports arriving— German troops with coal-scuttle helmets sitting facing one another in open trucks. They looked most frightening and very confident; after all, they knew it was only a small force causing the aggravation.

We managed to make it safely back through the woods, entering the village from the other end. At last we made it into the yard of Pierre's house. We felt ten feet tall!

We burst into the kitchen and were greeted with the sight of a very distraught Madame. Pierre went to her at once. His face changed from elation to shock. His daughter Marie had disappeared.

Peter sent me upstairs to change my clothes, wash my hands, and remove all evidence of onions, etc. I had a good clean up, feeling that surely there would soon be a house-to-house search. I examined my French boots. The soles had a pattern which would be formed in the frosty road. I burned the soles as best I could.

Peter came in and said the gendarme had just called to take Pierre to the village for questioning, "Just to make it look good."

"But where is Marie?" I asked. He shrugged.

"Let me go back and look for her."

"No, don't make things worse; the main worry now is whether or not Laura can get through to report."

We did not eat that night. It was very cold with the atmosphere tense. I could hear Madame crying in her room.

In the morning, I went down to the kitchen and looked out into the yard. My chicken friends were having difficulty in pecking the ground. There was a maze of visible footprints and crisscrossed cycle tracks. One very clear tire track had a regular gap about every four feet and led alongside the house but not out of the yard gateway.

Madame appeared; she looked rough. Peter joined us, and we started a solemn meal. As we ate, the back door opened and in walked the gendarme. He spoke French and I was aware that both Peter and Madame looked at me.

After the gendarme had left, I said I was worried about my bike. I should still have it and take my onions for a walk to dispel any notion of my connection to the raid. But Peter waved that idea away, saying that the big worry now was the fact that Laura could not make contact with London nor with the local Resistance leader.

"We are to get a message soon from the group leader or he may even visit us here. Anyway, there is more you should know."

He then explained that my sabotage job was only a minor part of a major plan, and although well done so far, was useless.

"Unless the man we have rescued gets on the plane tonight it will all have been in vain, and we will have to scatter to avoid the Gestapo!"

"Which man?" I ask in alarm.

They explained that the Resistance had rescued a British agent who had been ill, nursed him to be fairly fit, and asked for the sabotage job to provide confusion during the landing and take off of a plane from a nearby landing strip.

It was all very involved, and my fear was of the Gestapo or police, in that order! Peter's worry, apparently, was Laura, her radio, Marie, and now Pierre, who was also missing. Also, Madame was hinting that she would no more help the Allies and would have to move, which was not easy, owing to work permits.

I slept little that night and, although scared for my own skin, forced myself to work out where Marie could be.

Next morning I walked into the yard and traced the track made by the cycle with the odd pattern. It looked as if the tire had something stuck to the tread. I examined the footprints. They were not clear, but at least they were all made by men's footwear. So, where were Marie's footprints?

I raced into the kitchen. Madame's face showed disapproval. I pointed to my shoes and said, "Marie." Her expression changed to one of alarm at the sound of her daughter's name.

I held both her hands to convey my friendliness. She relaxed a little and worked out I wanted to see all Marie's shoes, then realized that the shoes she wore "when taken" would not be in the house anyway. I went back to my room and laid down.

I must have dozed. Voices below roused me. I crept down the stairway, went in, and saw Peter, Madame, and two strangers, both in field clothing. They looked me up and down.

"These men are from a neighboring area," Peter said, "and have taken charge of our man due to fly out. We will take orders from them from now on."

I asked for a drink to get Madame out of the room and, as soon as she had gone, I quickly explained that I had an idea that might get our missing father and daughter back, and possibly get us a prisoner. But I would have to talk without the French lady being present.·

She returned with a bottle of wine, and much to my surprise, banged it on the table and did likewise to her door.

When the wine was poured, one of the strangers turned to me, saying, "I am Ajax and would be pleased to hear how you assess the situation."

I lit a French cigarette, had a cough, and explained that, in my opinion, the French policeman was not one hundred percent pro-British, in spite the assurance that he was, and that, as soon as he had got us into the factory for the raid, he came back here, took Marie by force, possibly carrying her on the handlebars of his bike. He took her to the Germans dealing with the raid and returned later, inviting her father to help look for her. But in fact, he had used the girl to extract information from her father. Something like that. I also said that if he, Ajax, or another of his choosing, would accompany me to the village, I would investigate my theory. Whoever went with me would have to speak French, since my cover was a stammer.

Ajax looked long and hard at me for some time.

"How long have you been in the organization?"

"Five months."

"This is your first op?"

"Yes."

He topped up my glass and said, "All right, you have two hours tonight and can try your luck with Cartier here," indicating his companion.

"During that period, we will endeavor to get our man away." He nodded to us all and left with Cartier.

I liked the look of Cartier; he was a man of about thirty, dark curly hair, five foot nine inches, and appeared to have had regular meals.

At dusk, he popped his head in the door and said "Ready?"

And we went.

I was wearing my onion-sellers kit, and with hands stuffed in my pockets, I led the way into the village. I said very quietly, "Did you know I have a very bad stammer?"

"Yes, so I believe, and you have the reputation of being useful in a certain Eastern art."

"You mean my liking for curry judo?"

"No, not really, but we had best be quiet now."

We turned left into the village. A Citroen was parked outside a house set back from the others. As we paused, I heard voices. One of them was the gendarme's.

I whispered to Cartier that I was going on a reconnaissance

behind the house, and that if anyone came along, he should take the line that he was helping me look for the poor onion-seller's bike that went missing on the night of the trouble at the factory.

"Be careful," he answered.

Sure enough, my bike was there in the yard at the back, both wheels buckled. Nearby was another bike. I felt around the front tire. Yes, there was an external patch! That proved my theory about the irregular pattern in the frost.

I made my way out towards the road and could hear loud voices—sounded like a row. I crept forward trying to get sight of Cartier, but it was too dark. I went forward and stammered a lot of rubbish. Cartier touched my arm and whispered, "Help me get these two out of the road."

I bent down beside him and discovered there were two bodies side by side in the middle of the road.

"Who are they?" I exclaimed. "Are they dead?"

"No, just asleep," he said, heaving up the shoulders of one.

"Let's take them in to the gendarmerie," I said. "Then we can have a look around."

"Christ! you are bloody mad."

"Yes, maybe, but I want to get that gendarme."

We went in twice with our loads. On the second struggle up the steps, we froze for two reasons. One was that we both heard the sound of an aircraft losing height, the other was that footsteps were approaching from upstairs. We parted either side of the gloomy hallway. A tall figure passed between us and stood in the doorway listening intently.

There was a quick swish of clothing, a thud and a groan with Cartier's voice saying, "And a copper makes three." He had chopped the policeman neatly from behind and caught him as he folded.

"A present for you—now what?"

"Come," I said and mounted the stairs two at a time. I did not know there was a turn halfway up and had a head-on collision with a wall. The noise I made was a blessing in disguise, for there was a moaning noise nearby. In a room, we found Pierre and Marie. He was gagged and tied hand and foot to a chair. The girl was lying on an old blanket, covered in blood, but alive.

Cartier untied the father and massaged his wrists and ankles while listening to a distressing account of what had happened. I found a taper and lit it. Cartier joined me and together we saw Marie's blouse ripped to shreds and one breast badly cut. Her eyes were closed and she was very pale.

I felt hot, cold, and sick all at once. Always work as a team, they said, unless you are a specialist; then you will have the backing of support. Well, I was the explosive wallah, but we needed a surgeon, blood transfusion, and goodness knows what else, not forgetting there were two unknown males down in the hall, plus one French policeman.

Suddenly I felt angry and no longer sick. I asked Pierre, "Who did this to Marie?"

"Gestapo and Francois," he said and clung to me and cried in a low, sobbing voice.

Back in my school days, they said we would be taught by Pitman's *French Without Tears*. They were wrong; I cried.

Cartier said he would try to find Ajax for help and would give the three bods a tap on the way out.

He did, too. I heard him.

I helped Pierre with his ankles and wrists, trying to get the circulation going again, but my sympathy was with the girl. I also thought of the three bodies down below—what if one of them were to come round and either escape or even attack us? Just to reassure myself, I crept downstairs and in the semi-darkness could just see them—very still.

Then I heard footsteps approaching and I melted into a dark doorway in the hall. There were voices whispering, and I recognized Ajax and Cartier. I joined them and saw they had a pram! No hood, just the body and some very bent wheels. They pushed past me, picked up the gendarme, and dumped him into the vehicle, head towards the handles and legs dangling over the front.

"Take him back to Pierre's house. Gag and tie him securely and put him with the chicken." It was Ajax speaking.

"Yes, sir."

"Don't call me sir!" Although whispered, the tone was sharp. "Now get going and bring back that contraption."

I made the 800-yard journey without incident, half expecting someone to see me at every corner and doorway. I heaved the policeman out of the pram, during which the thing fell over on its side. I dumped matey on to the straw, grabbed a long-handled pitch fork, and only just restrained myself from giving him an inoculation.

When I returned with the pram, the other two men had been trussed and gagged.

"Is he secure?" asked Ajax.

"Hell, no, I forgot."

Now, just in case the Archbishop of Canterbury reads this, I will refrain from relating his answer. But I will say I was dispatched back to the chicken house with all speed, with the words ringing in my ears, to "sit on him till I get there."

I cautiously opened the door. The chicken cackled a little. With the pitchfork I had a prod. Yes, he was still there, moaning quietly to himself, mostly, "Mon Dieu!"

There were footsteps outside and I held the fork in the on-guard position. The door opened and faint moonlight was reflected on the tines of the fork.

"Get him into the house and upstairs," said Ajax.

As I helped Cartier with our lanky load, I noticed several people in the yard, and to my unasked question, Cartier simply said, "Resistance."

Between us, we dragged the copper through the kitchen and up the stairs. On the way, I noticed they had brought Marie home and she was lying on a couch, being attended by a man I had not seen before. He took no notice of the two men on the kitchen floor, nor did he appear perturbed with Cartier and me heaving a slack body through the room and up the stairs with a British officer holding open the stairs door for us. I assumed it was a normal occurrence for him.

Upstairs, Ajax produced a bottle of wine. He, Cartier and I drank.

"Now, young man," he addressed me. "Have you ever sat in on an interrogation?"

"Only in training."

"Well, hang on to that bottle and drink up, for you have done a first class job, and no hard feelings on the way I spoke to you earlier." We shook hands.

Suddenly, his attitude changed as he turned his attention to the gendarme, Francoise. He held the Frenchman's jaw with one hand and shook it vigorously. The eyes fluttered open. Just then, Pierre opened the door and spoke a few words, which included the name "Marie."

"Go down and hold Marie's hand," Ajax said.

Below, the girl was sitting up with the aid of cushions. She was well strapped up across the chest and had a shawl around her. Although very pale, she managed a smile for me. Madame was there and she was all smiles and tears. She held me tight, murmuring, "Mon ami, mon ami."

Pierre did his French kissing bit, and in his best English explained how much they owed me for finding them and getting them out of the gendarmerie, adding, "It is not safe, mon ami; the Gestapo will be searching. You must hide."

"No, I take my orders from Ajax now."

Three things then happened all at once. Marie extended one arm toward me, Pierre slid a chair under me near Marie, and Madame produced some food.

Cartier appeared from upstairs and told me I had missed the "question-master" at work, but never mind, I would get another chance soon perhaps. I replied that Pierre feared the Gestapo making a search for us, to which he replied, "Never fear, you will be on your way back to London soon."

"Non, non," from Marie.

"Oui, oui," from Cartier, kissing her on the forehead.

I then noticed the absence of the two gents that had been under the table. Cartier explained that our doctor friend had taken them away to another village.

"If he is stopped, he will say they are ill and his papers will get him through a check."

Ajax nodded and said, "Well done. I feel we may work together again. Meanwhile, you will be pleased to know the doctor says that, although scarred for life, Marie will make a good recovery. The knife just missed the part that could have been fatal, some kind of artery, I don't know exactly. But she held out until she fainted. As a result of this mission being successful, with the main task of getting away an important man, plus the damage you did in the factory, we are withdrawing all Resistance contacts from this area, leaving Pierre and his family with a little more peace and a lot less worry. Your work, in connection with the gendarme, plus finding the others, will be noted in London. You will almost certainly get a cup of tea!"

We shook hands warmly and with Cartier made for the door. I followed them out into the crisp night air, asking, "Where is the bastard?"

"Back at police HQ Why?"

"I'd like to carve my initial on his chest."

"Leave that to the Milice," he said, and with one last slap on the back, he was gone.

Back in the kitchen, there were more bottles of wine on the table and Peter was once again in charge. He sat staring at his watch. He looked ten years older than a few hours ago and ten times more worried. Yet, we had done the job. Hadn't we?

Pierre spoke in French to Peter and I heard the name Laura. I had forgotten completely about her. Not surprising, really, as I was very confused as to what was going on.

It seemed that the gendarme put the Gestapo on to Laura, who somehow managed to avoid them getting her radio. They took her away on the night of the raid.

The doctor removed the wireless, along with his "bodies" and by now Ajax had contacted London and we waited here for a message. All the answers to these questions were given in a flat, expressionless tone by Peter.

Poor Laura.

I looked across at Marie. She was asleep. Her color was normal. She could have been my sister and I felt I matured a bit with that thought. It made me wonder why we were punished at school for some minor misdemeanor, yet that bloody man could get a British girl handed over to the enemy, stick a knife in a fellow countrywoman, and possibly get away with it.

I must have looked sullen after that and Peter noticed. He asked me what I was thinking. I matured a little more as my reply was almost authoritative and certainly confident.

"Peter, have you access to a quarter pound of P.E. and a pressure switch?

"No, but I could try and get it. Why?"

"I want those items now—tonight, before we leave."

Much to my surprise, Peter left the room without a word. He reappeared through the back door with a small canvas bag, which he placed on the table. The contents were exactly what I required.

"How long before we move out, Peter?" I asked.

"If they can fix the landing strip, it should be 02.15 hours."

"Good. Can I take Pierre down the road from about half an hour?"

"Why?"

"Oh, just to stretch my legs and have a last look round."

I winked at Pierre, who looked puzzled, but who, nevertheless, followed me through the door. The air outside was keen, the kind that made the eyes water.

We walked in silence toward the village. Suddenly, Pierre stopped and held my arm, saying, "It is dangerous for you to be here, mon ami. Why is it so?"

"I want my cycle out of the gendarmerie."

"Ah, oui, but why the explosive?"

I did not answer, but moved on. There was no time for talk and I knew it was a bit dodgy. We reached the police house. There was a dim light on one side of the house, but the alleyway leading to the rear yard was in shadow.

We crept into the yard and, sure enough, there was my bike, the wheels buckled so badly they would not turn in their forks. It had not been moved since the night of the raid. Pierre made to straighten them with his foot and made a noise. We froze, but all was quiet.

"Find the police bike," I whispered.

"Mon Dieu! You English!" was the reply, as Pierre moved

away to the back of the yard.

I took my explosive from my pocket lining and rolled the stuff into a sausage shape, thinking that the nervous tension that kept the body temperature high kept the material pliable.

Suddenly, Pierre touched my arm and whispered, "It is there."

I suppose he pointed, but I could not see in the dark. I followed and at last got my hands on the bike. I felt around the front tire and, yes, there was the external patch! I fed the P.E. into the tube of the saddle pillar and prepared the pressure switch. My hands were hot, but fairly steady; my heart was thumping and I feared I might fire the whole lot.

Pierre was shuffling beside me, feeling a bit edgy with nothing to do. One last feel and I was satisfied it was as good as I could get it. Pierre had held the bike fairly steady in spite of his agitation and he was no doubt relieved when I told him to put it back exactly where he had found it, but I think he nearly dropped it when I whispered loudly, "*Don't lean on the saddle.*"

I wiped my hands on the bag. They were quite damp and I felt a little ashamed of myself for being so nervous until I realized there here I was being a naughty boy and risking goodness knows what, whereas on the factory job I was under orders and had proper support. Anyway, it was a relief to walk softly out into the village, feeling I had revenged Marie to some extent. When we neared Pierre's house, a figure emerged from the darkness.

"Where the bloody hell have you been?" It was Ajax!

In silence, we entered the house, and once inside, Ajax ranted on about leaving without instructions, etc. "Had to stretch your legs and have a last look round! Do you think you are on the last day of your holiday? Do you realize you could knacker-up all our work and that of others to come? Whoever vetted you in London must be the biggest fool in the entire organization."

When he had finished, I looked at Pierre. He had his mouth open and was staring blankly at me, not the speaker! All of a sudden I relaxed and burst out laughing. Tears rolled down my cheeks and I felt in my pocket for the cloth I used as a handkerchief, after first removing the explosives bag.

When Ajax saw that, I thought he was going to burst. He waved his arms about and spoke in fluent French to Pierre who, when he could, said, "Oui—oui, oui—non—oui—non."

Madame appeared in her nightclothes and looked alarmed. After a word or two from her, the voices dropped to a more subdued level. Calmer now, Pierre spoke, and I could tell he was explaining to Ajax in greater detail the purpose of our little "walk." I watched Ajax as his eyes darted from the speaker to me and, near the end, I detected the flicker of a smile on the leader's lips. Pierre finished speaking with a typical lift of his shoulders, arms held away from his side. They flapped to his thighs in a final gesture.

Ajax gazed at his watch. Instinctively, I did the same and held out my wrist for Ajax to see. He nodded; it was 01.30 hours. Madame had returned with coffee for all. Pierre sat with his face in his hands. Suddenly, we were all very tired. In the half-hour we had been in the kitchen together, many words have been spoken, and all I had contributed was a long, uncontrollable laugh.

Ajax looked at me and said, "You have a lot to learn, young man, but channeled in the right direction, you may do well—I hope. In the meantime, remove all evidence of your stay here and leave quietly with the two men waiting outside. They will take you to the strip. Please wait with your escort until after the plane has turned. They will tell you when to approach the aircraft, which will be after a passenger has safely gained cover.

"Now go, and hope that whatever happens as a result of your reckless action, those of us who remain here for the next few hours or days will be able to move out safely from this area"

He turned his back on my proffered hand.

Pierre saw my emotion, and said, "I will go with you, mon ami."

Outside two figures joined us and we walked quietly along the path by which I had come a hundred years before.

Pierre said, "Why did you risk us?"

I replied with another question. "Do you understand all the English meaning of my language?"

"Mostly so, mon ami."

"Then I hope you know what I mean when I say that if a person runs with the fox and hunts with the hounds, he deserves to get his punishment."

We turned into the woody area near the strip, and I continued, "That police officer was trusted by the British and on the night of the raid, he played his part and got us into the factory. During the action, he decided to become a double traitor and, knowing you housed the raiders, took your daughter to the Milice. You went with him because you thought he was going to help you rescue her; instead, he used his police house to torture your daughter to attempt to make you talk. She could have died, since he also alerted the Gestapo, who no doubt would have treated her even worse. No Pierre, cutting a girl's breast is not "cricket" in my country. You understand?"

We were now sitting on the edge of the strip. The grass was damp, the clouds low, the moonlight subdued.

I continued, "I hope he goes over a nice big bump when he next rides his cycle. If you hear the bang, it will be for your Marie."

Pierre was silent; I could not see his face. I felt I had done enough and wondered just how much he understood and felt sick at the thought of myself as a murderer.

Someone with hearing sharper than mine suddenly made a move. Sure enough, the sound of a light aircraft grew louder. Torches forming one half of an arrow were switched on, and after a few moments, the plane was down.

I got my signal to go. Pierre ran with me. A figure with what looked like a hold-all passed in the opposite direction. I climbed into the plane, with Pierre crying and hugging me. As the last part of me was about to tuck in, he shook my foot.

The engine noise rose and I feared that all of France and Germany would hear. As we climbed, it looked like we were heading for some trees. I closed my eyes, and that did the trick. We missed them.

The ground looked very black down below, and my rescuer was not "Old Whiskers," who had brought me. This one said nothing at all. No matter. I was thinking of all that had happened—in only five days! I was hoping nobody borrowed the gendarme's bike. Too late now, unless Ajax had the device removed.

I closed my eyes, feeling I never wanted to do anything like this again.

CHAPTER FOURTEEN

Back in London, in a museum of all places, I sat in a small room and was asked questions regarding the operation. Every detail was required. Nothing was said about the booby-trap under the cycle saddle, but I knew they knew. No praise either. At the end, I was dismissed, but before leaving the room, I mentioned I had done my best.

My reward was, "Of course, dear boy!"

Shortly afterwards I was on leave at home. Dressed in civilian clothes, I walked the same route I took when I went to school, but this time my destination was the local pub. On the way I passed a large house now occupied by Canadian troops, two of whom are standing on the porch. As I came opposite them, a voice said, "No wonder we have to come over to a dump like this while guys like him dodge the war!"

That was 36 hours after Pierre had shaken my foot.

On returning from leave, I found many new faces in the museum: French, Canadian, and Polish, plus a few others I could not place at all. It was clear that we all were on the same "wavelength," but certain groups were in differing states of mind. Some were waiting for the word "go," the decision perhaps merely resting on the light of the moon many miles away. One of the things I really appreciated was that we showed our respect for each other by not asking questions.

The day following my return I was summoned to the "bass," and was pleased to see that Sue was still in charge of the tea-making department. When we met in the outer office, she grinned and shook her head slowly from side to side, which I interpreted to mean that she knew of the cycle saddle bit.

Then I was in front of the man himself and was prepared to get the biggest blasting of all, even worse than Ajax's. But no, he spoke in a very conversational manner, after shaking my hand. Not at all the same atmosphere that existed when he had shown the files in the steel cabinet. It was odd, really, but I felt he was not so much a superior as before.

After chatting about nothing, he asked if I read many novels based on spies and cloak and dagger themes. I said I had recently picked up the odd book passed on from other group members, mostly relating the adventures of Lemmy Caution and a few other characters from the pen of Peter Cheney.

The No. 1 said that, although that might be fiction, it was not, in fact, so far from the truth. He then became very confidential and said there was a very serious situation existing within the network in France. He went on to say that the SOE operators were limited by the members of the French Resistance available, and while they did invaluable work as a team, there was, nevertheless, a need for another force to execute specific tasks.

We had more of Sue's tea, and when she was gone, he said the Germans had been very successful in very quickly tracking down our men, and our force was becoming a mere fraction in effective numbers. It took weeks or even months for a man to "play himself in" and gain the confidence of someone who might be prepared to be a bit slack regarding integrity. And time was not on our side. However, a plan was being formed, he said, and I might find myself on a short visit to the north of France in the very near future, this time without any explosives. "It would be—well, just a little job."

He went on to explain that some Special Force had to exist that could be in and out before a lead could be gained, someone who could do the work without having to live the life of strain dodging the authorities. A nucleus of "daring madmen" and—suddenly a red light appeared on the desk. He picked up a phone and spoke a code name. The only word he said was "Roger."

I was asked to wait outside, but before I left I overheard him ask Sue for the next code name to be established.

The outer door opened, and in walked a man of about thirty. He was well built, about five feet ten inches, with dark curly hair, and a pleasant disposition, by my judgment. Without ceremony, he knocked and entered the top man's office. No waiting for "Come in" or for Sue to do the announcing bit. Straight in. I was invited to join the small gathering. The No. 1 introduced me to the man as "Tom," who shook hands as though he was suspended over a cliff and my hand was all that stopped him from falling.

The boss said he had every confidence in the pair of us but it was Tom who would be held responsible for the job. Then he added that if, for any reason, Tom was in any doubt regarding our ability to work together, I would not be going.

"But do a good job and you might well find yourself in a very select team of operators."

We were dismissed with the usual wishes of "Good luck" and "Keep in touch."

Outside in the street, both in civilian clothes, we walked out of step and silent. Tom was a little heavier in build than me, otherwise we were about the same type. He was also a few years my senior. In a Midland accent, he suddenly said, "Let's have a pint."

I let him pay. After all, he was senior. Not only that, he had the grip when he held anything, so he could carry the drinks to the table I selected near the window. I sat facing the door, so that I could observe anyone coming into the bar. When Tom arrived with the two pints of beer, he sat with his back to the entrance. I made a mental note that he did not follow the training in this matter, since he could have sat beside me.

I was determined not to speak first and looked out of the window at some workmen clearing rubble from the pavement. A cat roamed over the pile of debris. Perhaps that had once recently been its home.

Suddenly, my companion said, "I've read your file."

"Have you?"

"You have a high sense of moral values."

"How do you mean?" I asked.

"You don't approve of people getting their chests cut."

"Oh! that—well, do you?"

"No, but there is no room for individual revenge in this firm. If you work with me, I want it clearly understood that if someone does the dirty on us, don't try and put it right—just do the job and get out."

"I can't promise that," I replied. "If anyone had a go at me and wins, you are telling me you would let it go? If so, you may as well get yourself another sidekick. If I decide I am on the same frequency as someone, then I stick. I'll say when I change my mind, and that will be only because you have said or done something that militates against my principles. I'll buy you a pint and we will be all square."

"You still have a lot to learn, but 'Cheers' anyway."

He lowered his drink by half, but he was smiling now and produced a packet of Players cigarettes.

"I get you all right, and like what I see—don't you wish to know anything about me?" he said,

"Only your specialty."

"Will a forger do?"

"Well, yes, it makes a pleasant change from noisy bangs, but I know nothing other than in the training about forgery."

"You don't need to. You are required to go with me to Cherbourg and leave a piece of paper behind—that's all."

"It's a bloody big piece of paper if it needs two of us!"

He smiled at this, and I felt a definite liaison between us. I was still smiling as he went to the bar. I relaxed at last, no longer on the defensive—but what did I see? Tom had three large whiskies in his hands. He dealt them out and one of them was in a position that would be natural for a third person sitting between us.

"Cheers," says Tom, and seeing me puzzled added,

"Go outside and ask that chap with a newspaper if he would like a drink with Tom. Well—go on then."

I looked sideways at him, half expecting him to turn into a pumpkin, but went outside, and foolishly said to a scruffy looking individual, "Er, excuse me, but Tom asks if you would care for a drink?"

In a beautifully refined accent he replied, "I'd be delighted, dear boy!"

After two pints followed by the whiskey, I saw things in a much clearer light, as I listened to the chat between these two, who obviously knew each other very well. But I felt a little upset, having watched the door but not the window. What a hell of a lot there was to this lark! I felt ready for anything and was not listening to the conversation going on, although I noticed it stopped when a car-man called at the table to collect the empty glasses.

I looked out of the window. The workmen had gone, but the cat was still there. Having a wash, no doubt smartening up for when his missus came home.

Suddenly, "old scruffy" rose, shook hands with Tom, and I, and left us alone.

"No more booze for you, my lad," says Tom, "but we will see what can be done at my place."

A short bus ride and a walk found us at the rear of a line of terrace houses. I followed Tom through a back yard into a house that was very untidy and then up some stairs into a room that was a complete contrast—very nicely furnished with good quality stuff. I said as much, and he winked and nodded towards a drinks unit. As I made my way over, I noticed a framed Indian ink sketch in over the "bar."

I asked if it was a good one, and he replied that it should be, as it was his own work. I let him know I, too, was keen on that type of work. I felt another bond between us forming and nodded agreement when he excused himself, saying, "Pour us a couple of drinks." I did this, and with my small whiskey, I again studied the line drawing, noting that it was dated 1938.

Suddenly, my head was jerked back and held. I felt a sharp blow to my spine, followed by an arm being twisted and forced up high behind me with the resultant collapse on my knees. I felt my senses slowly going and knew I had to do something. Where the hell was Tom? The stranglehold was getting tighter. I had to act quickly, and bending forward and sideways, I made a grab at my assailant's hand and luckily got a hold. Forcing two fingers apart and back, the pressure around my neck was relieved. I fell on top of the man. He yelled and I was just about to chip him when I saw it was Tom.

All this took only a few seconds, but the explanations lasted well into the evening, with Tom massaging his fingers and me doing neck exercises. Tom explained that whenever he had to work with someone new, he found it paid to get some idea of their reflexes, hence his attack on me from behind. It seemed he once had to watch a colleague be strangled simply because the reflexes were slow and his pal was too trusting and slack with his own discipline.

"Will I do?" I asked.

"Yes, you bloody well will!"

He then outlined the entire plan.

He and another would be backing me all the way, it seemed, but he would not tell me exactly what I had to do, when to do it, or where it would be done. I had to be satisfied that the less I knew the better the chance of success. But, and what a *but*, there would be no false papers, no cover, no false identity, and so on.

"If you are caught, you are on your own!"

"What about you?" I asked.

"Don't worry about me, I have friends and contacts."

"Well, then, why the hell don't you do the job yourself? You seem to have all the necessary help."

"Because I have friends and contacts. You are not known, so I can back you."

So began the story of my first operational drop by parachute.

CHAPTER FIFTEEN

There is no doubt about it, everyone is scared. Even experienced people get the jitters, and that includes the instructors who to some extent tense up.

I lost count of the number of times I found myself tugging my static line clip to make sure I was hooked on, and Tom, who seemed to disregard his line once hooked, was constantly checking his harness. Then the light went on and Tom went out and so did I— the icy blast, followed by the thump when the canopy opened; the crazy swing and the strain of looking into the darkness ready to brace for the landing; the hope that there would be a magic mattress. Then the ground that comes up—too fast—and the knees bend, and then the fall sideways and the grab for the lines to smother the air-filled monster that opened when it should, thanks to the packer, perhaps a young girl—no doubt very pretty—the quick rolling up of the life-saver and looking for a place to hide it, hoping no one heard a British plane arrive over an open space, linger, turn, and head back home.

Then Tom's voice, "Come on, let's get away from here."

The dock area was a maze of shipping gear. That surprised me, as I imagined the enemy would have taken all metal objects for salvage; but no, there were more heaps of metal than enemy personnel, very few of them in uniform, thank goodness.

Not far from the dock were many unoccupied houses, this no doubt owing to the proximity of the target area, but it was in such a place that Tom and I made contact with a man known as Landau, who obviously knew Tom very well. He said nothing to me, just set off along the street, followed by Tom, who, after a few yards, beckoned me to follow. We finished up in the basement of a very occupied building. I say that because the kitchen was a shambles, with piles of dirty crocks on the draining boards. The room was hot and stuffy, the air was a mixture of stale smoke, cooking aroma, and strange smells. I assumed it was some kind of boarding house or pension.

Someone produced coffee laced with rum in small glasses. Very good. It was followed by fried eggs and French bread. Very tasty!

I felt strangely confident. I had no idea of the part I was to play, although I knew the overall plan. I had a smoke and watched some overweight females enter and leave the kitchen through two large swing doors. The doors were polished in one place from the women's habit of opening them with their backsides. They had no "rule of the road," and sometimes would sandwich a door between them, with a resultant torrent of abuse toward one another. This constant procession amused me, but I wondered why Tom and I were ignored. I also wondered why I was not scared and had to admit that Tom exuded great confidence. Even so, I could not help asking if the building we were in was a hotel.

He laughed and said, "You'll see!"

Landau reappeared shortly and had a few quiet words with Tom, who went to the door and motioned me to follow. We went up the basement steps to the pavement. It was nearly dark and I kept close to Tom. My confidence slowly faded now that we were in the street, and it disappeared altogether when we passed two German soldiers, who were talking and smoking. The rifles slung on their shoulders looked frightening, but we passed them without incident. I tried to get an idea of my bearings, but could not see any particular features and gave up all hope of ever returning to the house we had left.

After two right turns, I reckoned we must be almost outside the front of the building. Pleased with this deduction, I nearly found myself alone with the crowd, for Landau suddenly dived into the "public gents," which consisted of an iron screen in a near circle shape with a gap of about two feet from the ground and chopped off at shoulder height.

I did not wish to "go," so I stood in a convincing attitude. Landau, however, appeared not to have been for several weeks!

Tom touched my shoulder and pointed, indicating the front of the house, which had a large porch-like entrance, under which glowed a dim, red light. So that was my guest-house.

Visitors to the toilet were in and out and I was sure that at least two of them were Miliciens (similar to Gestapo, but French); a sort of sixth sense, I suppose. But at last the three of us were alone. It was then that Tom gave me an envelope, saying, "Put this in your inside pocket, and in another pocket keep this money. There is 150 francs and some loose coins."

"What now?" I asked apprehensively.

"When I tell you, go into the foyer. In front of you there will be the pay-box with the Madame in charge. Ignore her, except to smile. Note the position of the staircase, and enter the room on the left at the foot of the stairs. Go to the end of that room, but do not hurry. Take a seat as close as possible to the trio playing music. Girls will approach you and encourage you to buy drinks; you can "Non-non," can't you?"

"Yes."

"Well, wave your arms about a bit and get rid of the girls, but sit tight. The risk is that a German patrol may appear, in which case you play it by ear."

It was a strange place to be briefed, because, apart from the drafty screen around us, every time someone came in to relieve himself, Tom stopped speaking. I thought of the stories I had heard of agents being given instructions in haylofts somewhere and bathrooms in London. I appreciated they were proper agents, and this made me wonder all the more what I was by title. A bloody fool?

"Well, what do I do and where will you be?" I asked.

"I'll be nearby, don't worry. Just wait for a girl to make you a private offer and go with her, probably to a place out of sight of the Madame. Anyway, go now and the best of luck."

"Hey! hold on a minute. Since when have the females joined in this lark?"

I was annoyed at this, but Tom was angrier. He told me sharply to "get cracking" and realize that the less I knew, the better.

I crossed the road into the unknown—hurt by the sharp tongue belonging to the man I would never give away—and I was at the entrance.

It was as I had been told. The Madame was in her pay-box, looking like she wore a mask. As I passed her to enter the room on the left, I saw it was very bad makeup on her face and her smile did not look very sincere.

At the far end of the room a trio of musicians were playing in waltz time. I took a seat near them, facing the way I had entered. A quick glance around the long room revealed several sofa-type pieces of furniture, most of them occupied by French soldiers with girls evidently encouraging the men to be unfaithful to their wives. There appeared to be a continual flow of wine being bought, and then suddenly two girls appeared and suggested that I go with them.

I was on the point of doing so, when another girl appeared, spoke sharply to the girls, and took their place as they moved off the seat. The new girl was considerably smarter in dress, cleaner, and, in fact, very attractive. She wore a gray skirt and a pale lemon, sleeveless blouse. She signaled to a young lad who, after a moment, arrived with a tray with two glasses and a bottle. I was tensed up and watching every move. I noticed some of the men looking at me with some kind of envy. Little did they know. Come to that, little did I know.

So far the girl had not spoken, but she poured two drinks with a steady hand. I noticed a thin bracelet slip down one arm to her wrist as she moved.

She handed me a glass. I raised it and quietly murmured, "Merci." To which she replied, "Up the Arsenal."

I nearly choked—beautiful English. She slapped my back. I drank. It was a very pleasant taste, rather like a liqueur, and I sipped some more.

The girl spoke again. "Excuse me for not drinking; it will be a long night and I am fed up with the booze, understand?"

I nodded. The accordionist started to play

"How would you like to be down by the Seine with me?" she said, right in my ear.

I suddenly felt as if I was down three days with the "flu." It was hard to focus and my head felt heavy.

The girl leaned close and said, "If you feel rotten, it is probably the lack of fresh air. Come and lie down for a while—you'll soon feel better."

She unbuttoned her blouse and fanned herself. I dimly heard whistles from the men as I staggered up some stairs, knowing I was drugged but unable to fight it. Someone laid me on a bed. It was soft and comfortable. My feet were lifted. I was lying flat and I went to sleep.

My head ached. I tried to open my eyes. They didn't seem to work very well. I could hear music. Where the hell was I?

I eased myself up on one elbow. The room was lit with about the light given by a candle. There was a figure sitting near me. It was the girl who had given me the drink. She came over and sat on the bed.

"How are you?"

I pointed to my head and she smiled and invited me to speak.

"Have a few words—in English—have a bloody good swear!"

"Well then, get me some strong coffee, six or seven cups of it—whoever you are."

"Ah! a south of England accent," she said. "How lovely, I was at school near Horsham. Hold on, I'll organize some coffee."

As she stood, I noticed she was topless. I realized just how effective the drug had been.

She pulled on a jumper and left the room. As soon as the door had closed, I made to get off the bed, but what a set of fireworks exploded in my head. I settled for the head between the knees position. Then there were voices. The girl was back with coffee; her companion was Landau. The drink made my heart bang and I shuddered as I drank. Then, for the first time, I heard Landau's voice.

"Did she take it?"

The girl said, "Yes," and at the same time asked, "Take what?"

"The envelope has gone as we thought, but the money was not taken."

I felt in my pockets and pulled out the bundle of notes.

The girl held out her hand. I looked at Landau, who nodded. The girl took the money, tucked it in the front of her jumper, smiled at me, and said, "Well done and good luck."

She went to the door, turned and smiled at Landau, blew me a kiss, and was gone. Not very much made sense to me at this time, in spite of the benefit from the coffee, but I had enough wits to know that there were some very interesting things in that jumper.

Now I had to get some sort of explanation and asked Landau what had happened. He replied that Tom would tell me; in the meantime, I was to follow. As we went down some stairs, the music became louder. The air was thick with tobacco smoke. Grins and leers from the men as I followed Landau past the Madame and out into the cold night air. I was unsteady on my feet and what those men thought was not what I thought.

The cool air did a lot to restore my senses. I realized I badly wanted to "spend a penny" and made my way towards the iron screen. Inside a young man was being sick and that made me sick, some of it going on Landau's trousers. What he had to say about that was a very long sentence—so long, in fact, that I had finished all my little jobs and was feeling better before he had exhausted the French vocabulary. Another man walked in and apparently asked what the trouble was. Landau started all over, and the newcomer tut-tutted at the soiled trousers, turned to the French lad, and booted him up the behind. He fell into the drain and rolled out under the screen.

After a short walk, we were joined by Tom, who asked how I felt.

"Bloody awful," I replied, "and not the slightest idea of what happened, nor why I had to do whatever it was I had done."

"You did exactly what was required, but the reason you have not been told of the purpose is so that you cannot talk. That is why you were drugged by Sally. Come on, let's get out of here. You'll be pleased to know we are going home by boat—I hope."

We did, too, but I was so woozy that I cannot remember much about the journey, except climbing down a rope ladder and getting into a boat, but whether that was the French or the English end, I cannot tell to this day.

I do recall the debriefing, with this time a few words of praise. The officer asking all the questions seemed a little bothered that I could not remember much after being put to bed so, since he was in a nice safe job while I was at risk, it was natural for me to ask him to explain exactly why there had to be anybody at all taken to France, drugged, laid on a bed, revived with coffee, and brought home. What the hell for? If it was just to let the enemy have a fake list of names to give them a lot of time-wasting work, why not just drop the list in the street, or plant in a place where it would be found and investigated?

He said that if it were necessary for me to know, I would be told at the museum. I asked Tom the same question and he was much more helpful. He suggested we had earned a pint. I settled for that!

Both Tom and I were at the museum next day, and much to my delight, so was Sue—and her tea. And the boss, bless him. He seemed to get friendlier each time we met. I really thought that the extreme accolade must be to walk in on him without knocking.

He knew of my question to the debriefing chappie and at once gave a satisfactory explanation. Briefly, it was that Landau was a Resistance man of high integrity, Tom was "our man in the North of France," and Sally was, in fact, a FANY who had been educated in France at a finishing school, and had elected to stay over there when the war started. Her mother was French and her father, who was English, had something to do with the War Graves Commission between the war. The reason for the operation was that (a) it would give me some experience, (b) it enabled Tom and Landau to observe which of the girls the enemy sent to relieve me of the paperwork, and (c) the lads working under Landau could follow the girl and see how she dealt with her list of names and to whom she made contact. Sally, the topless one, was "friendly" with both sides, and tipped off the girl working for the common enemy that a visitor would be in the brothel that particular night, and so on.

After a few words of praise, Tom and I were dismissed and had a few more beers before parting for the night. He told me he could not wish for a better partner and hoped I felt no offense with his method of testing me. He added that, to many, the episode with the bike saddle was a big joke, but Ajax had ordered the cycle to be removed from service. Tom added that Ajax regretted his action later, when he learned the gendarme had handed over three female wireless operators to the enemy. Ajax shot him dead.

Apparently my stock in this elite organization was quite high so far, so when Tom said, "Have another, then we will call it a day," I responded, "Good night Mr. Perkins."

He nearly exploded. "How did you get hold of that name? Have you seen my file?"

"No, but I remember the sketch you have in your room. It is signed with your name!"

Tom said something to the effect that I would do, and we went our respective ways. We had a week off from possible duty, and before that week was up I learned that I was a half of what had become a new "Secret Weapon"—*The Terrible twins*!

CHAPTER SIXTEEN

After a good night's sleep, I wandered down to the East End, near Bethnal Green, and found a pub that did a meal. I had planned going to the Windmill to see a show, but always backed out, promising myself that particular pleasure as a form of celebration one day.

Back in the pub, I ordered a meal and settled down with a pint. I sat facing the entrance near the door that led to the private part of the pub. Through this door, I heard voices that grew louder and louder. Suddenly, the door burst open and out shot a man, a suitcase, and an overcoat. Toilet tackle skated across the bar floor, followed by a lady who owned the female voice I had heard. She told the man to go away, not those exact words (just in case the Archbishop does read this).

She then opened the street door and kicked the items out onto the pavement. As I watched this, I thought how nice it was for someone else to have a problem for a change.

I was in civilian clothes, and this fact was noted by the "center forward" as she approached the private door.

"You look like another bleedin" spiv. My boy had to go to help keep dodgers like you safe at home."

I was pleased with myself, as I felt my natural defense quickly give way to my newly-acquired nature, and feeling not at all offended, quietly asked the lady which service her son had joined.

"Army, of course."

"Which regiment?"

"London Irish."

"So am I," I lied.

She calmed a little. I drank up quickly, saying I would not be long and left the pub.

Believe it or not, I was training. I was using this kind of incident to practice gaining someone's confidence. I would give myself marks of—Good, Bad, or Hopeless— at the end.

I took a short walk down the street, looked at my watch, paused, then slowly retraced my steps to the pub. When close enough, I made a mental note of the name on the sign. A quick glance up to the top of the door gave me the name of the licensee, although the sign was faded and faint.

Back in the bar, I ordered another beer and sat down at the same table I had previously occupied. When the "footballing" lady appeared with my food, she called out to the man behind the bar saying, "'Ere is that one I said about who said he was in the same lot as our boy."

I spiked a couple of meatballs, and asked, "Is his name Hardman?"

"Yes—that's 'is name, you know 'im then?"

"I think it must be because he said he lived with his parents at a pub called The Wheatsheaf."

"'Ear that 'arry—'ear that. This young bloke knows our Charley, don't yer mate?"

"Oh, yes, I know Charlie; that is why I called, but when I sat down you were busy kicking out another spiv, so I said nothing."

"You ain't no spiv mate. Not if you knows our Charley, is 'e 'arry?"

The man joined us. "You AWOL then?"

"No," I replied, "got a civvie pass. Been sick."

"Oh! 'ave some apple pie, Dearie?"

"No thanks, must be going. I'll tell Charlie I've met you."

I slipped a shilling under my plate and stood up, ready to leave.

"You don't 'ave ter pay," they said, and went through the bit again about knowing our Charley.

I asked if they had a message I could pass on, secretly hoping it was not likely to be of any great importance. Yes, they said, tell him we've had another gassey.

"A what?"

"A gassey, mate. Don't cher know what a gassey is?"

"Well, no, I don't"

"That geezer I kicked out 'ad stayed 'ere for two nights, and pinched all me money out of the gas meter. 'e's dunnit before, only 'arry, so bleedin' soft, lets 'im in again."

"Oh! well," says Harry.

"I'll give you 'Oh well,' my lad, now I've lost me rebate, the gas don't work proper anyway 'cos of the low pressure and you won't be gettin' any dinner mate."

I left them to it and made my way to a bus stop to get back West. I awarded myself a fairly good mark, burped a couple of times as my stomach became accustomed to the meatballs with beer, and noticed a commotion near the bus stop. Getting closer, I could see a policeman struggling with a man. The crowd was increasing and some of them were telling the lawman to "leave 'im alone." I joined in the throng and guess what? He was the "Gassey."

I could see the copper had one side of his handcuffs locked but not the other, and the gassey was flailing his arm around, using the metalwork as a weapon. I made a dive and put my foot behind his knees. He lost his balance and sank down to the ground. The copper said, "Thanks mate," and click, the cuffs were on.

The small gathering booed this and I felt the atmosphere could become hostile. Not only that, I should not risk getting into any kind of trouble, so without too much thought, I found myself saying, "Take this one to the station; I'll see you there later."

Much to my surprise the policeman saluted, and said, "Right, sir!"

The crowd parted respectfully and let me through, all five foot eight and one-half inches of me!

I awarded myself a good smile and a few more marks.

CHAPTER SEVENTEEN

It was nearly time to be at the place arranged for a possible meeting. At the arcade near Trafalgar Square, I waited for a contact to be made. A newspaper man called out with regular timing, "*Star-Standard*—real all a'baht it, 'itler 'opping mad." This went on all the time I was strolling up and down the arcade and I recall thinking a guise such as paper-seller would make a good cover for passing messages, and after allowing an extra half-hour in case my contact had been delayed for some reason, I at last bought a paper and made my way towards my abode.

Security prevented me from writing home, and knowing I had time to myself until the next evening at the same place, I made slowly for the mobile canteen staffed by those very brave ladies of the WVS.

I contemplated my cup of tea. My mind was clear of all concern except for my parents and sister. They lived in the country, but nevertheless in a vulnerable area, being near a fighter station and a Fleet Air Arm base. I also spared a thought for our black cat. He was a good friend, always clean, very affectionate, and judging by his purrs, grateful for his food. And very amusing. I had no doubt that at that very moment he was fast asleep—with one eye open. But whatever he was doing, he caused a lump to come into my throat.

"Come on, cheer up Dearie, it can't be as bad as that."

I awoke from my thoughts and had another cuppa. But the mood persisted. Why was I here? I had joined the Army as an ordinary soldier, was part of the British Expeditionary Force, and endured the rigors of that very cold winter of 1939-40, got my head and one leg bandaged, and returned to Blighty via Dunkirk. Had rapid promotion to sergeant, became instructor at a training battalion, and then it was all different. I was not in the Army; I was not myself. I was whatever some group of people thought I was. One thing for sure, I was leaning against a vehicle in very dim London, holding a cup of tea. Had I really been to France after the Germans had secured occupation? Did I actually prepare a deadly booby-trap to blow the guts out of a man who did not play to the rules, only to later learn he was saved from my punishment by a British officer, allowed to go free so that he could endanger the lives of English girls, then be shot by the same officer?

Had I really walked a string of explosives disguised as onions around a French village, stuffed some of it up a pipe in a factory, and done it a bit of no good? And had this interference with the occupation routine caused enough chaos to enable an Englishman to be rescued? That is what I was told. So what the hell was I doing leaning against a tea-wagon in London in the dark? People were dashing along to their homes. Homes? Yes, they had homes, like bloody rabbits, in their burrows, provided by the underground rail system. Nice cozy concrete mattresses, tiled toilets, plenty of stale air blown down the tunnels, nice stairways for old folk to practice going down instead of up to bed, stairs that were ideal for GPO messengers to take telegrams to folk who, because they were British, laughed, until they opened the envelope: "The War Office regret to inform you that . . . ."

I took my cup back to the serving area, and strolled in the direction of my bed. I caught up a group of men who were playing dodge the blackout with a pub entrance. I caught the eye of the last man going in, and followed as he held open the door.

The men I had in front of me apparently knew each other and were also known to the landlord. I was odd man out, which was ideal for my new profession, except that I had to bear in mind the advice that it was best to give the impression that one was not in the Secret Service.

My pint of Ind Coopes old ale was dispensed with a smile by a pretty girl. I took it to a table and made up my mind that, if anyone questioned my solo presence, I would be waiting for a friend. That seemed to work very well, since everyone was apparently waiting for someone. My seat was on the route to the gents, and as the men passed they would remark, "She won't be long mate," or, "Drink up and forget her, she won't come now."

The barmaid collected a few glasses from the ladies who were keeping the gin firms solvent and brought me a full pint of "old." Apparently it was free, from her to me. This system was maintained until closing time. Then she said that if I would like to bring my drink through, I could have a bite to eat with the family. I offered to pay for the drinks, but she said forget it. I was doing fine with my own thoughts until one of the gin brigade treated me and insisted I drank with her. That was fatal, and I knew it would be as soon as I tasted it, for gin makes me very morbid, and does not mix well with my beer. It seemed an age before the landlord called "time."

Instead of appraising myself, as I had with my cup of tea, I went back to the Training Battalion days and the bloody gin took control, as I feared it would. I went back to the last night in the sergeants' Mess. They had no idea of my impending move. Come to that, neither did I, as it all happened in one day. But the night before, everyone was in good spirits. Even the RSM was present, with a glass.

It was all so clear—the small serving hatch with a bar top just large enough for two pint glasses and two elbows. The old piano and the equally aged pianist. The dart board, the wireless that was loud and clear at news-time—if the sergeant.-majors' shooshed everyone to be quiet—the window overlooking the barrack square, and across the hall, the dining room, that on alternate Friday nights became a small dance floor, where guests and members' wives could enjoy a few hours relaxation, everyone treating the other with the greatest respect. Where I, as emcee, would do my best to keep things going, and enjoyed the link with the six-piece band of semi-professional musicians led by a pianist who played mostly with his eyes closed, but opened them when I indicated there were six pints of beer down near the loud pedal.

Feeling close to tears, I went into the gents' to avoid breaking down in front of the other drinkers, but I was not alone. Two men were chatting about some mushrooms, and then the air-raid warning sounded.

The anti-aircraft guns started thudding and we all knew by instinct that the dreaded noise of bombs screaming through the air was shortly to come. And it did—a stick of four passed over the pub and crumped their destruction about three-quarters of a mile away. Then, with a jangle of bells, the rescue lads went to work.

I forgot about my memories when I left the gents' and heard a man saying, "Bloody Jerries! I'll have to go Charlie. My missus gets in such a state, she nearly goes mad. Only tonight I said to her, I said, 'Why don't you have a bottle and get pissed,' I said, 'then you won't get so flaming worked up.' But no, not 'er, won't touch a drop. That's the trouble; I go 'ome half cut and not carin' and she is all sober and scared, so we argue. Well, got to go, see you in the mornin'. Goonite all."

It signaled a general drink-up and a scamper for home; it was closing time anyway. Everyone shared a common thought. Scared, apprehensive regarding their own safety, and concern for dependents, with hate for the man in Berlin, who had bred the philosophy that if you are due to cop it, then you will. Loosely called fate by some of the upper class. Man-made bloody indiscriminate slaughter, I called it.

I did not have an un-expired portion of beer to carry through to the pub folks private part, so the girl gave me a new one. I went through the bar flap into a small room where a table was laid for three. The smell of something frying was a pleasant change from the thick tobacco smoke in the bar. It appeared that the room was not normally very tidy, but conditions had been made worse by the vibration of the nearby bomb explosions. Cursing Hitler, the tubby landlord picked up various scattered oddments.

Spam, sausages, and two eggs each had been frying. The man and his daughter had plain bread. I had butter. I asked if she had any sauce. While she was out of the room, I switched her plate with mine and winked at the man. The sauce arrived and I shook the bottle and offered the girl first go. She had a little; I had a lot. She cut her bread and butter and implored us to start. The landlord looked a thank-you at me and then loud and clear the sirens sounded the all-clear. Those who were not killed or injured relaxed and London lost the sick feeling. For a time. Until they came back. And they would.

When the girl realized she had bread and butter, said she was sorry, she intended for me to have it—must have laid the table wrong—not in the habit of having one extra— fed up with the bombing—wished Dad would pack up the pub, then they could go back to Kent.

"What is the use of going back there?" Dad said. "The Jerries fly over our old place to get up here. It's just as bad. Anyway, there is too much to remind us of your Mum in that house."

I looked in silence as these two sorted out their problems and a sense of admiration grew as they went through the jobs to be done tomorrow: mend the black-outs, chase the brewers, try to see Steve for some whiskey, and try to get a few more glasses. The girl must really try to see poor old Mrs. Maxwell—all three sons killed and she herself in hospital with a leg injury, but cheerful with her knitting when she can get enough wool. And meals for old Mr. Dixon. Go to that shop up West on Saturday and try to get those clothing coupons back that the stupid girl tore out of the book—three too many she took. Course it was dark in the shop.

As a serviceman, I had none of these problems, and I learned a lot by listening to these two. It made me feel all the more bitter about war and all the more determined to do my bit. But how? Then they turned to me and said they were sorry to "crack on like that, so what about a nice cup of tea?"

As I enjoyed my tea, I felt awkward having to lie about not being in uniform. I claimed my name was Roy and that I was on leave from the Merchant Navy. They accepted all that and I steered the conversation away from me and back to the landlord.

He had been in the Army. Did most of his time and finished up in Quetta. Was there when the earthquake split the place apart, got discharged with a leg injury. Worked on a hop farm in Kent, was married, and lost two babies at birth. When the war started, his wife came to London and lived with her sister. They both drove ambulances. One night, during a raid, a wall fell onto an ambulance, and that made the landlord a widower.

The telegram that gave him the news was a permanent trea-
sure in his wallet. As I read it, I could feel he wanted to talk. I was
pleased to listen. I knew it helped. The problem arose when he, Bill,
had his daughter, Jane, bring in a very precious bottle of Scotch and
some cigarettes. All this gave Bill the fire he needed for his talk. For
me, it was a question of punishing my innards. On top of beer, I had
had gin, tea, and now whiskey. Thank goodness for the meal to help
the drink.

I felt a fraud being called Roy and did not always respond
quickly when they mentioned the name, but I felt very humbled as
they unfolded their story, and I very much admired the way they
respected each other as they alternated their conversation, each nodding agreement with the other.

Four years after being married, Bill and his wife had lost two
babies and had tried to adopt two older children. This was not to be,
owing to the war starting, but they were able to accept two girls who
were evacuated from London. These children were happy on the farm
in Kent and Bill and his wife grew very attached to them.

Late one evening, a police officer called to tell them that the
children's parents had both been killed in a raid. The authorities made
the necessary arrangements and Bill was now as near to a real father
as possible for a short time.

When the Germans started the VI (Doodle-bug) rocket attack, nearly all of the part of Kent that was on the way to London was
now a dangerous area. Since Bill occupied land in this sector, he
found that his new family were going to be evacuated to Canada.
The tearful farewell was indeed good-bye. The Germans torpedoed
the ship carrying hundreds of children and the couple were alone
again, with two spare beds and lots of photographs.

To try to forget, his wife joined her sister as an ambulance
driver. The telegram that announced another episode of sadness for
Bill lay on the table as the story was told, and I noticed that when
either of them spoke, their eyes were fixed on that piece of paper, as
though they were talking to it.

I followed the story in silence. The whiskey bottle was only
half empty at this stage of the narrative and I was puzzled as to how

the pretty young lady on my left became a part of the family.

The story was that she had appendicitis and was in the ambulance on the way to hospital. The ambulance was doing fine until a stick of bombs imploded and blocked the road. When the driver reversed and mounted the pavement to turn around, a delay fuse fired a bomb and a wall collapsed, killing the driver. The patient was transferred to another vehicle with her nurse and was saved. When Bill sorted it all out, he found he was the only visitor at the girl's bedside. She said she had lost her father at Dunkirk and her mother had gone away with another man earlier in the war. She loved her dad—really loved him.

She took up the story.

"He went over to France early in 1940, just after Christmas, and came home once on leave. One day we heard on the news that the Germans had made advances toward the north of France. He realized that his unit were either on the run or had been captured. He left two days before his leave expired and we kissed good-bye in a way that was different. He told me he had made me his next-of-kin and I had to ask someone what it meant.

"I was just seventeen and had left school. I did the best I could with the housework, but the rationing business was too much for me to understand and all the official people kept saying that my mother must do this and do that. I didn't have the guts to tell them that the bitch had walked out on us.

"Well, Dad was in the Army. What could he do? He worried, I know that. I told him not to cry so much, that I would be all right until the war was over. He said it depended on how long it lasted, and I told him it would be all over in six months like the newspapers said.

"He said that Hitler was not going to be satisfied until he stood up in a tank and ploughed his way up the Mall and crashed the gates of Buckingham Palace, and all that would take longer than six months.

"Oh! Roy, I loved that man." Then she cried. I was not falling out of my chair with laughter, either.

Bill then took up the final part of the story.

He offered the girl a home with him and she accepted. He

had her name changed in court and she became his daughter. She was nearly seventeen then and very grown up. Her new dad was just over forty.

Bill still owned the property in Kent and had to get nearly drunk before he had the guts to enter the old home. It was all right for Jane; she didn't have any memories of the place.

"Christ! I've never looked at another woman since, but Jane— she is like a kind of angel sent to help me. You wouldn't know, you're only a young bloke—but to be my age and done what I've done and had the luck I've had and finish up with a pretty young girl who insists on looking after me. She could be up west with the Americans now instead of being a proxy barmaid-cum-cook-cum.

"Oh, hell." Then he cried.

After a while, my two hosts composed themselves.

Bill said, "Find some coffee, Luv."

I saw Jane in a new light; she was lovely. She had answered my question and the question of millions of people: "What is love? It is Jane and girls like her. Girls that do things for other people—for years—then become women and are still looking after relatives. Or Bills.

More whiskey for me and I found a bitter hatred for the enemy burning a hole in my heart—but for him none of this would happened. The current saying of "C'est le guerre" was only a bloody excuse for covering up mistakes and taking advantage of the situation. Oh! Yes, I loved Jane—for what she had done for Bill in the circumstances.

It was late. I had to get back to my room, and said I had very much enjoyed the company and the very kind, friendly way I had been entertained.

Bill saw me off the premises. As we stood watching the searchlights weave the slim beams of light across the sky and listened to the drone of enemy bombers, with the now familiar flash of light followed by the "crump' of the exploding bombs, I could feel the alcohol start having its effect. I recall shaking hands with them both and setting off along the pavement.

I found myself marching along at 120 paces to the minute

with a large military band behind me, the thud of the bass drum keeping me in time with the band.

We did "Old Comrades" and after a few bars went into "Liberty Bell." At that point, I met some people approaching. My pace was so determined I barged through them, knocking over the poor trombonists. Suddenly the big drum signaled the end of the music and I relaxed. A little too much. I fell over.

I felt as though I was in a hammock swinging from side to side. There was a very loud noise in the sky. "I know what that is," I thought. "They are coming to bomb me, all of them."

A voice said, "Poor chap, not very old, had a shock."

I could see a lot of legs; further up I could see some little heads. Silly fools, I thought, with their heads up there they will get flown into. One of the little faces said, "Let's get him up on the wall and give him a drop of gin. That'll put him right."

I knew by the stumpy spigots of metal, left behind by the salvage teams when the ironwork was burned off, that my wall once had iron railings. The spigots served as a kind of anchorage for me. The world stopped swaying.

A Thermos cup was held to my mouth. I smelled gin and sipped a little. I was implored to "Drink it up, Dearie." The mixture was not near explosive and in a fuzzled way, I dreaded anyone lighting a cigarette, but someone did and gave it to me. It tasted good, but I knew the gin would make me morbid soon.

The searchlights had several bombers well lit up now and the guns were firing. Pieces of shrapnel whistled down from time to time and clattered off the houses. The alcohol was making me a bit daft.

"Come and get me," I shouted. "Bomb me if you like."

They must have heard me, for there came that sound of the air whistling through the tail fins of a bomb, getting louder and higher pitched as it neared the ground. There was a bright flash, an explosion, debris clattering down, then silence, dust, the smell of soot, groans, voices, distressed voices, the jangle of bells getting near, and me, back to where I started—on my back. Jerry had forcibly detached me from my friendly spigot on my wall and I thought, "To hell with this," and stood up. *Stood up!* Ha! you should have seen it.

You should have seen a young man stand up in a circle.

I weaved my way toward the street, where the damage was causing all the vehicles to assemble. The road was a carpet of rubble, the smell of brick dust and soot was heavy in the air. Rescue men were climbing on top of what, a few minutes before, had been a home, where now the bedrooms were street level with no snores, only moans of pain and shock. I was sober at once. Shocked into it.

It all came back. Coventry, Birmingham, and Liverpool. The same destruction and smell. The same kindness from the people who helped. The rescue parties, calm when calling for silence so that they could search for buried people trapped and faintly calling for help. The women who appeared from nowhere with blankets, hot water, and comfort. Women of all ages, even girls of sixteen, helped. They were all gifted with magic. With just one smile, they could produce a cup of tea. Frequently there were the same comments, "Never mind about me; have a look at so and so," or "It'll take more than a few bloody Jerries to get me down, Mate."

A policeman was kneeling in the road. Thinking he was hurt, I went to help him, but saw that he was beside a motorcycle talking to the rider.

"All right, old chap, hang on; we'll soon have you safe."

The police torch lit up a young man dressed as a dispatch rider. He had a pouch on his belt and was half lying on it. There was a strong burning smell, the same as I had encountered when a pilot was trapped in his cockpit enveloped in flames—burned flesh. I took the police torch and saw the exhaust pipe was on his leg, just inside the thigh. Between us, we gently lifted the bike off. The pouch had the crest and GR on the flap. When the enemy took off a few hours earlier that had been a brown leather pouch. Now it was red. Near his belt a large piece of shrapnel was embedded in the poor chap's stomach., "Christ! can you get it off?" the copper said. "I'm going to be sick."

Although dazed myself, I shut my eyes, unbuckled the strap, and threw the leather gear at the policeman's legs. Then I was sick.

Someone straightened me up. I felt a lot better now; the shock I felt earlier had cleared my brain and now vomiting had cleared the drinks from my system.

"Come on, Mate, and 'ave a cuppa. My missus is on the van, you'll be all right in a minute."

My new friend wore a steel helmet. With his arm around my waist we approached a tea canteen. "Put a drop of sugar in, Luv." So there I was again, contemplating a cup of tea.

In the distance I could hear the ack-ack guns firing at other bombers. Although feeling my old self with little or no ill effects from my booze-up, I still felt very bitter about the enemy's attack. I imagined the German pilots reporting back their successes and, no doubt, getting applauded for their skill—a very helpless feeling.

In my mind, I can still smell that flesh, see the old man's head sticking out of the rubble, his gray hair moving slightly in the breeze, the lady's legs still kicking slightly, the nerves not yet quite dead. Poor devils. To think they were alive only a short time ago. Little did they know the fate in store for them and I had no idea while listening to Bill and Jane that I was to witness this unnecessary murder and destruction. I appreciated that we bombed Berlin, but would we have done so if Hitler had not marched into Poland?

"Come mate, have another cup, then we can all move off," the warden said. "Mind you, this is as good as anywhere to stay; they never fall in the same place twice—well, not on the same night!"

He had a cup with me in silence. Suddenly, he said, "Seventeen injured and three dead. Knew one of the families." A further silence, then, "Come on, we'll take you home."

Within twenty minutes, I was in my bed. It was all too much to sort out. Then blessed sleep.

CHAPTER EIGHTEEN

The next day I made contact with Tom in the arcade. It transpired we were both going to Scotland as armed escort to a gent who had been of use to our Intelligence and was to be entertained out of the way for the duration of the war. Apparently he had reckoned he should be allowed to go free in return for his information, but someone said no. Hence the escort.

Tom and I had seen the boss, had some of Sue's tea, and collected our guns. We met our man at the station and settled in a carriage. Tom was in charge and he arranged us so that the "prisoner" sat in a corner seat. He indicated that I should sit next to the prisoner while he sat opposite us. I was a little disappointed that we were not free to chat about our exploits since we had last met, but Tom had a plan to overcome the boredom. He produced a pack of cards, and shuffled the pack on the small table top that separated us.

The train started slowly with, then gained speed. After belting along for about twenty minutes, we slowed to a near walking pace. The windows were completely covered and it was not easy to refrain lifting the blind to look out. I don't know what good it would have done, but it was a compelling thought.

During one of the slow periods our man asked if we knew any card tricks. I did the only one I knew, which, I dare say, they knew as well. Tom baffled me with his three tricks and then the man took the pack. He did one of those professional stunts—squirting the cards from one hand so that they piled up in the other, then pulling them up one arm and getting them to turn over and return as a pack. He did a series of these moves, and even sitting beside him, I failed to learn much. Suddenly he asked us to take a card each, remember it and replace them in the pack. After a few deft movements, it seemed I had the five of clubs in my top pocket and Tom had the ten of diamonds inside his jacket.

The magician said softly, "If I were on escort work, I would not have allowed anyone to find my ten of diamonds so close to my gun holster."

"Yes, well," Tom replied. "We are both armed, just in case you made a dash. Don't mind you knowing, but best for the public not to see."

"Rubbish," said our charge. "You were slack in allowing your jacket to expose the leather. Just because it is hot and stuffy, you should not be so careless. I recall when I was training, I accompanied a senior, both of us armed as you are, each with a shoulder holster, and I was posted outside a busy store with instructions to watch for a certain individual. The man we were after was known to be dangerous and the orders were to shoot to maim, if necessary. I watched everyone, so I thought, and was absolutely staggered to have a boy of about ten years old stand in front of me and stare. I put up with this for as long as I could and then told him in effect to 'go away.' He did, but not before asking if he could have a look at my gun! I called him back and asked why he thought I had a gun. He said I often patted my chest near my breast pocket!"

Tom and I looked at each other, as our man added that more than once I had given my top jacket pocket a reassuring pat.

While all this was going on, I had lost track of the progress old chuffer was making. It seemed to be fairly steady, perhaps 40 mph, and all seemed well. I decided I would visit the gents and asked Tom if it was okay to leave the carriage. As he said, "Yes, go ahead," the train slowed rapidly and stopped. There was a fair bit of clanking with the buffers clouting themselves. All was silent for a time, except for the noise of escaping steam, then the corridor on the side of the train began to get busy with passengers going up and down, trying to assess the cause of the of the sudden end of travel.

I was enjoying this job. It was simple, yet important. Tom was there, in charge, but most of all, I was looking forward to the return journey, so that he and I could have a real natter. So I entered the corridor and "excused me" toward the toilet. I spent my penny and returned along the narrow path. A man with a very fruity voice ventured that I should not have used the toilet while the train was stationery and, any way, why was a young man of my age not in uniform?

I replied that that rule only applied when the train was standing in a station. To which he exclaimed, "You mean we are not in a station?"

I said that while in the lavatory I had a crafty look through the black-out. "Take my word for it, we are in the middle of a large field, but not to worry, when the summer comes, we will have a delightful view of the Kent countryside!" Although the lighting was poor, I felt he gave me a funny look.

The engine had regained its strength while all this was going on, as slowly the chuffs got going faster and faster and it occurred to me that, if the speed was maintained heading north, we would shoot past the top and finish up in the sea.

I worried for nothing, as there was a halt when the train stopped at Crewe. It was there that Tom made a mistake. He sent me off to the Railway Transport Office to report our presence and then to organize some refreshment for the three of us in the station buffet. While I was doing this, he escorted our man to the gents. When we next met outside the buffet, he was minus our man. Tom's forehead was so wrinkled with concern that, if he had been wearing a hat, he could have screwed it on his head.

So, as we shared one and a half snacks and three teas between us, I decided to keep quiet and learn from the expert. I must admit that I had a quiet smile to myself and wondered if he would be able to walk into the bass's office next time without knocking. I was sure that Sue would be well informed!

We had bangers, egg, and chips—three times and three teas. Tom chased his bangers around his plate to such an extent that I felt sorry for the poor things. He missed one entirely on one circuit and his stab with his fork was vicious.

I would like here to point out that on more than one occasion these episodes were accompanied by quite a lot of booze of some kind. Always when we were off duty, of course.

It wasn't until much later, at a place near Jedburgh Castle, Scotland, that we learned from "our man" what this was all about.

The boss had needed two men for a special job, one requiring extraordinary physical resources. The men needed to be a pair of villains who worked well together, were skilled with silent weapons, and were specialists in the use of explosives, including booby-trap devices. They had to be in top condition and mentally alert to the highest degree. Once selected, a plot had to be hatched to get them to Jedburgh.

I once mentioned Jedburgh to an ex-officer, who claimed that no such place existed. I can assure anybody that it did indeed exist— and anyone who went through the assault course knows it was dreamed up by the devil himself. Anyone who says it did not exist obviously was not there.

Tom and I were the two selected, and "our man' was, in fact, a SOE officer with orders to give us the slip if he could. Which he did at Crewe station.

While I was busy with the eats, Tom had escorted our man to the gents. Tom finished first, and while he waited he kept an eye on all the brass coin locks to see which were vacant and which were occupied. From time to time, men would come and go until, in the end, he was a bit confused as to which door he was supposed to watch. In the end, he discovered he had lost the prisoner.

This is what happened. "Our man" was out of the loo as soon as he was in, joining those who only needed a pee. Watching careful-ly, he walked out of the gents, chatting to a stranger while Tom was doing his patrol up and down the doors.

For once, I had the edge on Tom. He was not too pleased with himself for letting our man slip through his fingers. He was less pleased when the Commanding Officer requested my presence— along with my colleague—in the Mess.

The commanding officer, a lieutenant colonel, was a kindly man, not at all the sort I imagined to be in charge of one of the tough-est training establishments. After all, if you were a Jed you were somebody. Really. Except that the world knew nothing of it. You could be a murderer, a rapist, or even Hitler himself, and be in the news. But a Jedburgh? No.

He invited Tom and I to join him in a drink, saying we would be with him for a week. We were welcome to have as much liquor as we felt we could enjoy, but suggested that when the training started we would do well to keep to beer since that, as opposed to spirits, could be sweated out. "In the meantime," he said, "please note we do not drink much whiskey, since we all prefer brandy." A white-coated steward brought me a large balloon glass. It contained some very good stuff.

We chatted for a while and he spoke of many things I thought were only known to London. He knew a lot about me and, in particular, the factory raid. I recalled that the raid was to cover the rescue of someone, which had apparently been successful.

The colonel nodded and suggested a few tasty sandwiches might do down well. They did, too, and coupled with the brandy and comfortable atmosphere, gave me the necessary opportunity to ask how he knew so much about the raid.

"M'boy, I should know. I was the person flown out while you and your colleague were dealing with the French policeman."

"You, sir?" I nearly spluttered my drink from my mouth.

"Why not? It had to be someone. My regret is that I missed all the fun. Anyway, please accept my personal gratitude for the part you played."

"Well, to be honest, I had no idea what was going on other than when I did my explosives bit," I replied.

"You did a first class job and according to instructions. The PM has details of the entire operation, so don't be too surprised if you meet the great man."

I kept to myself the fact that I had already done so, although not in connection with the raid under discussion. The colonel then asked Tom to join him and then invited the other members to listen to a few stories from "our friend." Our friend turned out to be yours truly, and I found myself embarking on what turned out to be a marathon of yarns, some true and others just plain jokes, some of which I recall quite clearly, starting with the occasion of my very first pay parade.

"In alphabetical order," said the sergeant. "A's up the front this week, "Z's the next week, and so on.

"So there was this chap wandering up and down the queue asking which letter was the initial of an individual's name. The sergeant decided to help by loudly asking the man's surname."

"Phillips, sergeant."

"Well, lad, get up there in the "F's!""

Another one sprang to mind. It was during a period while I was a raw recruit; I was one of many due for a "jab." The orderlies lined us up in a long queue. With shirtsleeves up, a quick wipe with spirit, and we were in the presence of the dreaded man, a Medical Officer with a reputation for blunt needles and lances. The man in front of me fainted and I caught him as he folded. It threw off the sequence so that he and I were the last to be done. As he jabbed me, the officer remarked, "This needle is getting blunt," and the poor chap who had fainted heard the remark.

To cheer him up and gain his confidence, the medical officer asked the chap's name.

"Stoney, sir."

The MO laughed loud and long. "That's good, that is, you're Stoney and I am major Broke. Dear me! That is good. Stoney Broke!"

Another one was concerned with swimming. The day came when, in a very old and dark pool, we recruits were told to separate into two groups: those who could and those who couldn't. I was a couldn't, so they slung me in at the deep end. I recall having a close look a the tiles on the bottom, and then being hauled out and laid on the edge of the pool with someone saying sternly, "Never do that again, lad!"

One of the stories I told was of the trials and problems that befell a young officer who just could not ride a motorcycle very far without falling off. "Follow me," he would say, and in convoy we would do so. You could bet as soon we all got moving, he would look back to see if we were with him and steer right off the road. He had some very nasty near misses, but always seemed to be unhurt and his bike undamaged.

Just before Coventry was attacked, my unit was engaged on Bomb Disposal. A bomb had failed to explode and the officer and I were detailed to deal with the brute, which we called a Herman. The case had a fracture near the fuse pocket and looked dangerous. We had magnets and other crude gear, and my chief makes a decision. "Let's get it onto the truck, sergeant, and we will take it to the 'cemetery.' That way we'll be sure."

Sitting snugly between sandbags, the bomb appeared quite comfortable. I placed our red flag in the wing socket of the truck and sat by myself in the passenger seat. Then I heard a bike start and the Lieutenant appeared by the driver's door, sitting on his bike.

"You drive," he says. "Follow me; I know a short-cut."

So I drove, not the shortest way to the derelict piece of ground that was known as the cemetery, where all services took explosive items to be destroyed, but directly towards the city!

I am not sure of the road names, but it was past New Street station. The cemetery was not far from Hall Green. Along the roads were permanent trenches, partly filled in to cover the service pipes and cables, always a long bank of soil. So we belted along with me in the old Guy motor with the back-to-front gearbox, my hand on the horn push, sweating, old Herman lying in the nest of sandbags behind, and up front a British officer leading the way. Everything going well, no falling off—until he looked behind to see if I was still there. Suddenly, he was in the trench, speeding toward workmen filling in the trench up ahead. In a cloud of the flying men shovels he finally came to a stop when he hit an uncovered pipe.

He was not hurt. His glasses were a little bent, otherwise he was quite normal. There was a bit of a flap later, after we had delivered our bomb, regarding the bike. We got a wigging for taking the bomb through routes without proper authority. I heard later that the officers' mess had an amusing notice on the board. Something about discipline in the trenches!

This episode brought to mind two other stories.

During the very hard winter of 1939-40 in France, when things were not at all warlike, our unit had a little training scheme. My officer had been sent out on a recce. and had reported that a certain stretch of water, a lake I assume, was frozen, and that troops could easily cross. There was some doubt about this idea, but he convinced the OC that it was possible, since he had ridden his bike across. This was considered one of the funniest statements ever made in the mess, since the speaker had been known to fall off when road conditions were excellent.

I was not in the maneuver, but I heard that he said his usual "follow me," and set off over the frozen surface. As he looked back to check on those following, he fell off, slid on his bottom, and came to a stop just in time to see the first 15 cwt. truck of his little convoy scrunch through the ice and settle in a few inches of water. When he did his recce., he assumed the troops would be on foot.

Much later, during the fighting just before we were chased toward Dunkirk, we encountered a Bren gun unit. The OC requested help in getting as many carriers away as possible. He was short a few drivers, so my officer felt duty bound to supply the required number of drivers. He had the first carrier, I had the last. A convoy of seven started off. A convoy of *six* rumbled along the road.

There was a lot of dust. Being at the end, I couldn't see the leader, so I stopped to have a look. When the dust settled, it was plain to see what had happened. The officer who couldn't ride a bike couldn't drive a carrier, either. He had rammed a small cottage, burst through the wall, and crashed through the floor, which was not built to support an army vehicle.

The property, which was not occupied at the time of the demolition, was now occupied by one very dusty Lieutenant, who appeared to be getting rapidly drunk. The cellar contained a lot of wine in bottles, now broken, and the air was very potent.

With some help, the officer was removed from his carrier and made a passenger in my vehicle. To try to catch up the remainder meant some fast driving, and I soon became very proficient with the tracks. The others up ahead could be seen over on our left and the officer said something above the noise which sounded like "Taa-a-a-ashor-r-r-rkut." This was interpreted as "take a short cut," so I did, but instead of slowing on one track and letting the machine change direction with dignity, as I had done on the hard road, I overdid the steering in my exuberance. I lost my sense of direction and opened up the throttle. We did a couple of quick pirouettes, and came to a abrupt halt in a steep downward position.

When we all got out and had a look at the problem, it was evident we would be walking from then on, as the thing was nose down in a well with one track broken. The officer prodded it with his cane and said, "Thash was a bloody silly thing to do."

We watched, fascinated, as the brickwork at the top of the well slowly crumbled under the weight of metal, and bit by bit the carrier upended itself until it was quite still, firmly embedded in the hole. It received another prod with the cane, with the comment, "You ken see now—why, why it went in the house."

Shortly after, a dispatch rider slowed to a stop on seeing us, saluted, and explained that the Jerries had landed a small force of parachute troops half a mile away, and did not recommend us to continuing in that direction. The officer climbed on the back of the bike and told the rider to "Take me to your unit."

The DR asked, "Has sir been celebrating?

"No, I'm just living from the fat of the land!"

It all came right in the end. The fighting started, and we were reunited with our unit.

At this point, I explained that this officer was a real nice man in every respect; it was just funny things that happened to him, mainly when he was riding his bike. Or catching a ferry.

They understood, but what about a ferry?

So I told about the time when, in Wales, we were marched toward the quay to board the ferryboat. As we neared the water, the officer called out to me to get the men to double. As we did our leader ran on ahead. Shouting and waving his arms, he leapt off the quay, missed the boat, and went into the water.

A crew member threw a line and called out to the little bridge. The captain went to the rail, took one look at the army cap, and shouted down, "Bloody army, can't you wait till we have tied up?"

And so it went on, into the early hours, the stories moving slowly from the truth to the type that men like to tell, each yarn reminding someone of another story.

For five long days, Tom and I sweated out with every type of body-building stunt man could devise, some quite dangerous. There were no social chats in the evenings after the training, for we were dead beat. But on the last day, things relaxed and the night before we left was a near repeat of the first evening, except that the CO and the major we had escorted gave us a very sharp lecture on being alert to everything possible.

"You have it in you, otherwise you would not have been selected for your work. Goodness knows how long the war will go on, but you will find yourselves being extended more and more with experiences that no other men have had, and you will become expert in subversive activities to such an extent that, if you survive, a group of you could form the most successful team of crooks in the world. On the other hand, you will find yourselves able to read people as though their heads were made of glass.

"In later years, again if you survive, you will be most unhappy, and you will be hard put to find or make friends that are compatible, for you will be very lonely even in a room full of people. Remember, to do your job, you have to be 'different' and your self-discipline will rub off in later life. You will always be different, and in my opinion, superior. I very much hope that some of us seniors will be able to form some kind of 'old comrades' association, so that we can keep in touch. What is more, I hope that we all find employment with lawful establishments. Personally, I would like to see an international force of emergency teams made up of you men, all specialists, but with the common basic knowledge, ready to deal with anyone who steps out of line, from politicians to mad dogs; store detectives would be suitable as employment for the older men. Believe me gentlemen, when they share out the spoils of war, there are sure to be many arguments, and being politics, the bad feelings will smolder for many years. Getting back into the incident at Crewe, let that be a lesson to you both, be on the alert at all times, remember you may be clever, but the one that wins is smarter, so make sure you do not allow people to take advantage of you, for it will be human nature for you to be so tolerant, that you will be robbed of all you have worked for, *except your memories*. This work will extract great inroads of your life one way or another, and your conscience will be your jury. Now come and have a drink, and let's have a few more of your stories, for we up here have been together so long now, that there is little new to tell."

The major from Crewe shook hands with us, and with a smile said he didn't think we would be shot at the Tower having failed in our escort job and hoped our cuts and scrapes would soon heal, although what little blood we had left behind on the assault course was not as bad as the bruises we had inflicted on some of the instructors.

So to the Mess and sandwiches, coffee, brandy, and more yarns, this time with Tom in the limelight. With his Midlands accent and shy manner, it was impossible to appreciate just how tough he could be in combat. Of medium height and build, he was just the man to have handy when there was likely to be trouble.

He had quite a fund of stories, but his best yarn involved a vicious male monkey that had escaped and found refuge up a tree in a private garden. Police and firemen had chased the animal out to the end of a long branch. An expert in these matters arrived with what he claimed as a very special breed of dog, one trained to bite and hold on to the private parts of any male. The expert issued orders and had four men hold a net under the branch. To another man he gave the small box containing the dog, and to another he gave a loaded gun. He then explained, "I will climb the tree and endeavor to shake the monkey down into the net. If I succeed, let the dog go as soon as the animal is in the net. If, however, the monkey shakes harder, before I start to fall, shoot the monkey. If you miss *shoot me!*"

Many more followed. It was well into the small hours when at last we finished. We said good-bye to all in the Mess, returned to our room, and after packing managed a few hours sleep. The next morning, after a good breakfast, we were boarded our train and said goodbye to Jedburgh.

CHAPTER NINETEEN

Our journey back to London could never be registered on a railway time-table, for we changed trains and belted over and under platforms that reminded us of the assault courses we had recently endured. At one stage, Tom ventured his opinion riding the train was really the reason we had to be so fit. He also exercised his new sense of observation and determination to be "alert at all times" by pointing out that he was sure the sailor kissing the girl on Platform 3 was the same man who kissed a girl good-bye on another station an hour before.

It was a relief to get the door of the boss's office in sight. I exercised the correct protocol and allowed him to approach first. I knew what was in his mind and I was right. He knocked. And waited.

Sue, bless her, opened up. Her smile, combined with a saucy look at the ceiling, told us that all was known about the escape at Crewe. The bass was busy writing when we entered and kept us waiting for a full three minutes. When, at last, he put away his paperwork, he said without looking up, "I know all about it; I am disgusted. Sit down and have your tea. Sue?"

"Yes, sir."

"Get on to the Ministry of Works and get them to provide some kind of ante-room or something, to prevent anyone from barging in here. I know we occupy these few rooms as a cover for our work, and I am well aware of the security men that are on duty, but once past them there seems to be an open invitation to Tom, Dick and Harry to enter. *Especially Tom.*"

"Now look here, sir, how was I to supposed know?"

"Never mind about what you were supposed to know. What

worries me is the attitude of your No. 2," indicating me.

I started to stammer some kind of defense, but was interrupted.

"I am of the opinion that the pair of you could not stop a pig in a passage. Do you honestly think that the enemy playing at their home ground would allow such slackness? Does it not occur to you that you were both entrusted with silent weapons to safely escort a man to the North, without hindrance from the enemy, and that you both sat close to him in a railway carriage confined in space, with the thing on the move. All this for half the journey, then as soon as you are out of the train, where escape is easier, you than halve the escort. The result, you know; he got away. And so would you, had you been in his position. Now do you honestly think your action was correct? Do you think this is a Sunday school outing? Do you think I can pass this off to my chief as a mistake? Well? Do you?"

He looked at me for an answer.

His long tirade had given me time to think. So I used my training, added my own character, assumed I was dealing with an interrogator, and replied, "You hold on a minute, Sir. Just calm down and appreciate just who you are talking to. We are on the same side. Tom and I knew our man was not a genuine defaulter, for when members of the organization are sent to the highlands for a spell or the duration, they are not sent with an armed escort. It was obvious he was a 'plant,' and although there was nothing in his behavior to support this view, there was plenty to start with. After all, we met him by appointment at the station, like an uncle seeing his son off to school.

"Come off it, Sir, Tom and I were approached by the 'defaulter' on the platform. He made himself known to us, shook hands, and said, 'Well, I'm all yours and ready when you are.' I am sure Tom will verify that."

The guv'ner looked hard at the pair of us and just as sternly explained that it did not matter whether we all met one way or another, even if our man was dressed as Santa Claus, the point at issue was the fact we lost him at Crewe.

At this, Tom stood and blew his top. Among his many comments were examples of the frustrations of our job. The tensions were terrific.

"Did you ever have to do any of these missions? No, of course, you didn't. You found yourself ideal for the job you do and you get the results, thanks to those of us who back you. But tell me—why were we armed? You know we can both instinctively, without aiming, hit even the cords that pull the bloody silhouettes set up for target practice. Do you think we would have shot at the man, even to maim?"

"Have you finished?"

"No, I bloody well haven't. I'd like to know why we had to sweat it out on that week of intensive physical torture you blandly call 'toughening up,' while you do a couple of miles shaking up your liver sitting on an old nag you get from the Guards' Depot. I know, I've seen you prancing up and down Rotten Row smiling at the nurses and nannies. It wouldn't surprise me if, when they see you coming, they say to themselves, 'Look out, here comes that bloke from that secret lot.'

"And another thing. How much longer are you keeping Sally in the Northern sector? Why can't she have a break? Why don't you get her back here and let her tell you what it is like for a lady to sweat? And, as for my colleague here, that you call my No. 2, let me tell you, he did as he was told and was in no position to stop old Happy Harry from escaping."

Tom exhausted himself and sat down. The bass pressed a button and Sue appeared. I knew then that we were to have some tea after all.

The tea was in cups with handles and too hot for immediate drinking. The room was tense. Tom blew his tea. The guv'ner frowned, so Tom stirred vigorously, until he had a hole in the center of his liquid so deep I wondered how he managed to keep the stuff from going over the top.

When it seemed no one would do doing any talking, I finally broke the silence. With colossal nerve, I asked the guv'ner if his apparent concern and worries were causing him to act like a very disturbed man.

After a few moments of thought, he spoke, explaining the

difficulty of being in charge of a subversive section such as ours.

The thought crossed my mind that the man was overdoing it, and I asked, "When did you last have leave sir?"

"That is none of your business and has no bearing on the problems I have at the moment."

"If you continue with these pressures for many more days, Sir, you will be out of your mind, so pack it in and ask your chief for a break. He must be out of touch anyway, not to know of your condition. And if you both think that we have endangered the country by letting Sherlock Holmes through our fingers, then why not let us loose in Berlin and have a crack at Hitler, or better still, two or three of his top men? The risks are the same, whether we are fiddling about with pieces of paper in brothels or general sabotage."

The officer's response was to slump forward with his head in his hands. Tom jumped up and pressed a button on the desk. Sue entered immediately, looking quite startled.

"Our boss is not well, Luv," Tom said. "Can you report to somebody and get him taken somewhere? We will go with him if you can fix things."

Sue evidently was capable of things other than making tea. She calmly asked us to leave the office and not let anyone in while she made a call.

Tom and I left the room, automatically taking up positions that would have spelled trouble for anyone trying to get in.

Sue opened the door and beckoned us in. She explained that she had taken appropriate action and had been told to ask us to remain in the office until instructed to leave. We were on no account to admit anyone other than a person who would introduce himself by his code-name "Bluebird."

We made the officer as comfortable as we could—tie off, collar loose, drink of water. He repeatedly murmured, "Thank you, most kind of you, so sorry."

Tom opened the door and looked outside. He popped back in and announced that someone was coming along the corridor. We listened. Suddenly, I said, "The man that we shall see will wear an eye-patch and walk with the aid of a stick."

I was correct. "Bluebird" was the officer who had interviewed me in the earlier days. I noted that he looked in much better health than when we first met. He shook hands, indicated the door with a nod, and said, "Ambulance. Go down and get the stretcher."

Downstairs, I was given a stretcher, with the query, "Wot's so bloody secret in there, mate?"

I grabbed the stretcher and said, "Nothing secret about it; just a suspected case of the first man to have a baby."

The officer was on the floor when I entered. We lifted him and Bluebird said, "Take it easy. He is not an emergency case in the true sense of the phrase." Nodding to Tom, he said, "They know where to go, but you go with him." To me: "You return here to me."

Back in the office, I found Bluebird seated at the desk talking to Sue. He stood as I entered and we shook hands again.

"Nice to see you again," he said. "Sit down and leave me to glance at the files and I will be more sociable."

Although I had been in that room several times, there were many details I had not noticed. This time I found the atmosphere different. I noted I sat in one of three leather armchairs, the type one saw in exclusive clubs. The desk looked large but quite ordinary, except that not all desks had four telephones. Neither did all offices have filing cabinets that looked like the strong room of a bank, or a plain door leading off behind the desk marked "Keep Out." Or a secretary that was as good looking, kind, efficient, unflappable, tea-making, smart, clean, and cuddly as Sue.

I thought back to Sally in France. She was very similar, but she was not a secretary. What she was, other than very brave, was a bit vague since my experience with her was also a bit fuzzy. Nevertheless, both girls had something in common. Then I looked at Bluebird. He was similar in manner to the man we had known as the boss, the guv'ner. This one used his one eye as though he had six. He still used a stick and still smiled a lot.

My thoughts were interrupted, for he said with a smile, "I would like you and Sue to join me for a bite to eat and a drink; that is, of course, if neither of you have a previous engagement." I accepted without thinking and looked at Sue. She had a bus to catch, but had nearly two hours to spare.

"Good," he said. "Lock up the factory, Sue, and let's go."

A short taxi ride, a few battles with some black-out doors and we were in the basement of a pub-cum-club. Whatever it was, it contained an enormous number of people, mostly service personnel of both sexes, much laughter, little lighting, lots of tobacco smoke, and, miraculously, a table for three and a waiter who acknowledged the officer as Mr. Bentley.

Between us, we had a bottle of wine and the only three-legged chicken in the country. Mr. Bentley evidently was well-known in this place, since there followed some brandy and cigars with a cigarette for Sue. The conversation during the meal and up to the brandy was between Sue and the officer. For my part, I kept quiet, but since I sat between them, it was easy for me to hear what was said. I learned a lot!

I discovered that the man we carried on the stretcher was known as "Blackbird" (a fact he kept to himself) and that he had been charged with the task rescuing an important ally. His man had been caught and quite a mess had been made of the chain of "safe" houses along the escape routes used by the RAF lads.

On top of that, he had recently discovered that his wife had left him for another man—one, she said, who came home every night from work and stayed with her at weekends. Not one who made excuses for being late or on duty, or who constantly looked at his watch or the moon, or listened to dry old programs on the wireless, or was in the Army but never wore his uniform.

While all this information was passed between the young officer and Sue, I felt a bit alarmed that they apparently insisted on conversing about what I thought was most secret information, while others were only a few inches away. Bluebird read my thoughts and explained that where we were was as good as anywhere to talk, but not to pass anything. Passing messages was best done in absolute privacy. He told me to have another and enjoy myself, because my next task would extend me to my limits.

What a jolly thought that was. Extend me to my limits? And what job? And enjoy myself? In what order?

Surely this was a funny way to run a sabotage unit, I thought, and again he was clairvoyant, for he added, "Don't worry, nothing has been said or done that will affect the outcome of the war." His smile restored my normal frame of mind and I realized he was merely conditioning me for the next task. A clever ploy on his part, but did he know that I knew his method?

Sue made the first move, saying she would have to go soon, and that ended the evening out. We shook hands all round, and when we were outside, Sue suggested that would be a good place to bring Sally. I said something about not being quite sure what Sally looked like, and anyway she was on the other side of the water, which brought the comment from Bluebird that the young lady would be in London very soon, perhaps next week, and he was sure she would be pleased to have my company.

I responded by suggesting that I thought she would set her sights on someone a bit better cut-of-the-cloth than myself, and received the opinion that the girl was a tough nut and would please herself, but could do worse by choosing me as an escort, bearing in mind that she was not being recalled to find a husband. She was coming over from France to speak freely on how best she could help with a problem, but what she did with her off-duty periods was her own business. Bluebird added I could learn a lot from this very attractive young lady, for she had a lot of experience and was a most precious member of our team, being one of very few females "in place." (This phrase was used to describe a person who elected to work for their native country, staying in place, and not returning home when the threat of enemy occupation was imminent.)

In bed that night, I thought of the events of the day, and wondered where the old guv'ner was; come to that, where was Tom? Was he still with him? I didn't know. Then sleep.

CHAPTER TWENTY

"How do you fancy keeping an eye on the King?" Bluebird asked. When he spoke, Sue was standing beside him and I looked at her for some kind of inspiration. She smiled her lovely smile. I looked at Tom, who was sitting beside me. He closed one eye in a friendly wink, then I looked at the young officer. He continued, "Well, you seem to have the approval of your colleagues, so what do you say? Will you do it?"

My reply came quickly, as was expected, and I put forward my view that I was under the impression that His Majesty had a body-guard, a private detective, plus goodness knows how many more people near him, and surely the police were involved as well. So what could I do?

It was his turn to smile.

He said, "Let me put you in the picture. Within the next few days, plans will be completed to prepare an area of Salisbury Plain, where the entire compliment of a newly-formed armored division of troops will parade in a route designed to pass a saluting base. His Majesty will take the salute from a raised dais.

"This platform will be supplied and erected by engineers in the Division, and as you will be aware, having been in the Corps of Sappers, a party will be detailed for maintenance. You will join that party. Everything has been arranged. You will be armed, you will wear denims, and you will be suitably briefed with regard to the individual under suspicion. I may add that this person is not British. Any questions?"

I replied that several questions sprang to mind and I was invited to state them one at a time.

"First, why let this person get so close before anything is done to protect the King?"

"That is because he will be more vulnerable out in the open than when traveling. Next?"

"If the would-be assassin gets within firing range, why cannot he be put out of action before he can do any damage?"

"If anyone is seen acting suspiciously, of course they will be arrested. That is not your worry. Any more questions?"

"Yes—why me?"

A smile and "Why not?" was all I received, so I thought it best to be quiet. Just as well, since Tom then had to pay attention. He was told to stand by, ready for some sleepless nights, for as soon as "37" arrives there would be many hours of planning.

Then, turning to me, he added, "And on your return from Salisbury, you will be required to join the team. You may then find out why it was necessary to spend your holidays in the Highlands recently."

It was like old times, being mixed up with the Sappers again. They had been told I was "in Security," and were not to divulge that I had once been one of them. The night before the big display was spent under canvas at Imber. As a guest of the Warrant Officers, I enjoyed the old Corps chat and was pleased that whoever had briefed them had made it clear that my presence was nothing to do with the host unit.

Before going to sleep, I recalled to myself an incident that caused me to "make a funny." A group of young officers were on exercise here at Imber and were due to take part in a night map-reading scheme.

A series of check points had been set up during the day, and after being split into teams of four, the officers set out with their prismatic compasses at fifteen minute intervals. Those of us who waited to assist had many tales to tell the next day. One story concerned a team that had a disagreement and split up. One team had a battle with some cows and managed to indicate his position by a series of regular yelps when he became firmly entangled with an electric fence.

In another incident, one team went missing—all four of them—and wandered around most of the night and, unlike the others, they at least agreed they were lost. Their leader was most apologetic, but when they found me and I said it was not a bad thing, providing they could give me the map reference of where they were now. They huddled and finally committed themselves to a reference. I checked the position twice, and could hardy conceal my mirth as I pointed out that, if what they said were correct, we were in the middle of Salisbury Cathedral.

Before sleep came, I reflected that I would never forget the words and tone of the briefing officer with regard to my task the next day, who had said, "Study these pictures of the man. Position yourself under the dais, adjust the tarpaulin to give yourself an unobstructed view within the area marked with tapes. When His Majesty arrives, he will meet several high ranking officers within the taped area. It is during this meeting of corps commanders that the attempt may be made. If you see anyone preparing to aim any weapon, shoot to maim. If, however, a shot is fired without you seeing the preparation, you will be expected to fire twice—*he will not miss and neither must you!* There will be other marksmen around to deal with the flanks and the rear, but only you will be concealed, *so hit the man that fires a shot. Understand?*" I understood.

In position the next day an hour before the arrival of the staff cars, I found myself pacing up and down under the dais, then going out to the area below the four steps leading up to the platform. I stood up on the saluting base to get an idea of what was possible, what was visible, indeed what was anything. There was nothing much to see. Away in the distance was an enormous collection of tanks and other armored vehicles, and as always, I wondered at the sense of forming such a lot of people in one place. What a target for a stray enemy aircraft; indeed, suppose someone had leaked out the fact that this parade was due to take place. It would not be a stray aircraft that would visit the Plain.

Slowly, as time passed, the route along the perimeter filled with officers, with those of higher ranks, generals and brigadiers, nearest to the dais, chatting and generally moving around within the confines of the reception area. I decided they were on our side and was puzzled as to where I would elect to be if I were the assassin, for opposite was an expanse of open country. No cover at all.

Suddenly, the "top brass" stood at ease in an orderly position. I saw the officers stand at attention and salute as the Royal vehicle approached. Things happened very quickly then. There were handshakes and saluting and while, smoking furiously, I paced up and down like a chicken in a run. Even though I had a silent weapon with a telescopic sight with the safety catch off I decided I had no chance of hitting any individual. The King was about seven yards from me and more or less surrounded by top officers.

In the distance, I could hear the whine of gearboxes as the heavy tanks approached and slowly the King of England passed from my sight, mounted the steps, and stood above me. The first tank appeared with its gun pointing at the angle of respect, the tank commander at the salute. It was followed by another and another. A continual grind on tracks and noise indicated many hours of moving machinery to come, judging by the number assembled in the distance. It seemed a hopeless task and I could see that the only position for the attacker to be would be in one of the vehicles, and he could never get away with that. It also occurred to me that it was not necessary for him to use a gun—why not a grenade?

But I worried in vain, for under the flap at the rear appeared the briefing officer, much more jolly this time.

"Stand down and relax," he said, and explained that the civilian police had arrested a man acting in a suspicious manner, and he turned out to be the man we were after.

"I have dismissed the others and I'm having a pee, then we can get out of it before the parade breaks for lunch. Come on, we can use the Royal latrine."

He took the rifle from me and cleared it of the six rounds, detached the telescopic sight and packed it away in its case. As this was being done, we heard quite a lot of movement from the decking above us.

"Quick," he said, "they are coming off the dais. Get into the latrine!"

We both did a hasty job of relieving ourselves, each smoking a cigarette. We stood at the entrance and he continued, "You hang on here and I will get my truck, then we can beat it before the rush to the dining tent starts."

Alone again, I stood a few feet away from the entrance of the latrine marked V.I.P. and Senior Officers Only. Around the corner appeared a Brigadier, and in one swift movement, I threw my cigarette to the ground, stamped on it and stood at attention, all as though it was a drill movement, even though I was dressed in borrowed denims, devoid of rank or insignia and no headgear and I stood and looked at him. Another officer followed—His Majesty. He was pretty sharp, as he had apparently noticed me stamp on my smoke, for he said haltingly, "Good morning. You need not have thrown your cigarette away for they are far too expensive—please, have one of mine."

He produced a gold case, Turkish on one side and Virginia on the other. Grubby fingers that only a short while ago were ready to squeeze a trigger on his behalf now took a cigarette. Other officers had now formed a queue, not daring to get ahead of the King. I stood my ground and could see there were a good many boilers near bursting point. Not only that, they all had their own idea of a suitable delaying tactic. Some were beating the living daylights out of their legs by nervous lashings with their canes. Others had thrust their sticks under the left arm and assumed a position of rigid attention, but with feet apart. Two had folded their arms and leaned against the back support of the dais, giving the impression that they had seen this all before. The Royal aide-de-camp shrugged his shoulder to the waiting group as much as to say, "There is not much I can do about it."

In the meantime, I had placed my Royal cigarette in my top pocket, holding the rifle between my knees as I did so. This prompted His Majesty to ask what type of weapon I had in the case, to which I replied that I didn't know, sir, as I was just looking after it while my officer was getting our truck. He seemed satisfied with this and said, "Good-bye. Thank you and good luck." He then turned to his aide saying, "I'm so sorry. After you." They disappeared behind the screen.

My officer arrived shortly and together we traveled away from the area behind a long row of tents and out towards the exit and on to the road.

I had not met this officer before he briefed me early in the morning. He was quite clear and concise in his manner, but when he joined me under the dais and announced the 'stand-down' his manner was most friendly. He said he thought we had earned some refreshment and knew a nice little pub. Within a couple of miles, we were in an old place that was indeed a nice little pub. Not only for its beer, but for two very generous helpings of bubble and squeak. It was smashing!

We arrived back in London in early evening. It was the first time I had seen the big city approached by road and was amazed at the large number of barrage balloons; there seemed to be hundreds in sight all at one glance. As darkness fell, they were slowly winched up or down. It seemed to signal another night of unknown dread.

In the museum, we met Bluebird and I was asked to explain about the incident regarding His Majesty. I did, and was surprised at the number of questions fired at me about the incident. I tended to treat it as if it were a "perk" to the job, but I was sharply reminded that there were many present who had the opportunity to harm the King, and "never mind about your precious cigarette."

There then followed a dressing down to end all dressing downs, conducted by Bluebird and directed at the security officer who had briefed me, bought me a meal, and driven me back to London. I felt rather sorry for him. Then I had to suffer the sharp edge of the new guv'ner's tongue and it seemed like the coffee at Camberley over again. I was supposed to keep an eye on everyone within the radius of the underneath of the dais, until His Majesty left the area in the transport provided, not wander about collecting souvenirs to show my relations—and so on . . .

I felt myself getting smaller as time went on and nearly disappeared altogether when Bluebird asked me how I knew that the man who briefed me was on our side? Did I not see a strong possibility existed that he himself could be the assassin? To which I replied that I had been told the man we were after was not British and this officer is British. "How do you know?"

"Well, I don't, but at least he is one of us—as far as I know."

Suddenly the officer, who had remained silent for a while, did a yawn and suggested we all packed up for the day, as he had driven a long way and had had little sleep the night before. He raised up both arms to stretch and yawn again as he spoke. Then, without warning, Bluebird had a gun in his hand, and saying as he pointed the weapon, "Good, now keep them up—Tom?"

From behind one of the large leather armchairs appeared Tom, who quickly had those arms pretty useless to their owner. Bluebird frisked the victim and emptied his pockets onto his desk. Tom had the protesting man on his feet now and was propelling him toward the door. I left my seat to open one of the two doors leading out into the corridor, and there were a couple of surprises awaiting my gaze. One consisted of a pair of very large men who took an arm each from Tom's protesting burden. One of the giants said something like, "You will accompany us to a place whereby you will be charged by acting with another in a manner that contravenes the Official Secrets Act."

The other surprise was to see Tom hasten a few yards and embrace a very nice young lady. It didn't last long, but it looked good. I knew that she was not a wife or girlfriend, since, without some means of identification, no one could get into that floor of the building. The puzzle was solved when I opened the door for them to enter the office. In the much better light, I saw Sue standing beside the guv'ner. As soon as the door opened, Sue flew round the desk and embraced the girl, saying, "Sally!"

With stick in one hand, and Bluebird joined them, and shook hands with Sally, turned to me, and introduced me to her as "Robin."

I looked surprised. My mental picture of the girl I met in France was different. I would not have recognized her here. I offered my hand. She knocked it to one side, gave me a playful punch in the midriff, and for the second time in half an hour, arms were raised. Hers went right round my neck and I discovered how difficult it could be to talk without moving one's lips.

When she released me, she said, "I'm so sorry having treated you so badly. I hope the effects wore off without any upset. You needed quite a dose to put you to sleep—you are a very fit young man, if I may say so."

I replied that my physical condition caused me no stress, but I was a bit confused mentally with the speed of events in this office. We were invited to take a seat. Tom and I sat, with Sally in the middle. My seat was still warm. Yes, it happened all that quickly.

I thought Sue could only cater for one guest with her tea. I was wrong. She seemed to have an endless supply of cups. She even possessed a tray! When we were all busy stirring, we all exercised our good manners and waited for Bluebird to speak. He was reading something and stirring at the same time.

Tom leaned across to me and quietly said, "When he has drilled a hole in that cup, he will have more than a saucer-full." I nodded agreement.

Voices brought Bluebird back to earth and he explained briefly, for Sally's benefit, the events of the day. These included the cover supplied to safeguard the King and the subsequent arrest of the Quisling type gent who left the office as she was waiting to enter. He did his best to look sternly at me with his one visible eye and said he still had a few more questions to ask about the Salisbury Plain job, and although late, he would like a few more details around the time the Royal party left the saluting base and the cigarette episode.

"It was, as I have already explained, Sir," I replied. "There are no bits and pieces to add."

"That may be so, but I have a report to write and I would prefer the details now, while they are fresh. Not only that, there is the business in France which concerns the three of you to deal with."

I went through it again. When I exhausted the details, Bluebird ceased writing and said, "Make one more mistake like that and you will not see your next birthday. You allowed this officer to disarm you, clear your gun and stow it away in its case. I appreciate he left it with you, but as a trusted member of a security section, posted in a prime position to deal with an attempt on someone's life, your behavior was not up to the required standard. How long would it have taken you to arm yourself? Ask yourself, if it was sensible to be in position an hour before time, is it not unreasonable to assume that you should have remained alert until His Majesty was out of your sight? Did you not feel it odd that, at the very moment when the party left the dais, the King was all the more vulnerable."

To that I replied that the man who dismissed me was the person who briefed me very early that morning, and I was not to know that he was not a genuine member of our force. "With respect, I may as well ask you to prove to me you are who you claim to be, and even with your answer, am I to assume you are not, in fact, acting for the enemy?"

I noticed that Tom and Sally shuffled their feet at this. Sue decided it was an opportune moment to remove the empty cups, and she disappeared into her "what-ever-it-was."

I could sense that in some circles it would be thought I'd gone too far. Insolence in the Army. On a fizzer—a charge, Section something-or-other. Left-right-left-right-halt and so on. In the Army, fair enough, *but you are not in the Army now*, they said. You are in a special force. You are different, they said. You will work with others of a similar character.

Bluebird interrupted my thoughts. He evidently did not think I had gone too far. He said kindly he could appreciate my view, knowing just how much I was told. He added that perhaps I might have noted that he had introduced me to Sally as Robin. This was a small form of accolade, inasmuch as I had now made the grade and had a file opened with the name I would be known as in this country—Robin Foster.

"With regard to the Salisbury Plain job, you were conned good and proper but, to be fair, so were we to some extent. I have been working on this for some time in conjunction with the civil forces. It was, and still is, of a political nature. You see, the information we had suggested that the threat was on the Prime Minister, since it was he who originally intended to take the salute. It was he and the Army chiefs who instigated the idea of an armored division made up of Guards battalions and it was he who would have reviewed the troops.

"Owing to political pressures, he was unable to be present, and when he confided his regret to His Majesty, the King immediately insisted on performing the duty, the PM agreed to this, but unbeknownst to the King, instigated a very strict security instruction. I was put in charge of this and one of my men happened to be in a pub and saw a very cute piece of message-passing. He very astutely worked out that a customer and the barman passed a message. This was done quite simply by giving of change. The customer had ordered a pint of beer; he proffered a £1 note. The change was in the form of a selection of coins and a ten-shilling note. All these were laid on the bar top with care to see that all the coins and the note *were face upward*, you understand. The heads were on top, each coin being placed down firmly, with a knowing look at the customer.

"My chap got the message before the man picked up his money, but when the penny dropped, if you'll forgive the phrase, the man drank up quickly and made toward the exit. I might add that he was discreetly followed and my man was able to get the address of the house and inform me of this and provide a good description of the suspect. This information enabled us to find out that a possible threat existed to the King. So far, then, we had the small fry. Now we needed the big fish. All men available, including you, Robin, were given specific posts in and around the area near the saluting base.

"Now we come to the part that baffles you. You see, we were hard pushed for personnel for this job, and then a young officer from SOE headquarters at Orchard Court volunteered to do the briefing. He had not quite lost the army system of getting all concerned together to 'put them in the picture.' Well, that's fine for the army, but not for the kind of organization we are. He was a little peeved when I refused to allow a bulk briefing. He could not grasp that, although I know all my men, many of them do not know each other. I allowed him to brief one chap, and much to my surprise, he stressed that it was the King's life at stake. I said surprised, *because he knew the prime minister was not to be present.* If he knew it was to be His Royal Highness, where had he obtained the information?

"You will recall, I asked you how you felt about keeping an eye on the King? Well, I took one man into my confidence. He was the one who was responsible for the yarn about you having to 'stand down' since we had the suspect. The rest you know—except that my man was on the dais, dressed as a Polish Brigadier, armed, with a name I invented that was so diabolical to pronounce that other officers took him on face value.

"I may add that, as trusted people, you would not divulge my admiration for the way he conducted himself and I only hope that one day his Corps will honor him, for you see, he was selected from the regular Forces, like yourselves, as a suitable type of person for this particular work and proved himself to be the person to which all credit will be given, if I have my way. Until he joined this type of unit, he was a Corporal in the Royal Corps of Signals. Now we have other things to discuss but, before changing the subject, any questions?"

Tom asked about the old boss. Was there any news? Could we visit him the hospital? The answer to that was that he had been relieved of all responsibilities for the time being and would be given three months leave to sort out his domestic affairs.

"He is in good spirits." There would be no visiting and no need to worry about him, as his welfare was well and truly under control. "He is to some extent vulnerable, so we have one of our chaps on the staff keeping an eye on his visitors."

My question had to do with the mention of Orchard Court. "What was it?"

They all looked at one another. I caught Sally's eye and she asked, "Don't you know?" She seemed more alarmed than surprised.

"Yes, I know," I replied, "but I have never been told officially. I suppose it is secret."

This remark prompted more laughter than I intended and it seemed to clear the air, for from then on we all got quite matey. Bluebird gave us a good idea of the proposed plan to try to establish escape routes to be used by Air Force crews, should they be shot down and not captured. In addition, we had to get a man back to England before he weakened too much. We were to fly in a Hudson and land with a fair amount of supplies to be collected by an organizer in command of a large group of Resistors.

"In the meantime," he continued, "you, Robin, will exercise your knowledge by instructing Tom and Sally in the finer arts of incendiary, booby-trap and other diabolical explosive devices of which your records show you to be capable. In addition, you will put them through the required amount of personal exercises you appear to be capable of administrating. Come to think of it, I'm of the opinion that you may do my leg a bit of good. On the other hand, you are really not very nice to know, if the comments in your file are correct, and they should be. No offense, of course."

I responded that I would like to have a look at my file in return for having a go at the leg, and I was surprised to hear Bluebird say that, as the Group Leader, it was his policy to read the salient parts of individual's records to the teams selected for specific jobs. He would do that tomorrow at 10.00 hours, when we would meet here again. In the meantime, he suggested we have a drink and get as much sleep as possible.

He did not join us for a late drink, but suggested that from now on we stick to beer. "Even you, Sally." Then he entered a taxi. I noted he did not get in with ease, and I made a mental note to get some of the stiffness out of that leg.

Sally, Tom and I found a pub. Tom said it was pints or nothing. Sally said a pint— providing it had a handle. He was a long time getting served. The pub poorly lit and crowded. An American soldier said, "Jeeze! You can't do it in here," and Sally laughed.

We found one empty seat and I offered it to Sally. She maneuvered into a position that left me in a sitting position with her in my lap. This arrangement was short-lived, as she spied Tom wandering about the bar with three pint mugs of beer looking for us. She left my lap to guide him to where we were sitting. Quite a natural thing to do in the circumstances, but no sooner had Sally left me, and before I could take another breath, I had another female on me. This one had had more than one drink and was feeling very friendly. She asked me in a French/English accent who "ze ladee was that go so queek, and would I pleeze do the same to 'er," for she would not run away.

I started to explain, but was not doing too well, the French girl apparently having more than one pair of arms. The sight that greeted Sally was not the sight she had when she left me. And she said so, in English.

When my new companion spoke, Sally was quick to detect the accent and there flowed a torrent of French abuse that could equal what a London docker might say to someone who had dropped a heavy weight on his foot. Only more so. The Anglo-French liaison between us parted company as the two girls faced one another, and I soon witnessed the degree of frustration that existed in the war-time alliance between the two countries.

The only place to park three pints of beer was on the chair. This is exactly what Tom did, and then very firmly suggested to the new girl to "allez-off." It worked. She did—right in the lap of another unsuspecting lad and there she seemed content.

It was almost impossible to raise a glass to the mouth without a nudge or barge in the back. The place was that crowded.

I felt unsettled, not sure of myself, not really wanting the warm weak beer I nearly had in my glass. I evidently let my thoughts show, for Sally said, "Cheer up! You are in London, not in a little French village looking over your shoulder every few seconds and constantly wishing you were in London. You are here now; make the most of it, for soon you will be under stress."

She slipped her non-drinking arm through mine to convey her point. We drank up, parked our glasses on the still vacant chair, and left the place. The air was decidedly chilly outside, but Tom had a remedy. He suggested we make our way to his place.

I had been there once before, and once inside, my eyes went straight to the line drawing in Tom's lounge. It was still there, but the signature had been cleverly obliterated. The craggy roots of a tree were now in the foreground. Very clever.

I had made up my mind to keep my eyes on Tom and to face the door at all times. Well—I didn't know—perhaps he was intending to have a wrestle with Sally. If he did, I wanted to have a good view. But no, he was a gentleman. Bade us sit and went to his little "bar" and served us some whiskey, then joined us for a few silent minutes.

I sensed a strange atmosphere and was puzzled regarding the lack of communication between my pals. Very sensitive to a change of environment, I inquired the reason for the hush. They looked at one another and came to a telepathic agreement. Sally confided their fear regarding the mission we were doing jn a few weeks time. Very dodgy, she thought.

"Bloody dangerous," said Tom. And Sally nodded.

"Well, cheer up, you two," I said. "Remember, you said that to me in the pub? Are we not in England, and indeed, in London, and with your combined experience, surely you have some confidence?"

Tom refilled our glasses, sat down on a chair, back to front, and leaned on the chair back.

"When I was with the guv'ner in the ambulance," he said. "He told me that Laura had been caught, tortured and killed. She did not betray anyone at all. Ajax could have saved her, but could not be in two places at once. He is brokenhearted about it, but is determined to find out who gave the orders and who exactly did the rough stuff. We hope to know of this before we three go over again. You are not supposed to know of this, in case you decide to do your cycle-saddle act again. Promise you will work with Sally and me. Then, perhaps, we can enjoy ourselves a bit. You must realize that now that you have a name, you are entitled to know how the land lies. Before, you were only required to do as you were told. Now you are one of us."

"Do you mean to tell me that I'm the cause of this gloom? Do you honestly think I will let you down?"

Sally laid a hand on mine. "No, of course we have no doubts about you, otherwise you would not be here. You must realize that Tom and I have two years experience with this sort of work, and of about thirty of us that started, we are the only two survivors. Not only that, at least once a week, we hear of someone getting caught and you must see the odds are getting lower."

"Yes, of course, I understand. What I don't quite get is this mention of when "37" comes over. And all these names we have, such as Blackbirds, Bluebirds and me—I am a Robin. What has "37" to do with it, or does it refer to your bust-line? If so, then I can quite see the logic of the ornithological idea for you two—Tom-Tits? or, if cold, perhaps Blue-Tits?"

This remark relaxed the atmosphere, and with the refilled

glasses, I secretly thought of applying for the post of Court Jester.

Sally and I left Tom after a while, and as we made our way toward our living quarters near Baker Street, I learned a lot. When we arrived at the old hotel, I found that, although I was well-known by sight, Sally, however, was not. In spite of her identity card, there was going to be some delay in her getting in. I suggested that, while the checks were being made, we push off for a bite to eat and be back before midnight, or later, if any bombing caused a delay. The security man gave me a knowing wink and agreed. I mentioned that the lady would prefer not to be put with the French section. To this, he ventured that she would have to go wherever it was thought fit to place her.

It was arm-in-arm to a little place run by the Sailors and Army, with eggs, chips, sausage and tea for a meal. They had a number system and we were number 117. They were calling out 91 at the time, so we had a wait. We were both in civvies, which caused some funny looks from soldiers, but it gave us a chance to talk.

Sally asked my real name. I told her and answered other questions, and without any prompting from me, she told me her name was Lee in real life. Sheila Ann Lee from Richmond, S.A. Lee— Sally, as near as one could get.

By the time No. 112 was served, we were old friends, and when she took off her coat and revealed that she followed the current fashion of wearing a sweater two sizes too small, I could also well understand why she had the number 37. I also wished I had not been so woozy after having been drugged there in France.

She read my thoughts and again mentioned quietly how sorry she was to have knocked me out. She suggested that perhaps next time we could half each of the tablets— that way we would be equal. I thought about this, and although it was a semi-jest, I felt sad, and reminded her of the fate of Laura.

Sally looked at me for a long time and replied, "You are too much of a gentleman to be in this war. Do you realize that one or more of us could be in the same position as Laura before long? You do know now, don't you, that it is doubtful if the three of us will return all in one piece?"

"No, I didn't realize that, and by your tone, you are apparently very concerned, and evidently know something I do not. Tell me, Sally, how is it you are not missed from your usual haunts in France? How will you explain your absence when you return? And how do you know so much of the mission?"

Sally moved closer, gave me a knowing wink, and said quietly, "Watch how you phrase your sentences—you never know—and anyway, our number is due next."

We ate more or less in silence, with no more mention of our type of work. After the meal, we found a pub. The bar was almost deserted and very cold and dim. We left after one drink and found another—well, we couldn't miss. There was a bit of a "knees-up" going on, and this place was just the opposite of the last one. Very crowded and very warm. There were as many civvies as there were uniforms, which made things easier.

"I'll have a pint, with a handle," said Sally, "and I'll find the Ladies."

My order was passed forward by those pressed against the bar. Two pints arrived, and I had no means of getting my money out. "That's all right, mate, all paid for. You look like a sergeant."

I couldn't wait for Sally to find me at a table, and when at last she approached, she was smiling, her jumper was fully alive. When she sat, she was very close. She picked up her pint, looked me straight in the eye, and said, "up the Arsenal!"

That brought back memories of the time I first met this girl and I took her free hand in mine and squeezed it hard. She squeezed harder, and it hurt. Lovely smiling eyes over the top of her pint glass looked a message. She finished her pint, smacked her lips and said, "That was smashing, I'll get the next."

I stood to protest, but a hefty thump in the chest had me back in my seat. I watched and learned how to get served in packed London pub. The first requirement was to be a female. The next was to be as attractive as Sally and very fit, able to draw in the waist and thus raise the bust line by the minimum of three inches, then slowly ease forward by turning sideways.

The pianist was playing a popular song I though very appropriate, "I'll Get By." And she did —sideways. Not only that, her drinks were a little different; they were whiskies, three of them. Neat. Trebles.

"What's the idea, Sally?" I asked, as she sat down very close again.

"Well, look at it this way," she replied, "I've felt rotten having given you a "mickey." This will help put it right."

"Yes, Luv, okay, but why three drinks?"

She just told me to drink up, wished me all the very best of luck in the future, and hoped that one day, if we survived the war, perhaps I would take her to the South of England, and show her the countryside in spring, buy a bottle—and celebrate.

She sipped her drink. She was very attractive and became more so as she mellowed into her normal self, without the overriding discipline of her job. I took that as a compliment and told her it was nice to be trusted and encouraged her to talk, if she wished.

The story began at the start of the war. She was twenty, with a French mother and an English father. He helped the British when the Germans occupied France. She had a sister two years older.

After Dunkirk, her village was fully occupied. One night, after the family was in bed, they were wakened by a loud knocking on their door. Her father opened up and in came two German soldiers. One searched downstairs, where Sally had successfully hidden.

"The other soldier made himself a great nuisance in Mum's bedroom, opening drawers and making himself objectionable, to put it mildly. Suddenly, from upstairs there were screams of, 'No—please don't!' These cries were from my sister, and without thinking, I broke cover and ran up the stairs. The downstairs soldier was surprised to see me pass him and chased as I made for my sister's room. We went in almost together.

"I was shocked, dead scared, and feeling sick all at once. On the bed, my sister was being raped. She was terrified. The soldier still wore his thick coarse coat and his helmet. My parents had by now arrived. My father leaped onto the bed to pull the German off his daughter, my mother was screaming ."

"The soldier standing threatened us with his gun and made us stand with our backs to a wall. He had his gun pointing at us but he was watching his mate. My mother held her hands over her face and I can see her now, as the soldier hit her in the stomach with his gun. She slid down to the floor, sobbing. My father was trying to push past the soldier. I don't know what I was doing, but I felt sick.

The man on the bed stood up and motioned to his mate to carry on. There was more screaming—the soldiers changed places, but the new one took off his helmet and coat. My sister rolled off the bed. She was hysterical, but was made to climb back. The new one grasped her nightdress at the neck and tore it off my sister."

For the first time, Sally found difficulty in continuing, but after some effort to compose herself, continued.

"My mother, father, and I were forced to watch this animal, this beast, and when the leering Jerry stated how good it was, my father leapt at him, but the German was too strong and used the butt of his gun to smash my father's face. It was awful. My father, who could speak French and German, reverted to his native English tongue with the intention of letting off steam, but luckily checked himself and gave them a verbal blasting in French, threatening to report the incident to their Commandant."

I heard most of this experience quite clearly, as Sally relived her thoughts, but some words were lost in the general noise of the environment of the pub. That was the gist of it, however.

In these kinds of circumstances, I have never been one to say, "Never mind, cheer up," and such stupid comments, since it is impossible to "cheer up" at such short notice. So I said nothing.

Suddenly, Sally lifted her glass and emptied a treble Scotch—in one go. She spluttered a bit, but it seemed to do the trick, for she looked straight at me and said, "Now do you know why I am in this organization?"

I replied that I could fully understand. "But why tell me? After all, there are many more suitable types in the firm to tell such a story. Some with authority, some with the means of consoling you—in other words, officers."

To which she said, "Shut up and drink up!"

So I did.

She shuffled about a bit and I had the nagging feeling that she either was half sozzled, or not the girl operator she was cracked up to be. Or she had found someone at last to confide in.

She answered my question. She drank a half of the third whiskey, handed me the glass, and said, "I'm prepared to share everything I have with you for the rest of my life."

Well, she was attractive, I must admit, but then so were other girls, and I personally felt no great desire to take any advantage. To be honest, I was far more concerned with the task that lie ahead. It was one thing to show sympathy regarding her ordeal in her home, but it was another thing to have an offer such as this thrust upon me. I did not take it too seriously and pointed out that we had just twenty minutes to get back before midnight. It took exactly that period for the whiskey to take effect.

She was very heavy by the time we arrived at our quarters. The security officer we had seen earlier was still on duty, and he raised his eyes in mock concern as he let us through. Once inside, there were still many people on the move along the corridor. One was a FANY major who did not express any mock concern. She read the riot act without a stop for a long five minutes. During all this Sally was leaning heavily on me, slowly slipping down until I heaved her up, giggling from time to time. Then it was my turn to listen to the voice of authority. I was irresponsible—getting a girl in that condition. At this Sally burst out laughing, turned, and hid her shaking face close to mine. But the FANY wasn't through.

"Who are you with? Which section administers you? How can we more responsible people conduct a serious campaign? Only recently we had one of our most brilliant men go down with nervous tension. I have girls that are at risk every minute of the day and night, possible torture and rape."

My cuddly companion left me as though I was electrified, took up a stance facing the officer, and loosed off in fluent German. The major held up a hand and shook her head. Sally started again, this time in French. I could tell by the occasional wince that Sally was getting home her point, and as my eyes darted from one face to the other, I could not help but admire the cool way Sally handled herself. A small group had collected in the narrow hall and those who could understand had a chuckle from time to time. Some looked a bit scared. I wondered how anyone could recover so quickly, having been almost unable to walk after drinking two pints of beer followed by over four tots of whiskey. That was another thing. How did she manage to get whiskey? Perhaps the Canadians had got it in.

Suddenly, Sally stopped talking, turned to the assembled group, and told them to "allez-off," held out her hand to me and said, "Come on, Sunshine, let's get some coffee."

"What was that all about?" I asked.

"Well, having enjoyed ourselves tonight—you know, 'Lambeth Walk' fashion—on the way home, and then being told by an old battle-axe about behavior and so on—fair enough, I suppose—but when she said rape, that got me. I told her how I saw things from my end of the job in France and as a civilian operator was not subject to good order and military discipline, and—Oh well! Forget it. Let's sit down in the corner."

I brought over four cups of coffee, two each. I spilled a little of each. She had a habit of looking over the top of her glass or cup and her expression was very appealing. I apologized for making a mess of the coffee.

"I thought you were the one with the steady hands," she said.

"Well, the cups were too full and hot, and anyway, you managed three glasses of more potent stuff in the pub. How did you sober up so quickly?"

Another long look over the top of her cup, her expression soft and caring.

"I brought over three glasses. Two were ginger ale, one was whiskey. The idea was to mix it how we liked, but when you invited me to talk, and when I realized you were suffering with me, I made up my mind you were the one for me. So you earned the scotch. I drank the ginger and half of the third one, offering you the remaining half, remember?"

"So, really, you were not pickled?"

"Not a bit, but I enjoyed the way you helped me along, which I wouldn't have so much if I had been under the influence!"

"Why, you . . . " She stopped my lips from ending my sentence.

I do not know what *she* looked like, but I had my eyes closed during this very pleasant interlude of the proceedings. When I opened them, I saw a group of young people watching. I noticed the men looked at me with some kind of envy, but the girls were evidently not going to give Sally any competition. They moved away when we resumed drinking our coffee. I mentioned my opinion to Sally, who replied that she was a one-man girl and I was her man. If I would have her.

To that, I said I felt we would be wise to wait until we had done the job.

To that, she said I had a lot more to learn, for there was little guarantee that we would return.

The sexes were segregated for sleeping purposes. At Sally's area, she told me to meet her tomorrow for breakfast, gave me a saucy look, and shook hands!

In the morning, after breakfast, we reported to the Museum, arriving at ten minutes to ten. Sally bumped her hip against mine a couple of times on the way up the stairs and past the many security checks, men in blue uniforms and men in civilian clothes who appeared to share a common opinion of the girl who held my hand. Without exception, these men of fifty or more all looked like they wished they were thirty.

Tom was already in the office when we arrived, and when we were all seated, the man behind the desk did as promised. He read the salient parts of our individual files so that we knew each other's abilities. He added that I had a report from one officer that contained just one word: conceited.

Bluebird looked at me and inquired if this bothered me. I asked the officers name and he shook his head. So I said, "Taylor" and he nodded.

Sally said, "Well, what a bloody sauce."

Tom said, "Didn't know what confidence is."

The young boss commented that some people did not know the difference between determination and stubbornness, looked at me and said, "Don't worry about it."

The next hour was spent dealing with the details of the task ahead for the three of us. As the plan sank in, I began to share the apprehension Sally had indicated earlier. It was a diabolical idea even to me, who had no previous experience, other than the brothel and onion jobs. But Tom and Sally had had two long years of this type of work and knew, or sensed, the danger.

I found out that at one stage of the operation I was to do a solo job while Sally and Tom dealt with another task. Due to lack of time, I would have to get back to the checkpoint, otherwise they would be expected to push on ahead.

We looked at one another and just shrugged to the inevitable. After a while, Bluebird said, "Now, when you are dismissed, you will be tempted to talk about this briefing. Well, you can. But please do so in here. Just talk among yourselves. Sue—tea.

Sue arrived with the tea, and a very happy smile. She had some sugar!

So we sorted out our problems. Details of details. Things the public never sees depicted in the cinema. No things here such as one unarmed man fighting off five or six of the enemy, with the transport manifesting itself just at the crucial time for escape—a transport that never needs refueling and weapons that seldom need reloading, and so on.

Tom's main worry was his ankle, and he wanted to know if there was likely to be much walking. He was told he had exactly seven days to get it fit for a medical, so rest it. In fact, all of us would rest as much as possible without risking injury at any cost.

Sally said she had only one problem. Within the next seven to ten days, the mission would be at a most inconvenient period. If we saw what she meant.

"What about you, Robin, what's your main worry?"

Three faces looked for my reply, and three countenances broke into a smile at my answer.

"I'm just bloody scared!"

Bluebird warned us to be very careful conversing about the forthcoming mission and reminded us of the current slogan, "Careless Talk Costs Lives."

"Be here at 10.00 hours every day for the next seven days for more details of how your reception committee is progressing out there. On the seventh day, you will each have a medical and three days after that—you go!"

He stood as we left the office.

CHAPTER TWENTY-ONE

Outside it was warm and sunny. It was nearly noon. Time to eat. We agreed on all that, but funds were low. I did not know how much my companions were paid, but I knew how much the going rate for operating in enemy occupied territory was in my case. It was £3/12. Three pounds, twelve shillings (£3.60). A week. No overtime. No bonus. No dirty money. Mind you, I saved nearly £1 a week by an allotment. Then there was income tax, to say nothing of 6d. (21/ 2p.) barrack room damages deducted.

So I fished out my pound note and some odd coppers. The others had a look, and between us, we had just over £4. So we three civilian-dressed young persons walked in uniformed London, past large mountains of sandbags protecting important buildings, and headed for a pub across the street. Little or no traffic to dodge, but plenty of funny looks from some people that thought we were of service age and should be in uniform.

But no funny looks from a man with a car outside the pub. His head was well under the bonnet of his Morris, and he was busy talking to the engine. I could not resist asking him the trouble, and without looking up, he said, "The bleedin' thing packs up every half mile and it's not short of petrol, 'cos me and me mate milked a lorry last night."

Suddenly, whatever he was doing went wrong, for his hand slipped, bringing forth a long series of unprintable words. This made Sally laugh, and her chuckles brought the man to a standing position. He wrung his hand, which had a slight burn mark, and apologized to the "lidy."

I suggested he give his petrol pump a sharp tap with a tool

after first switching on the ignition. He did this and the pump clacked into life. I advised him to remove the large cork float and give it a coat of shellac. He said he would dq that in the shelter tonight.

"Thanks guv, you're a toff. 'Ere, have a drink, and 'ere missy, have some of these."

I found I had a nice white £5 note and Sally was holding two pairs of nylon stockings.

We protested at this, but he said we were welcome.

"You will be called up soon, by the look of us. Anyway, I do all right with my scrap."

He looked at Tom, who watched all this with hands in his pockets.

"You fink you ain't got nuffin doncher mate? Well you can have the job of fittin' on the stockin' on the missy!"

He drove off happy and laughing.

We laughed, although I had to admit to the nagging fear of the forthcoming task. But the drink and a nice meal mellowed me into some confidence, aided by my two more experienced companions.

During the afternoon, we visited the armory, and I showed them how to arm incendiary devices of a type to insert in a pocket, explosive cigarettes, and other tricks. Outside we were able to fire off some of them, which was far more impressive and prompted Tom to mutter, "Rather you than me with your fireworks." He added, "A fine pair I have—one with the bangers and the other with the dopey booze."

This prompted Sally to talk about her knockout drops. She said she had often been asked how it was possible to drug a drink without the person seeing it doctored, and what would happen if the drinks were swapped over? The answer was simple.

She recalled an instance where she got her man alone, having enticed him to a private room with expectations of a sexual interlude, and offered him a drink. The man was a professional, with the information she needed. He knew it, so was on his guard. She left the room, leaving the door open, had a quiet drink, and returned with a tray on which was a full bottle and two clean glasses. She had lowered her neckline a little and was none to demure when she sat, not seeming to notice her skirt was a bit high.

The man was too tough to be impressed by this, and was expecting the drink to be tampered with when she poured. Sally stopped talking at this point and I asked what happened next? She laid a finger on my nose and explained she found out what was expected of her. She added that the trick was to drink the antidote, which neutralized the dope, adding that it was a dodgy business, but better than playing about with those fireworks that you call "easy when-you-know-how."

Did I say that?

CHAPTER TWENTY-TWO

I think the take-off place was Croydon that was, or was it Dunsfold? For sure it was very dark. We were taken into a hanger and it was obvious the plane was far too large for just the three of us. We walked around it, ducking under the wings at each circuit. Sally, I noted, seemed to regard the wheels as being important. Tom would adopt a stance from time to time with hands on hips and contemplate the cockpit canopy. I know what I did. I looked at the part that I would look at today—the engines and the propellers. But one thing was missing—the pilot.

I asked one of the RAF chaps where he was. The reply was to the effect that he was probably still in a padded cell, as he and people like us were all mad. I asked if he and his mates had ever prepared a plane for this kind of work before? His reply to that was that he had done so many times, but never when the "kite" had to land.

"Other times," he said, "you crazy sods only jumped."

Inevitably, the three of seemed to agree that this plane would do the job for us, as though we had a choice of aircraft.

There was a flurry of action. Men appeared and heaved and pushed the aircraft out into the blackness, and I could not help thinking how small it now appeared. We climbed aboard, followed by two RAF men, obviously the pilot and navigator. The navigator had charts and maps; he was also a sergeant. That pleased me. He sat in a seat with a small table. In front of him were a lot of instruments, all slightly aglow. Another man entered and announced he was the dispatching officer. He pointed a torch at us, counted that there were three of us, and said, "My chaps will just check the cargo, then you can be off."

The cargo consisted of about a dozen large supply containers, each one having several cells. These were apparently to be dropped en route to our place of landing. Quite an involved scheme, since a reception party had to be present at each place.

The waiting was now getting the better of us. This was my third mission, and although very much junior in experience than my colleagues, I found myself again making a study of the two veterans. Tom inspected his watch, and from time to time, tried to get into conversation with the navigator, without much success. Sally was sitting next to Tom and was, of all things, having a bother with her hair. This was odd, since her medium length blonde hair managed to look good in a gale-force wind, but now it was apparently trouble-some. She caught me watching her and smiled, then left her seat to sit beside me. This left Tom with more space on his seat, which enabled him to transfer his interest from his watch to his boots.

Sally transferred her interest from her hair to my welfare, and sitting very close, she whispered, "You will be careful, won't you?"

I replied that I would, to which she added, "But you don't know just how bloody dodgy it might be."

"No, but it looks as though I'm going to find out!"

Just then, as though by magic, the plane rocked and an engine started, followed shortly by its mate on the other wing. The three of us exchanged glances. *This was it!*

The engines revved up to an even note, the plane ceased shuddering, Tom crossed his fingers, Sally's left arm slipped through mine, and we all braced ourselves for the big moment.

We didn't move. The engine note died and finally cut.

The pilot came through from the front, the navigator removed his headphones, the door slid back, and the head and shoulders of the dispatching officer appeared in the gloom saying, "It's all off for twenty-four hours."

Sally said, "This is the worst of this job, all stop-go, and bloody anti-climaxes."

We spent the night in a Nissen hut with an enormous combustion stove in the center. Someone had a supply of fuel and the smoke pipe was red hot in places. There was also an endless supply of cheese sandwiches, which were toasted to a nicety after a technique was evolved. These were washed down with light ale via enameled service mugs.

Later we were shown our sleeping quarters. A RAF Corporal looked at Sally as she deftly made the three camp beds comfortable. She confused him even more by saying, "We often share a room; tomorrow night, with a bit of luck, we may sleep in a ditch!"

When the business of the latrines was sorted out and I went to bed, I realized that I had sheets. I called over to Sally to express my thanks, and she explained that we all had them, to which a sleepy Tom muttered, "They wear pajamas, too."

We were, of course, comparing the fact that, in the Army, there were no sheets, just blankets. No doubt the beer helped, for we slept till awakened in the morning, this time by a RAF sergeant, a much older man than the one who saw us the night before. He brought bacon and egg with coffee, and having set up a table, laid the meals out with expertise, saying knowingly, "I know what you lot are in, was once in them myself, until I spoke out of turn."

Tom propped himself up on his elbows, said thanks for the food and added, "And you have done it again."

Halfway through the breakfast, we had another visitor. He was an officer who gave a smart salute saying, "Good morning, Ma'am and gentlemen, I am Group captain Browne with an 'e.' We have a Brown without an 'e,' but he is a Flight sergeant—very confusing."

Tom said, "Very."

The officer continued, "I am to apologize for not entertaining you in the Mess, but at a very late hour we received very confusing signals as to welfare. This seemed to be the best we could do in the circumstances. Perhaps this evening you would join us?"

Tom's reply to that was that we would be delighted to do so, if we were still here.

Later we were shown the parachute packers. Young girls deftly, but carefully, folding and packing those large, unwieldy pieces of material with confident care.

We also had a chance to see our plane in daylight. It all looked so different now. We kept together, more silent than anything, collecting some funny looks from the camp staff.

Dinner was brought to us in the hut and the two orderlies noted the empty bottles from the night before, one of them asking what we were doing?

Tom said, "We are on an exercise and have to lay low during the day."

The orderly then asked what were we in?

"Coldstream Guards," said Tom. We were sitting at the time, but when we later stood, not one of the three of us could make more than five foot nine inches, and even then one of us was a female.

During the afternoon, Tom went off to have a chat with the dispatching officer. Alone with Sally now, I asked what she thought we would have been doing at this time had we flown out the night before. She studied her watch and thought we might be with some Resisters in a wooded area. That meant little to me until she added that Pascale was nice, to which I replied, "Who the hell is Pascale?" A lady, it seemed, who was a very tough nut. She had her own way with men—if she was attracted, she had her own way with men.

"And I have to meet her?" I asked.

"You have to work with her for a few hours, but there will be no time or incident that will cause me the slightest jealousy," Sally replied.

We had been strolling along the perimeter of the airfield while talking. In the distance, we saw three officers approaching. Sally changed the subject abruptly. The three men smiled at her and scowled at me! Also approaching was Tom, who appeared to have acquired a friend, for he was accompanied by a very small RAF officer, who, because of his stature, walked with very short, sharp steps.

Tom introduced him as Flight Lieutenant Worthington.

"D.F.C.," added the officer.

Tom said he was sorry. The officer said there was no relationship with the brewers.

Our new friend joined us in our hut and explained he was from the Met. Office and that we would definitely go tonight, even though conditions were not ideal. It seemed the reception party could not hold out any longer as things were desperate.

None of this waiting, walking, talking, and the general activities that had gone before had removed the dull, sick feeling that persisted in my stomach. The fear of the air crossing, the landing, the conditions existing from being in enemy-occupied territory, the instructions, the false papers, the language problem, the hopelessness of not having enough information, no authority—all this made me wish I had never joined.

I was scared.

CHAPTER TWENTY-THREE

Not being an expert, I suppose the take-off was smooth. At any rate, we were in the air. Those who have won medals, or played in the Cup Finals, or achieved anything on the same order will know that, looking back, they were not entirely aware of what was going on. It is the same when one gets married. The Service, the reception, cutting the cake, hearing the telegrams—to me, just a blur. Mind you, out of that lot all I can claim to have done is the getting married bit, and a bloody great blur that was. But not this flying job. This was no blur. It was a cold, uncomfortable, tense, dark, frightening journey.

The activity that preceded the canister dropping found me unmoved, and the action as they disappeared into the darkness left me cold. Literally. Not only that, I needed to have a piddle. And I said as much. In the gloom of the fuselage, I could see Sally, Tom, and the two RAF lads who had done the heaving-out of the containers. Only the girl answered, "You should have gone down the hole." Even she was confused, since it was a door.

The navigator was busy having a chat with the pilot, the plane appeared to change course, and the navigator and Tom were together now. Things were happening. A slight movement in the tummy indicated the loss of height and then the pilot did what pilots often do. He increased the revs, making more noise. Fine, if that is the technique, but why make such a racket and draw attention to the fact that three English agents were about to land so deep inside France. However, I thought that gliders would have been noisy in the circumstances.

The takeoff had been from a billiard table compared with the landing. This resembled the Grand National course, except it was dark. And raining. I noted that German-controlled rain was much the same as English rain, but this somehow was wetter.

So, out of the aircraft, on to the sodden grass, giving the front of the machine a wide berth to safely avoid the props that were still moving quite fast, even though the engines were throttled back.

The three of us had quite a lot of kit. A very heavy radio, some explosives, lots of money for some local leader, field dressings and general medical supplies, lots of tubes of Bostik, a black adhesive used for a multitude of sticking jobs.

And I still needed a piddle.

So I stopped stumbling along, undid a few thousand buttons, and added to the water on the soggy grass. I felt a new man, and made good time towards the direction I imagined my colleagues would be. But I had lost them! Left and right I weaved, peering into the gloom, but with no luck. The strap of one of my loads was cutting into my shoulder, so I let it slip to the ground and sat on it. I thought how easily the situation could change, for not many moments previously, I had appreciated the presence of my two companions, as opposed to my first venture when I was alone. But now? I was alone again, sitting in the middle of a French field in the dark and in the rain. A good place to stop an episode of a serial, I thought. *Watch next week . . . what will Robin do next? Poor thing.*

I think it was Tom that sniffed me out, and for sure it was Tom who asked what the bloody hell I thought I was doing and didn't I know it was hard enough as it was without me playing hide-and-seek, adding that it was not so much that they needed me, but they had to have the stuff I was carrying.

"I suppose, you still have it, or did you decide to leave a trail?"

Tom's voice led Sally to us and there we were, all together again. After a few moments silence, Tom asked, "Are you all right now?"

"Yes, thank you."

It all turned out to be a blessing in disguise, since our voices had alerted the reception party, who made themselves known and relieved us of our baggage. In single file now, we started into a wooded area, but many small things can go wrong, in spite of experience and training. One of the Frenchmen up front of me stumbled over a surface root and twisted his ankle. Instead of a helper, he was now a liability. What was more, I wound up carrying his load. In the sort-out, I lost contact with Sally, having followed her so far.

We walked nearly half a mile, I estimated, before we stopped, and we were then under cover at last. The old hut had no windows, and every gap was sealed with sacking to prevent any light showing through. Not that it was much of a light, for it smoked so much it defeated its own purpose. But still, it was good to sit on the coarse blankets provided remove the wet boots and socks with great speed. There was no heating of any kind and I thought back to the night before when the stove was hot. I also recalled that Sally had indicated we would be in a wooded area. She was busy in conversation with what appeared to be the Resistance leader. Tom was dealing with the wireless, one of the Frenchmen was practicing with the Morse key although it was not connected to the set.

I had no specific duties, so I changed my socks. Well, doing nothing at a party like this was worse than anything, but all of a sudden, they crowded round and "Robeen" had his back slapped and hand shaken, to say nothing of a kiss on both cheeks. I thought he was quite pretty really!

I would have enjoyed a nice hot cup of coffee, but the only liquid available was wine. The eats consisted of plain bread and the assurance that breakfast would be more than substantial.

There had been five Resisters in the party, now three of them left the hut. The two remaining wrapped themselves in their blankets and settled down in the gloom in a corner. Tom came to me and motioned his head towards the door. Outside we jointly relieved ourselves. I whispered my concern about Sally.

"What happens. Do we stand guard for her, or what?"

"Didn't you know?" replied Tom, "they seldom go, they last for days on end! Come on in."

Sure enough, when Tom asked if she was going out, she shook her head!

The floor was the dry earth. It smelled musty and was not at all comfortable, but using one of the hold-alls, I managed to make some kind of support for my top end.

Nobody said good night—we were all busy with our thoughts. We had been told our tasks would take a week and that we would be back in London easily within ten days. I tied a single knot in one of my laces. That kind of thing meant a lot to me; it was my talisman and I would savor the moment when I untied it back home.

In the dark under the blankets I also fiddled with my watch-strap. It was a French watch and strap, non-luminous. I longed to call out to Sally and ask the time; even if she did not know. At least it might start us talking for we had hardly spoken since we landed. I kept quiet, then dozed. Not for long, as I could plainly hear the noise of a train in the distance. It seemed to be moving very slowly. It caused me to listen intently, and I sat up sharply when I heard foot-steps getting louder.

Sally whispered, "It's okay; probably our new guard. Don't worry."

"How long have you been awake?" I asked.

"Most of the time; been waiting for you to speak," she replied.

"None of us slept." This from Tom over on the right, adding, "Why don't you two get married?"

There was no comment to that remark, and anyway, the environment of the hut changed sharply, for the door opened to admit four men with lanterns, which they lit. I was pleased to note they were of the non-smoking type.

After some long chat with Sally and Tom, we got ourselves ready to move before daybreak. This was easy, since we only needed to put on our footwear and pick up our baggage. The two lads in the corner came to see us off, one of them being the owner of a swollen ankle and very content to receive the administrations of his friend.

So off we went, in single file, through the trees for at least another half mile, until the woods opened out into a clearing. Here we all assembled in a group, augmented from time to time by Resisters who apparently appeared from nowhere. They looked a formidable force, mostly dressed in a kind of green denim with woolen head-gear or the traditional berets. I noticed they had almost not shaved, for they sported, not beards as such, just two or three days stubble, and having arrived at the appointed place at the correct time, they very confidently squatted in groups of two or three using trees as back support. As I said, they exuded confidence and their numbers made me feel the same.

More consultations, then a decision at last. We were going to have breakfast . . .

In a derelict railway building, we enjoyed coffee, eggs, and lovely French bread. Afterwards, we had a wash and I had a cold water shave. On my return from my ablutions, I saw a sight that stopped me in my tracks, for there among the men was another woman. Although dressed like the others, this one had a green shirt that was stretched tightly into a broad leather belt. The waist was about thirteen inches smaller than the chest. Not only that, at least four of the shirt buttons were undone. As a point of interest, buttons were spaced a considerable distance apart. I looked at this arrangement until the button's owner met my gaze. I then looked at Sally, who was watching me. I started toward Sally, but was halted by the new woman, who said, in very good English, "You must be Robin, yes?"

I nodded.

"You will work very closely with me this evening."

Before I could acknowledge that, one of the Resisters made a remark in French which caused quite a lot of laughter. I looked blank at this and feeling the joke was on me, asked for an explanation. It seemed the comment was to the effect that a short session with this lady would soon give Robin a red breast.

I gathered this young, confident woman was Pascale and it soon became apparent she held a very authoritative position.

We were now all sitting wherever it was dry enough to do so, and for clarity, Pascale spoke in French and then repeated herself in English. At the end, her attention was directed at me. While I was at last learning the details of my specific task, all of the Resisters moved off, leaving Sally and Tom to listen to my brief.

I was to accompany Pascale to a safe house, there to be dressed and kitted out as a railway line maintenance worker. Together with others, I would help repair the track. The others would be Resistance men, who would indicate where it was planned to blow the line. I would do the preparation at a certain time shortly before a train was due and then get back to Pascale. As soon as the explosion was heard, she would escort me back to a place to join my colleagues.

"You understand, yes?" She was in the habit of getting a "Yes" it seemed, but on this occasion it was a "No."

She stood silently, ran her hands around her waist inside her belt, which required her to breathe in, thus lifting her bust to even more prominence, and asked with a definite sneer why I should question her instruction.

I asked why I had to do a simple rail fracture, which was, after all, basic training. Why couldn't the other men do this? She approached me as I stood. I swear her bust was no more than an inch from my chest. She had almost hate in her eyes as she said, "You bloody English promise this and that and when the time comes you parlez around. Pick up your kit and follow me."

As she moved, I made a grab and held on to a nicely formed arm. She swung inwards, and with a smirk, made it very plain she would welcome that inch to become zero, but I held her other arm and moved back a pace.

"Well, this from the Bloody English," I said. "In my case, if. you want my help you bloody well ask, not tell me, for I have quite enough people telling me how to risk my neck without having a bust-conscious Mademoiselle joining in, and to me it looks pretty certain that if you ride the high-horse too much, you will get captured. Then you will have plenty of attention."

She stalked off. I picked up my canvas bag containing mostly explosives and followed, having given a backward farewell to Sally and Tom. That lady could certainly move, for she strode in an easy relaxed manner, her hips moving beautifully. I made no attempt to catch up—as a provocative female, she held no attraction for me. I was far more concerned with the job.

On a road now, with the railway running parallel and some houses in sight, my leader slowed her pace. Finding myself gaining, I, too, slowed. At last she stopped, and turning to face me, adopted a stance with feet apart, hands on hips, stretching that shirt tighter. She held out her right hand, and with a slight smile, said, "Not many men say 'No' to me."

I took her hand and explained I thought she was a very attractive girl and if the remainder of her body was as good as the parts visible, then she must have many admirers.

Walking side by side now, much slower, we continued chatting, something about my statement regarding the "other parts." I suggested that her legs were hidden in those very unladylike trousers. She smiled and indicated the railway.

We crossed the road and looked down the cutting. One single track on a bend to left and right, with the rails not too bright, indicating that not many trains used the line. Away to the left, I could see a tunnel and more houses. Still holding hands, we slithered down to the line. Here she let go to explain that the track would be under repair along this stretch. I would be expected to prepare the charge where told and show the Resisters how it was done. I asked about the language problem, but she said talking would not be necessary. Just show.

As we scrambled up to the roadside, she again held my hand, and but we both knew this very fit young woman could go up the side of any mountain without any aid.

Across the road now and into a house, unoccupied, but with evidence of subversive use, none of which was hidden. Bandoliers of ammunition, emergency food tins, clothing, first aid kits, and all manner of haversacks, and in a corner, obviously used as a seat, a full-sized tin sporting a faded but clear label: "Huntley & Palmers, Reading, England."

I pointed this out to Pascale and expressed my concern regarding an English article and the consequences if the Germans made a search. She told me there has always been biscuits in France from Hunter & Palmers.

Through the rooms we went and up the very dodgy stairs, into the first room and there were three of the Resisters I had seen earlier. They each gave me a leering grin. One of them got up and gave me some clothing: dirty, smelly, coarse trousers and jacket, a greasy cap, and a pair of boots.

Pascale was no longer the hand-holding girl. I could tell she had to be in authority, for with bust raised, and hand on hips, she said, "Put them on," then added a few words in French to the other men. I tried to put the trousers on over my existing ones. It was not easy, as the inside legs rode up and jammed the effort. Pascale spoke again to her troops, who then left the room, then told me to undress properly. Then she, too, left the room.

Much more at ease now, I got myself dressed in this filthy garb. Strangely, it was not the presence of the girl that made me try to double up on the trousers. It was the thought of having those things so close to my body. But there it was. All part of the job. I started to itch immediately and the smell of that old jacket was terrible. I thought I would have preferred a hired coat from Moss Brothers with a large Union Jack on the back.

Pascale and her men returned, looked at me, and nodded. The Resisters had the same clothing as before, but were now without carbines. Instead they had shovels, iron bars, and other line repair tools.

Pascale studied her watch. We synchronized and moved towards the door, all faces tense. I felt it, too. This was it. I moved with my bag of explosives, faced Pascale, and asked how long the fuse should burn. She shrugged. I asked again, explaining I needed to know. Again she shrugged, this time the bandolier she wore found the position it sought between her breasts. It was hopeless.

CHAPTER TWENTY-FOUR

Not a soul was in sight as we walked to the line. Down by the track we split up into pairs, Pascale staying with me. After a few minutes, a train could be heard. I was sweating; my clothes were now giving me hell. I made to move, but was restrained by the girl. A small tank locomotive appeared round the curve, its speed decreasing. The engine pulled one flat truck on which six or seven German soldiers sat. Some of the Resisters waved their arms in salute. The soldiers ignored them.

"A pilot train to test the track for sabotage," said Pascale to my unspoken question. I was disappointed, for I thought we had left too late to place the charge and could pack up. But no. This was *it*. For up-track came a signal and the order, "Right Englishman, blow the track—*here*!"

Pascale indicated the place with a vicious stab of her foot, and as I suspected before, climbed the embankment like a gazelle, without a hand to hold.

On to the line went the two charges, staggered to cause a shearing effect. Primers in each charge, followed by a detonator crimped to two feet of safety fuse to give one minute burning time.

Next a problem. Should I light it? Where was that girl? I talked to myself. The Frenchmen tried to follow my words. They were wasting their time, for I was not talking about the explosives. I was telling myself how bloody stupid I was never to learn that women just cannot be relied on in this caper, and I was right when I said "No" earlier on and should have insisted on a different arrangement. All very well, having your tits bursting your shirt, a wide belt pulled in tight, but what about now? Where was the bloody girl?

I said something that sounded like, "Oo a le femme?"

The bloody fools understood, thought I could speak their lingo, and started waving their arms and talking all at once.

This was crazy. I thought for a second of Ajax. Decided he would have had a baby in these circumstances. Then reality. The bloody train was coming. Pascale was coming. The Frenchmen were going.

"*Pouf!*" said the girl.

I lit the two fuses. They smoked so much I felt sure they would be seen. The two of us scrambled up the slope and made it safely to the top. Pascale was running on ahead. She did not know about always walking away from a charge. But the circumstances were so very different now. I did a cross between a fast walk and a slow run. There were seconds to go.

"Down!" I shouted, making an effort to catch her up. We went down together. Not much fear of getting hurt, since the charge was below us. The engine was chuffing hard and getting louder. I wanted to look and turned my head. The girl pushed me back and left her arm around me. The exertion of our retreat had increased her breathing. Her chest was close and alive.

Two pounds of explosive when fired has a short, sharp noise. A train at speed, when suddenly deprived of a continuous track, makes a hell of a noise. This was badly timed, for the engine was well past the charge at the time of firing. Even so, the cut in the line left a gap of about eight to ten inches, with the fractured ends curling in opposite directions. That was why the fourth and fifth trucks fell over. The grinding, ripping, splintering noise seemed to go on and on.

Resisters pounded down the embankment, jumping over the two of us. I started to laugh; Pascale withdrew her arm very suddenly. I thought I knew how it feels if you fall at Beechers.

I waited for the sound of firing. The only sounds were of men shouting and a hiss of steam from the engine. It seemed like hours but, in fact, was only a few minutes that I laid beside this French girl. I made the first move and asserted myself. I announced I was going back to the hut and find Tom and Sally. Pascale joined me for the rest of the scramble up to the road, suggesting that I would need to change back into my field kit. This meant going into the house, the difference being that all the Resisters were engaged in dealing with the stricken train. The girl and I were alone.

Again, as I ridded myself of the offensive trousers and jacket, she left the room. I must admit I felt it odd, since she was either highly sexed or a tease, but whenever the opportunity arose, she made herself scarce. I still had the itch, even with my better French gear on, but at least I had lost the smell. I waited for Pascale to return and badly needed to get back to my colleagues and have a drink and a smoke. In that order.

At last, footsteps.

The person that opened the door was almost a stranger, for it was a very attractive female, hair loose and brushed, a short-sleeved blouse with puffed sleeves showing very nice arms. A low, round neckline showed the bust to perfection. A very short skirt, at least seven or eight inches above the knees, showed very well proportioned legs. A wide black belt pulled tight—one I had seen before. A trace of perfume that was a pleasant contrast to the sweaty odor I had lived with during the past few hours.

She stood, not with hands on hips, but with hands behind her back. Not at all arrogant. Almost shy. I went toward her and held out both my hands to say sorry about my attitude, thanks for what you have done and what about getting out of here.

From behind her back, she took a bottle of wine and some cigarettes, So I had two of the things I needed.

Pascale sat on the Hunter & Palmers tin, which meant that her bottom was low and her knees high. It also meant that she had to listen to my more rational mind pointing out that this was neither the place nor the conditions for any form of affection. Also, what about the original idea of my getting back to the group as soon as the explosion was heard?

Her reaction to that was to upend the bottle and drink long and loud. She wiped the neck with her hand and held the bottle toward me with outstretched arm. I went forward and took it from her. Now closer, my eyes were drawn to the legs that were visible, the skirt having ridden almost waist level. There was no sewn hem. It had been cut. In a hurry.

She opened the pack of cigarettes, took one, and made to put the pack in my pocket. I restrained her so that I could have a smoke. Our hands touched and she drew hers away sharply.

"No—please do not touch me. I have to do this for myself."

I made no sense of that, but lit my cigarette and had a swig from the bottle; I walked to the window. Not far away was the de-railed train. I could hear voices and a transport moving. I was edgy and not very confident. I did not wish to be in a room in France with a girl who was neither one nor the other. This one was not a Sally. This one was a something I had never met before. I turned as I heard a slight noise behind me. Pascale was still sitting but was crying with her head nearly on her knees. I looked at the bottle I was holding. She had drunk about a third in one go, but it was poor stuff. Surely she was not feeling the effect?

I went to her, and bending down, asked what the trouble was. The tears were genuine enough. They had made several trickles down her cheeks and washed away some of the dirt from the work we had done; even so she was a very lovely girl. I tried to hold her hands, but on contact she pulled away. It was hopeless.

I left the wine beside her and made for the door. As I opened it, I said, "I am going back to the group; my job is done. Thank you and your lads for the help you have provided. Good-bye."

Before I had got halfway down the stairs, she was behind me. I turned and more or less caught her. She hung on tight, and me, being a practical type of chap, thought what a stupid place to have a party. She took my hand and placed it inside her low necked dress. She dived up from below. It was semi-dark, so I couldn't see, but I could feel. I had a hand full of soft paper.

She sat on a step of the stairs and sobbed. She said she had to pad herself to form a non-existent bust line. She dared not let anyone touch her. She was as flat as her brother. Her father was dead. Killed by an English saboteur. She knew Sally. She had begged Sally to get her to London. Sally would not try. Sally had let it be known her boyfriend was in the same sort of work. His name was Robin. You are the Robin she loves. You are the one that does me good and tells me I have a fine shape but cannot see my legs in my field trousers. You are the one who does not tell me I have the legs, yes? I cut off the dress for you and you say nothing except you want to go back and see Sally, yes? Well, go and find her, and I hope the Gestapo find her first.

Self-preservation was natural and I felt very compelled to make a hasty move. I felt very sorry for the girl, but also felt I should insist on an escort back to my proper place. I still could not grasp how it could be possible to cause an explosion and derail a train that had been proceeded by the enemy with a small army of searchers. But it appeared to be possible, since there were no troops or police. Even so, I was on my way.

Being under the impression I would be escorted back, I had not made any particular note of landmarks. It was fairly safe through the woods, and although perhaps not by the same route, I made it to the building.

It was empty.

No sign of anyone having occupied it the night before, so I went outside, wondering if I was at the place I had left. It was the same place. Back inside I found a dry patch in a corner, stretched out, and lit one of the cigarettes. I thought of Pascale. Thought of possible capture. Thought I should have taken more advantage of the girl and hang the rules. Hang Sally.

The door crashed open.

One of the Resistance came to me and handed me a piece of paper. I recognized Sally's writing. It said they could not wait and had to go on. The bearer, Paul, would escort me to them. Bring any unused explosives with me, and bloody well hurry.

We left immediately. Not in the direction of the derailed train; in fact, quite opposite, to the right. I determined I would try to memorize the route. Assuming my escort could not speak English, I kept quiet. He was much taller than me, well over six feet. He carried his carbine in his right hand and I noticed a silver ring on the small finger of his left hand. I was pleased with this, for I felt superior to him for some reason. I suppose there were no other people in charge. At least I did not feel nervous.

It was late afternoon, with rain to come shortly. Our route was parallel to the narrow road, a few yards inside the woods, and after nearly an hour, I decided to ask how much further we had to go. He lifted his chin to point and said, "Un kilometre." I asked if he spoke any English.

"Yes, bad," was the reply.

Nearly dusk now, and over to the left, as the road and woods curved together, I could make out what looked like a village or a small town. Before long I could distinguish a church, so assumed it was a sizeable place.

Right on the outskirts Paul bade me wait. He did so rather like getting a dog to sit and stay. So I sat and stayed.

It was damp and chilly and dark enough for making it difficult to find me. I risked a cigarette and had to strike several times before getting a light. The smoke made me think of Pascale. Poor girl, she had to put on that show of arrogance to offset her paper chest. Surely there were other ways of being feminine. I hoped I might meet her again, Sally permitting.

I heard the swish of leaves and the occasional snap of a twig and quietly stood, feeling for a tree. I put myself with the tree between me and the noise. A man, just discernible, went past, treading stealthily. I almost called out, as it was obvious he was looking for me, but did not, remembering the training never to assume. On the other hand, if he was looking for me, what was the point of letting him go on?

Blast it! They don't tell you things like this in training. All very well, saying "Good luck laddie, and you are on your own," but what to do? Why the hell was there not a signal like a prearranged whistle? Too late now, the fella had gone and I could no longer hear him kick up the leaves. I hopped from one foot to the other and was very indecisive. I began to sweat a bit. Seconds were going by. I was letting them down, *again*. I should have returned to them after blowing the rail instead of fiddling about with a girl's—wait a minute! Surely she did not delay me on purpose? If so, why?

There was no time to work out those possibilities, as quite clearly came the sound of more leaves being scuffed, this time quite quickly with no attempt of stealth. Also a chanting which, as the sounds came closer, was in Tom's voice repeating, "The North wind will blow and we will have snow . . ."

Knowing how sharp Tom's reflexes could be, I dared not risk getting clobbered. I waited until he had passed, then softly called out the first word that entered my head, "Redbreast."

The footsteps stopped and slowly got closer. Still behind my tree, I repeated the word.

"Where the bloody hell are you?" It was Tom.

I told him at once about the other man who had passed and he explained that that geezer was a baddie and has to be put to sleep. Permanently. This was because the Germans had a search party out, with check points on all roads. They were everywhere. He said Paul had told him where I was, but he, Tom, had to make a wide detour through the woods, hoping he would join the track before he reached my position, hence the delay. Also, that there was a check point within half a mile this side of the village.

I asked after Sally and was told she was in the church, where a priest was "one of us." We had started to walk back the route I had taken with Paul, back toward the hut not far from the derailed train. I felt safe with Tom. Until he said it was good to have a buddy.

I mentioned Sally's note and Tom asked where it was? I said it was screwed up in six inches of mud along the track. I dare say he nodded.

He was half a pace ahead of me and suddenly held out an arm to check me. We both stopped and listened. Getting closer was the noise of the leaves, someone moving quite fast, almost a run. He was panting and from our position with our back to the woods, it was just possible to detect the silhouette of the crouching figure, bent low to avoid branches.

Tom whispered, "Dive for his legs, I'll do the top end, don't shake hands."

I took off and made contact with both arms around one leg, getting a hard knock on my forehead from the following boot. He fell over my left shoulder as I laid hanging on and buried my face in the leaves. The shock and the fall made him grunt and a strangled groan from Tom's end kept him quiet and still. I extricated myself, spitting out most of the French woodlands and rubbing my head, which had a swollen lump above my eye.

"All right, mate?" I asked.

"I think so, but I am bleeding from my arm somewhere," Tom replied.

"Let's have a look."

"Bloody fool!" was all I got for my concern in the dark.

He was bleeding, no doubt about it. A sticky mess from his wrist higher up. These Rugby tackles were all right on the playing field, but in the dark against an enemy was a different thing. No set of rules.

"We have to get back to Sally in the church," said Tom.

I followed. But blimey! I was hungry, and had not squatted for the last twenty-four hours. Oh, yes! We had to eat and squat and piddle when it was necessary to do so. Even those few of us chosen to operate in this kind of work were human beings. Of all these, I was hungry. They once said that the best fighter was a hungry fighter, but in my experience, the best one was the one that was well fed and content. Still, that was the grown-ups' idea. No doubt confined to the boxing ring; certainly not in my case now. I was just bloody hungry, and where was Mum to prepare it for me. She was miles away. Food rationing or not, she would have had a Christmas dinner for me any day. Every day, if it came to that, for weeks. She was real. These figures in the night were only bad dreams, but by "the right," they were real.

The films at the cinema, the war stories of landing craft beaching on undefended shores, the officers who indicated with one arm, "Follow me." Ah, balls to all that. What did the public know of this? Did they think that they would put it right, while they sloshed back the weak booze? Did they?

Not every Mum had a son or daughter in the woods of enemy-occupied France that night, alone, except the very few that knew of our job. And they were very few.

In any event, I was still bloody hungry, having not eaten since the breakfast before daybreak. That was a fact.

Back to the church to Sally was an adventure in itself. To get there, Tom and I went a long way into the trees to avoid the Germans. But we got to the church and we found Sally. She nearly gobbled me up with her welcome. I thought to myself, she was only human, for she liked me, really. I didn't know why, but she did. She said hello to Tom as well, but not quite the same show of affection.

It was late in the evening when I met the priest who was "one of us" and I must admit I cottoned on to him. He spoke in what I call ordinary English, albeit with a refined accent. No matter, it was his attitude I liked. He understood.

So, we were together again. Tom, Sally and I. So? I had done the track blowing job. What next? Well, what next was impossible, for it should have been done yesterday. It seemed we should have had a Father Martineaux in the church, but we didn't. We were as many minutes or hours adrift as was equal to the time taken to dismantle Pascale's bust-support, leave her, and stagger back to the hut. Was it my fault?

Whether it was or not, I was still hungry, and no amount of codes, false identities, and games of hide and seek would alter that. Nevertheless, the three of us were together, even if bomb-blasted London was sixty or seventy miles away. To do the job a fella had to eat, and since there was no food evident, I suggested we should do something about it.

The priest responded and we had a fine picnic with wine. It was not very comfortable under the church and I noted that there were many boxes of ammunition, including grenades. Much later, I learned these items had been taken from the derailed train. The holy man said it was not stealing—it was spoils of war. Besides, if it had left out in the open, it would be ruined if it rained!

This Father Martineaux had a brother who ran a large school some ten miles away. The church and the school provided excellent cover for all sorts of activities. The school had a very good wireless contact with London, and with a staff who were scholars, there was not much bother with languages. The Germans had a teacher on the staff just to make sure there was no hanky-panky.

I learned this during our meal, and no doubt would have gained more information had there not been an interruption, for clattering down the stone steps came a rifle. It slithered to a halt, and before the nearest person could get to the bottom step, the rifle was joined by an empty can.

I suppose it was the wine. It was very good, and I had drunk a bottle and was well into the second. I had two more—my reward for the rail job. I mention this so that it is understood that those of us doing this type of work did get something in return.

Sitting on the hard stone floor with my unexpired portion of explosives beside me, I leaned back on one elbow to observe the action taken to deal with the two items that had noisily manifested themselves. As a student of facts, I noted that a carbine, being long and thin, travels over the extreme edge of stone steps, whereas a cylinder, being the shape it is, tends to roll around its own circumference, then drop suddenly onto the next step and repeat this motion until it runs out of steps. It appeared to be offended at this, so stopped doing anything. It just laid there, snug up against the gun.

Putting my two unopened bottles in my bag, I stood up with the idea of going up the steps to investigate. I was shushed and motioned to be quiet and sit down. I sat, had another guzzle, and as all eyes were on the steps, I looked as well. They went up and round to our left. At the top they finished at the back of the church not far from the font. That much I remembered from my entrance. Other than that, there was very little to observe. I had some more wine and had a look at Sally. She was sitting crossed-legged at right angles to me, rather than on her own, I thought.

I aimed a cork at her. She looked at me with a negative expression. Keeping a straight face, I winked. She picked up the cork, looked at it, looked at me, and then concentrated on the steps again. She kept the cork in her hand, passing it around her fingers, and generally fiddling with it.

So there we were. A priest, three Resisters, Sally, Tom and I, and sure enough, I needed a wee. I whispered to Tom, who semi-crawled over and laid beside me. I told him of my problem and asked if he or the others needed that tin. He said he didn't want the bloody thing, what of it? I said I would take it into a corner and fill it up.

Tom explained he didn't care what I did as long as I made not the slightest sound of any description.

I asked why we had to have all this hush and I learned something the remainder knew without discussion and I learned by being asked in a whisper, "What would you do if you suspected the enemy was down here and you wanted them kaput?"

I put my mouth to Tom's ear and said, "Grenade."

"Exactly. That's the reason for the tin coming down. Up there are the Boche waiting for a noise, so boil it."

"I couldn't," I replied, slowly got to my feet, pussy-footed to the can, and picked it up. I think they all stopped breathing during this, which was rather like removing a Zuss 40 fuse from a bomb. In a corner with my back turned, I took aim. The tin was about eight inches high and five inches in diameter. Capacity about three pints, I thought. No matter how I tried I could not perform without a little noise. To make matters worse, it was all I could do to stop laughing.

I placed my hot wine quietly in a corner and returned to my place beside Tom.

The lighting was dim, but at least I could see the other folk present. Unlike me, they showed no desire to use the tin, but then, unlike me, they had not had the wine. Then again, they had not blown a nasty slice out of a rail track and as I had. That's why they gave me the wine.

Comforted by this logic, I laid down, closed my eyes, and ceased to be interested in watching stone steps that had been there without moving for over a hundred years.

My rest was short-lived. Tom, who apparently had been in very quiet consultation with the priest while I dozed, nudged me to say I was to go with the priest to the school to make contact with Father Martineaux. I was to take a written message and get them to send it to London, then lay low until dark and bring the Father back here.

Awkward Sussex cuss as I was, I had to query every aspect of those instructions.

"Why couldn't the priest take the message on his own?

Answer: "He dare not be caught with a message."

"Supposing I am caught?"

Answer: "You are not a priest, you are not French, and you have had training. If though, you are caught, you pay the penalty for being over here."

"Do you think he can get me safely to the school, wherever it is?"

Answer: "No, he knows the way, *you get him there*."

"What about the geezers you thought were up the top, waiting for a noise?"

Answer: "They may still be there; you will leave by another way, with the priest."

The Reverend gentleman, in a black gown and hat complete with tassel, stood and stretched himself. Tom, in conjunction with Sally, wrote the message. I could just make out the block letters. Tom folded it and handed it to me. Folded once more, it fitted the slit in the lining of my jacket. I eased it round away from the opening. The priest laid his hand on Sally's head, held his other hand to the ceiling in salute.

Together, he and I left the crypt with one last look at Sally, Tom, and then at Sally again. It was to be the last time I would see them alive.

CHAPTER TWENTY-FIVE

It was just as well I knew nothing of the events befalling the little group during the next three long days, otherwise I would not have felt so confident with my new friend. I wondered about him and vicars as such in general. Did they not feel any fear? Indeed, did they not fear pain and torture? After all, anyone in our job could be killed at any time. Providing it was instant, there was little fear, but to be wounded or tortured. Well, to me that was most frightening.

This line of thought came as soon as we left the church, for it was not quite light and having been told by Tom that the Germans were all over the place, I assumed they were behind every bush. We did not see any, but I kept a pretty sharp lookout just the same, for I reasoned that the longer we went without seeing one, the more chance there was of one popping up.

Eventually we were on the road out of the village, having cut through the woods. The priest veered off the track, making for the road. I pointed out that it was better to take advantage of the cover afforded by the trees, and explained that Paul and Tom had both used the track the previous evening. Not only that, I wanted to see if matey was still where Tom and I had clobbered him. I also hoped to see as best I could the hut and building we had occupied earlier. Perhaps a crafty look at the train. Perhaps Pascale would still be there.

My white-collared friend gave me a shock when he said we would get a bus better on the road than in the woods. I thought we were walking all the way.

On to the road now and daylight increasing fast. An odd farm worker here and there passed the time of day with the priest. Further on, the Reverend gentleman had a busy time patting the backs of a small herd of cows, one of which took fright at the dark flapping robe. The animal went off in the opposite direction of the main herd; in fact, it was going our way, but before going out of sight, turned sharp left and into a field.

When we were level with the beast, she was quietly grazing and apparently content not to be milked.

The sound of honking and tooting came from behind us and the priest said, "The bus!" I was not too happy about this. Although I had false papers, I had not as yet suffered the awesome experience of having them examined by the police.

On the bus were about a dozen workmen, unshaven, weary looking, tired, and no doubt hungry. Some were smoking those cheroot-type things that smell like an old bonfire. At least the fog made some kind of smoke-screen, and I was grateful for any type of cover.

Nobody asked for the fare; in fact, there was only the driver and he was very intent on keeping his vehicle on the road for the steering appeared to be in need of attention. He worked hard at the wheel until, with shrieking brakes, we stopped at the outskirts of a town. Here the men got off, leaving my colleague and me alone.

The driver spoke to the priest, who replied. I decided to retie my laces, which gave me the chance of being occupied. The priest stood up and motioned me to follow. Off the bus now and walking towards the town up ahead, where German troops were visible. They were a small group and were being inspected by an officer. I came over all peculiar at the sight of this, but kept pace with the now-smiling churchman. Onwards we went and passed with no trouble, him still smiling at everyone and me trying to send a message to my heart imploring it to stop banging. This was my test and I was no good, If caught, I had good papers. Why be so scared? Even the dumbest man at a checkpoint would be suspicious.

Too late now. I told myself that Tom and Sally and dozens of other operators had been through worse than this. "Keep your eyes open laddie, one step on is one step towards the end."

I calmed down, did a grin at the priest, and looked about me. The street was coming alive. Quite a number of old women, a few elderly men, and many children. They showed signs of not having the benefits of the foot and cloth rationing scheme that existed at home. Apart from their clothing, the standard of which I was not an expert, I could tell by their faces. No doubt about it, they were suffering under German occupation.

The priest and I walked slowly on and on until we reached a drive that led us off the street. At the end of a long straight gravel path I could see what turned out to be the school, a massive place in the distance, even bigger as we approached the entrance. I was a little surprised to see the priest walk in, holding a large door open for me to follow. He seemed to know the way, for after a long way through corridors, we were at a door that obviously said "Principal."

A man left his desk and embraced my friend, kissing him on both cheeks and saying, "Dominic, how good to see you. And your friend."

Now I was the friend!

After a short conversation in French, they both turned to me and explained that we would rest awhile, have something to eat and then, after dark, make our attempt to get Father to the church.

An attempt? Surely that sounded a bit doubtful.

I queried our chances. They mumbled something barely audible and shrugged their shoulders in typical French fashion.

It was about 00.02 hours when we left the school, having eaten well and rested as best we could. Father was an elderly man, spoke very good English, and obviously was a man of some considerable substance, for he was destined to go to England for some important reason.

As far as I was concerned, all he had to do was to get himself back to Tom and Sally in the church.

Now with two companions in clerical cloth, it seemed easy to trot along between them. I felt inferior, for with no great knowledge of who knew what, I had no option but to be just a passenger. I had no idea what I would do in an emergency, except that I was armed. The situation was not at all clear. I had handed over the message from Tom and had a reply from London for him in the lining of my jacket. I also wondered why on earth, if these Reverend gentlemen were privileged with regard to checkpoints, I had the message.

I asked quietly if they could sail through checks on account of their profession. The elder man said that often they were detained and searched, since it would be an easy garb to wear if one wished to travel with ulterior motives. He added that, should we be stopped, he thought it wise if I made myself scarce, forget them, but get that message to my colleague. With luck, we should get there in about three hours.

One thing pleased me. They knew the way, for the route we followed was not the same as the priest and I had used in the early morning. I was lost! No idea at all! What was more, it was very dark most of the time. Occasionally, the clouds allowed the moon to give a little light, but not often.

I longed for the company of my friends. The job was nearly over. The track had been blown and here on my left was the man required for transport to London. I felt I was halfway through my third operation. I had seen armed Germans and had walked past them, had the scare from the items sliding down the of the crypt, helped deal with one of the enemy in the woods, and had met and worked with that strange girl, Pascale. That was an education in itself.

I wondered exactly what her rank or position was in her group, for she seemed to have quite a lot of authority, and at no time, did I see or hear of anyone her senior. In fact, she appeared to have the edge on Tom. Ah, well! As they had often said, "What you do not know, you cannot talk about under stress."

All these thoughts got rid of two or more miles. It also meant that my young bladder needed relieving of the many cups of school coffee I had enjoyed. I mentioned this fact by saying nature called, and veered off the road to the verge. The two others apparently were of a similar mind and also stopped. The clouds parted about this time and we were bathed in clear moonlight. Having few buttons and starting first, I finished first. Slowly making my way toward the two men, I had the doubtful privilege of studying the problems they have on such occasions, for, although there was no wind, they each had quite a battle with their clothing. I could quite appreciate why they did not do this very often, for it appeared to be quite a performance.

In the end, with three bladders now relieved, we made good

time. We started to chat and I thought how simple it was to break down the barriers of reserve. Another burst of light and I saw the field the rebel cow had entered earlier, then the house that had been Pascale's undoing. Further on, the hut that had sheltered us on arrival. But were the Germans still all over the place as Tom put it? Indeed, were they at the top of the crypt steps as Tom feared?

I was feeling tired now, for what with the mental strain from the events of the day, plus this long walk, I was not feeling at my sharpest. Easy to make a mistake, I felt.

The last few hundred yards back to the church was done in a very stealthy manner. A very wide detour until, after a long confab between them, the two priests suggested I waited under cover while they entered the church to see if all was well. They added that they hoped the enemy had now left the area.

They left me seated quite comfortably among the branches of a fallen tree, with the assurance that one of them, or perhaps Paul, would collect me within about forty minutes.

I eased off my French boots and let the night air cool my hot socks. I let my mind wander back to England to my home, knowing roughly what they were doing, but certain that they had no idea where I was or what I was doing. They probably thought I was at Chatham. They most certainly would be most surprised and alarmed if they could have seen me propped up by the branches of a French tree, all alone, in the dark. I thought of a week ago. Of how Sally had warned me just how bloody dodgy it would be.

Ah, Sally. What of the future? She and I certainly worked on the same wavelength. She must have some faults, but I could think of none that mattered. It was my intention to do my full regular time in the army. I supposed she would join the ranks of a soldier's wife, married quarters, for the use of.

Of course, it would be wonderful to be at peace again, but not all service men and women were doing quite the same as us. It would be a little tame after this, and I could quite see what was meant when we were told that, after a few years at this work, we would make first class crooks. I concluded that it all depended on how long the war lasted; at the moment it looked like going on for years.

My thoughts were interrupted by the approach of someone from the direction of the village. I quickly replaced my footwear and tied the laces, keeping my secret knot intact for when I arrived back in London.

It was Paul. He said nothing, but placed a guiding hand at my elbow. We went almost directly to the church, none of the detours we had practiced before. When we went down the steps of the crypt curving to the hideout, in better light than when I left, I saw an appalling sight.

On the floor were four very still bodies, their faces covered but their legs distinguishable. Two pairs of feet were French Resistance men, one pair was Tom's, and the others were unmistakably Sally's. It was to her I rushed, grabbing a lantern as I moved. I gently pulled back the cover. Her eyes were closed, her expression not really relaxed. I could see no mark on her face nor neck, and pulled the cover right off. I could see very little anyway, for I was crying, and felt very sick. Her hands were together, arms on her chest, and in spite of the lantern being beside me, I could still see no sign of injury. It was no use, I collapsed beside her.

I felt a hand on my shoulder, a soft voice suggesting I stand. More than one person gently led me away, and through the blur of tears, I allowed myself to be taken into the opposite corner of the crypt. They sat me down, someone held a glass to my lips, and I tasted cognac. I dried up as best I could and blew my nose. I sat with my arms on my knees, head down and shivering.

It was a long time before I could admit to myself that both Sally and Tom were dead, and coward or not, asked for more brandy. Paul poured with a shaking hand. I made to help steady it, and he, thinking I wanted the bottle, handed it to me. I offered him my glass and he gratefully took the lot. After one or two drinks, the sick feeling left me to some extent, and I asked Paul what had happened, not really wishing to know.

Paul laid his hand softly on my shoulder and walked away, returning shortly with the two priests. Between them they tried to explain what had happened.

Shortly after I left with the priest, the three Frenchmen, Sally, and Tom, firmly believing that the enemy were above or close, had the problem of what to do about the carbine and tin that had slid down the steps. Well, the enemy was close, and Tom was the one who found out. How, I could not work out, for the only one I was really interested in was Sally. Hard, but true.

Apparently the Germans suspected, quite rightly, that the damage done to the track was executed by someone hidden in the church. They assumed it was the work of Resisters. Since they had not the slightest suspicion that any British were involved, they were not interested in taking prisoners. They immediately fired and hit Tom, sending his wounded body down the steps. As he laid moaning at the bottom step, Sally raced to him. Her blond hair, in view now from the top of the curve, drew two Germans down to the bottom few steps. Paul sent his two friends up and out of the crypt, with orders to deal with the enemy from above. They were all a trigger-happy lot. The two Frenchmen opened fire at the two Germans and missed them, their shots ricocheting off the solid stone walls. One of these hit Sally in the back. The two Germans turned and fired upwards with automatic weapons, killing both Resisters.

Paul observed this massacre from a dark corner, not daring to shoot, but hoping the two Britishers would be left alone.

One of the Germans dragged Sally away from the bottom step into the light near the blankets. She screamed when moved.

At this point the priest stopped talking for a moment, then said, "There is no need for you to know any more, Mon Ami, for I can only recount the action as told me by a very upset Paul."

"I want to know all of it." I said, feeling sick again.

"The German with some care," the priest continued, "undid her clothing, possibly to attend to her wounds, but could not see too well. He had his friend bring over another lantern. The girl was conscious and could see the German uniforms and feel her clothing being tampered with. For some reason, she screamed in personal anguish and not, I assure you, in a cowardly manner. She appeared to Paul to have an aversion regarding help, for as the soldier ripped her shirt, she made the fatal mistake of screaming, "You have already ruined my sister, isn't that enough?"

"Unfortunately, she used English words, and whether the German understood or not, at least he knew the language. I'm afraid, my friend, he went berserk, for he fired his gun."

He was near to tears.

"Please go on Father, I said."

After a long pause, he continued, "Between her legs. At the bottom of her stomach."

The priest left me, and slowly walked into the shadow. His place was taken by Paul, the young French Resister. He sat beside me.

"My English is good to hear, Mon Ami, but very bad to speak. I could not help. I was afraid; I could not move. I could see the blood come out of her mouth; she would not, no could not, lay still. It was not good for me to see. They went up the steps to the chapel. I see them tread on your friend, he not yet dead. He made a noise, so I come out to see them. The English girl is all bloody. I go to the man to help somehow. I cannot leave. You and the Father have gone, my friends are shoot, your friends are shoot, I am alone, then I hear talking and down come the Boche more and I run to hide and see them. The same come with tool and they pull the fingers nail of the girl, then the man, with screaming, comes the nails out. He is not yet fini dying, you comprez, Mon Ami?"

I dare say I nodded, for he continued explaining that he was too scared to come out into the open, but waited until the two priests returned.

"They saw the bodies and cleaned them, laid the two English ones side by side. How you say? Mort? They ask me how it happened all, and I tell them, but I am not well when I say. They tell me you all very brave men and lady, and without you they have no stomach to come from the school. Now, they say you are one, with your friends go. You are now as the Germans say, "kaput," oui? My mother and father help the English in Annecy, long way off here, they say the English good people who will come one day and give us back our France. I think no, the Germans shoot too much of you. I am sorry not to shoot."

The two priests joined us and I realized I was hungrier than I thought. They gave me some food and some wine, and I felt better, but still sick. I knew what I wanted to do, but could not bring myself to do it. I had to see them again. They were lying in the dark about twelve or fifteen feet away from me.

At last I got up and walked slowly to the bodies, covered from their faces to just below the waist. In the lantern light I saw them. Very still feet.

I eased down the cover from Sally's face. It was peaceful now. I lowered the light. Her hands were as I saw them before, but now black and blue, no fingernails, just black congealed blooded stumps. The right hand I had seen hold a pint of English beer in London. The right hand that had shaken the hand of President de Gaulle at a quiet English house, when he had presented her with the Crois de Guerre. The right hand that had more than once held my left hand. The right hand that had done a thousand things. There it was, a stumpy black mess, its fingers intertwined with those equally stumpy left fingers.

I removed all of the cover. She laid in a dark red stain on the stone floor. Her clothes were stiff and I did look below her waist.

Was this the Sally I knew in London? Was this the girl that had said, "Up the Arsenal"? Was this the lovely girl that had teased me, hugged me, kissed me, and encouraged me to become one of an important team of operators in France? Was this the girl, all twenty-four years of her, that had seen her sister raped by two Germans and sought not revenge, but some sense of justice? Who was loving and caring, honest, and with compassion cared for those who could not fight back?

Next to her and very close, laid Tom. The one who did the sketches. The one who attacked from the rear to make sure his victim was quick to defend himself. The one who said, "Go and ask that old chap if he would like a drink with Tom." The one who had said, "You'll do."

He, too, had black and blue hands and wrists. And like Sally, he, too, was very, very cold and stiff.

I left the church, concerned about what would happen to the bodies. Our training, to my knowledge, had not covered this kind of situation. In the dark, I wandered to where the priests were quietly in prayer. They knew I had approached and both joined me. The elder, Father Martineaux, kindly put me on a straight course.

Slowly he and his companion, the priest, I never did know his name, reoriented me. Gently, they led me to accept the fact that, at least for the time being, I was the sole survivor of an experienced team from England, sent to disrupt the railway, rescue an important French priest, and send and receive messages to an end that would ensure the arrival of an aircraft to take the three of us, plus the father, to London.

Father Martineaux, the senior, was very kind, for when he thought it was prudent, he asked me if I had a message?

A message? How could I have a message? They were dead, surely. There was no one to send any more messages.

Gradually, I returned to reality and realized that in my jacket lining I had a message from London—for Tom.

I maneuvered out the folded paper and gave it the priest. He read it, refolded it, looked me straight in the eye, and said, "Leave this with me for today, have some more cognac, come with me, and sleep. Tomorrow you will be a new man, and surpass yourself. Now come, drink, and sleep."

I recall being led, as if half asleep, half shocked, or even half intoxicated, into a corner of the crypt. There were some blankets on the stone floor. He helped me down. I was twenty-four years old, and he was at least fifty or more. He settled me down. He began to pray. After a while he asked if there was anything I would like to say. Inwardly, I knew he hoped I would answer in a religious manner, but I asked for two things.

"What are they, my son?"

"I want to see Sally once more, for one thing," I replied.

He helped me to my feet, now without the French boots. We slowly made our way to the bodies, four now with the two Resisters. I knelt beside her. Her short cover was just below her waist. I felt in her pockets. Nothing in the left, but in the right was one single object: *the cork*.

Back in my blankets and with the cork clasped in my hand,

the Father asked about the other request. I could not think of what else I ever wanted, for I had the cork, hadn't I?

He repeated his question, adding that now great things were expected of me. Finally, I recalled my second desire. It was a desperate situation for me. The one thing I now needed more than anything was *a cup of tea*.

Thank goodness there was no set time to awake next day, although up to now, having left England, all the days and nights seemed to be cockeyed. Fortunately, nature has its way with these circumstances. I slept, although the physical effort of the long walk and the traumatic experience of the deaths made my sleep uneasy.

CHAPTER TWENTY-SIX

It was nearly 10:00 a.m. when I awoke, and although there was no daylight down where I was, I knew it was day time. I soon recalled the events and felt rather like the period after a funeral. A kind of acceptance of the facts, with the future of things a little uncertain without those who created the circumstances. A little unreal, a little unfair, for I had been the one at risk. Tom and Sally were safe, under a church, with thick walls and earth and Allies and priests— yet they were dead and I was not.

I knew the trouble. I just could not accept the fact that they were gone forever. Why should I be straining to come awake? Why was it that I could not just be a training instructor at Chatham? Why did I have to meet people like Tom and Sally?

No one in London or Scotland said anything about colleagues being shot. Caught, captured, and even tortured, yes, but this set of circumstances, no.

The dull, sick feeling returned as I realized it was not all a very bad dream. This feeling tended to loosen my bowels, and there being no lavatory in the church, it was a question of doing as we all did. Go to the woods. And that meant the risk of being seen. With the exception of blowing the track, all movement had been in the dark or semi-dark. Now it was mid-morning, and ironically, the sun was shining.

I asked the younger priest what he did in these circumstances and was told that he had already escorted the older man to a house near the church, where both had washed and attended to nature, and he would be pleased to take me. This was done quite openly, no question of posing as anyone else. Mind, I kept a very sharp eye open for soldiers or police. I was offered breakfast and coffee. I ate, but did not enjoy it very much. I was glad to get out, because the French lady was very scared to have me there, for good reason. The Germans sometimes searched houses near a church. Evidently the priest had told her he was sheltering me.

Back in the church, I felt a little more secure. The two priests, Paul, and I did not go below, but sat in the vestry, and I made a note that the only place to hide in a hurry was behind the masses of gowns that hung on one wall. Not very effective, but the best I could see.

Everything now, however small, was important, I felt. I also felt very insecure, for I had no leader, no means of getting back home, no nothing. It seemed hopeless and I felt very, very uneasy.

The three Frenchmen stood, sat, and wandered around the small, musty-smelling room. It was nearly 3:00 p.m. A glance at my watch prompted the others to do the same. They seemed to tense up, which worried me. At last, I stood and asked all the questions that were buzzing through my mind.

"What are we waiting for? What happens to the bodies? Supposing the Germans return? Surely, the troops that had done the killing had to report to their officers? Why does the Gestapo not want to examine the English dead? What was on the message I brought back? How am I to get back to London?"

With a hint of a smile, Father Martineaux held up a hand to stop my torrent of words.

"Soon," he said, "very soon, we will know the answer to some of your questions, and when we know those, we can plan to overcome this unfortunate position. You have, I understand, already met Pascale. Shortly she will be here and will help, for she has many contacts. The need for leadership by the British is not appreciated in London, and I hope to impress them to that effect. That young lady had done yeoman service to the cause, and should not be at any time underestimated, for she has to work very often on her own initiative. Believe me, never has she needed more help than now."

So, Pascale was still in the running of things? I had, to a large extent, dismissed her as some kind of freak, mainly regarding her bust, I admit, but then, suppose she had more or less confided in me? Perhaps she wanted to get that part of her life off her chest! Thank goodness for an English sense of humor.

Father Martineaux motioned Paul to the door, closing it behind him. Two priests now paced the small area of the vestry. I sat still on some kind of seat. Secretly, I knew that soon I would need another piddle. It could be nerves or the weather, but I seemed to perform more naturally than these two churchmen.

All thoughts of such relief went with Paul entering and holding open the door, through which Pascale almost marched.

Instinctively my eyes went quickly from her eyes to her bust. It was full. Recharged. Firm. Very firm.

She avoided my eyes and stood before the senior priest.

"The situation is grave, Father," she said in English, "for I am unable to contact my organizer. My only suggestion is that you, or another, return to the school and inform London of the situation, and without seeking advice, demand an aircraft to land at Blearaux with an organizer and take you." Here she paused. "And Robin to London."

The senior priest smiled the smile that all priests do when confronted with young French patriots insisting on aircraft from across the Channel, especially if they need the help of those that live across the water. But this suggestion of getting back to the school? Were they all going to look at me?

Oh, no, I though, not again. I have lost enough in this lark. If anyone has to travel in France, then let it be a Frenchman, because if I attempt it and get caught or killed, what would be achieved? A ten inch gap in a railway line. A delayed train, the death, and not quick, of two British agents, plus the de-papering of a young, albeit brave, French girl. Blimey! They could have fiddled about among themselves and achieved more.

But they did not look at me. They decided I was to go, without looking at me. I was to go with Paul. In a cart, under a load of something I could not understand. I was to be hidden with the message in my good old lining. And we would leave very soon. But I still needed to pee.

Things moved fast. I peed. I laid in the bottom of a cart. I was joined by Pascale, who, for at least five minutes looked me straight in the eye. Then assuming a female attitude, said she was sorry about Sally. Really sorry. And Tom. But Sally. She looked away from my gaze and continued, "There is something about you that my education and knowledge cannot understand. You are somehow different, yes?"

She still said the yes as if everyone had to agree with her, but this time I also said yes.

She knelt down beside me in the cart as they piled hay on me. She made me move so that some of it was under me, and between us we formed a bed. It was an itching, sneezing, erotic affair, for I believed I might be one of the few who knew her secret. When the cart was finally loaded, I knew that indeed I was the only one to share her secret, for she told me it was almost impossible to get off the cart since she wanted more than anything to stay with me under the straw. It was hay, really.

At last she left, Paul burrowed his way into the hay, the cart moved, and I had the chance to study the traction of two wheels that I calculated were about four feet in diameter and about twelve feet, nine inches, in circumference, give or take a little.

This study was the result of having observed the size of the wheels before getting in the cart and listening to the regular beat of the metal tire on the road afterwards. The action was slightly up and down and side to side. This continued about an hour. Then there were voices, indicating that the contraption was either holding up traffic or driving on the wrong side of the road. Whatever—it was caused me some worry. But then we passed and the voices died down. For me, the trip was not easy. Any of it. Without being able to see any potential danger, I knew we would be right in it if things went wrong. And the thing that would be wrong just had to be some bloody inquisitive Jerry with a desire to see if there was anything under the hay. Even I knew the best way of doing that. Something long thing with a point, for instance—like a bayonet.

We jazzed up and down and swayed side to side in a rhythmic manner until, suddenly, we stopped. There was silence for such a long time that I felt tempted to have a look.

That would have been fatal, for even an operator like me could not explain why I needed to hide in hay, having good papers. Papers? *Where were Sally's papers?* There was only the cork—*our cork.* Blimey! What a place to suddenly think of a thing like that. What a useless twit I was.

There was still no sound from outside; it was as if the driver of the cart had left us. Well, perhaps he had. There was only one thing to do. Stay still and stay put—and I was content to do this until a volcanic eruption in the hay put a knee or something equally hard on my cheek. It was Paul, who could no longer contain himself. He had to look, bloody fool.

Still silence and no movement from my French companion and I was trying to get smaller and smaller. All of a sudden, a hand touched me near the part of me that normally only I touch, but being French made no difference, for he found his way up on top of me, swished the hay about, found my ear, and said one word: "Boche."

My heart has never been the same since. I thought if they were alongside the cart, I would prefer to take my chance, and bluff my way out as to why I was hiding, having produced good papers. So I sat up, had a couple of sneezes, and what did I see? A long line of vehicles of various sorts in a long queue, and sure enough, a couple of coal-scuttles either side of a car about fifty or more yards away.

I asked Paul if he would leave the cart and make a dash for it. He said, "Non," so I said he could stay under the hay, but I was off. And over the side I went, meaning to run and hide where I could, but on getting out realized the driver was sitting on a perch between the shafts. I changed my mind, went to the front of the horse, grasped the bridle, and just stood there.

I don't know what the driver had been told, but he took my action in stride, as though it were quite a natural thing to experience. Hooded lids over his eyes, a very smelly cheroot in his lips—well, he didn't know if I was English, French, or from Timbuktu.

It gave me the chance to size up the situation, and having done so, I decided I would rather risk it than be under some hay and not know the situation. This was far better, I felt.

I estimated there were fourteen people to check before it was my turn. I secretly went over my cover story, who I was, where I was born, my school, my job, and my last employer, plus many other details, to say nothing of a cool manner and a very casual attitude, as though I had seen it all before.

Well, I did my homework and was fourth to go. The French driver was half asleep, I was very wide awake, and Paul was very still. Too late now for him to avoid the prodding. He had done his bit, I felt, for he had seen Sally die and that was something I could not even now imagine, although I could be caught within the next ten minutes. But I felt, in some way, secure because I could see the enemy. None of this behind-the-back business.

I must have been born under a lucky star or something, although I had more than my fair share of worries, for a man with an old motor vehicle in front of me was the last check made that day. The Germans stood to one side and waved me and the remainder of the little convoy onwards through the checkpoint.

I recall having the sauce to give him a thank-you nod as I passed. I felt a tightening of the chest as I went through, for the fear turned immediately to a restricted elation. Mind, I had no idea of where the turning to the school was, but I led the old French horse along, hoping I would recognize the way or old Frenchie would emerge from his hay to tell me, for to be sure, the driver was not to be relied on by the look of him.

Such was my luck that shortly after this, the two German soldiers passed me and the cart and actually grinned and spoke as they presumably went off duty. It was a very exciting experience and I felt good, but sad to think that there would be no Sally or Tom to tell.

My luck continued my way for, suddenly, Paul shouted out.

I stopped the cart, went to the rear, and adjusted the load, at the same time asking Paul to repeat his call. He had apparently found a knot hole or gap in the side of the cart and was observing our progress, so was able to indicate that we should turn left shortly. I admired him for that and also for having the guts to stay put when I felt I had to leave the cover of the hay. But then, I always had preferred to drive than be driven. I liked to be in charge.

CHAPTER TWENTY-SEVEN

At the school, I more or less followed the route and pattern the priest had followed and knocked on the door. But, Oh dear! It was not the principal who bade me enter. It was a teacher. A German. What's more, I knew he was and even worse, he knew I was neither a priest nor French. In fact, he as good as said in English with a German accent, "You are English."

He was a very clever man, for he employed all the tricks there are to demoralize me. He smiled when he should have been stern, he was stern when he joked. He knew he had me by the short and curlies, for I had no mental weapons to fight with. He had cut the ground from under me.

It was a diabolical situation, with just the two of us in the study. He was in his rightful place, with all the backup needed at his command. And me—a Sussex lad miles away from home, with no leader or boss, in an unexpected situation with this man like a cat playing with a mouse.

What I did and why I did it was later criticized, and to my knowledge at least one officer was decorated as a result of my action, and *he was bloody well not even there*, because there were only the two of us and he had the more comfortable chair.

There was no way I could get out without him alerting the authorities. I had a message in my jacket lining and he knew it. Self survival was the priority, but that could only be achieved if I could get the message through, for London knew nothing of the deaths of Sally and Tom, unless the priest had got through. That was the trouble. There was no proper organization. I was a puppet with too few strings.

I made up my mind I was done for and decided that to be killed by a German was going to be an honorable death. I felt that I could put up a good show if I could get my hands on him, but he was sitting at the big desk, at least four to five feet away from me, with his back to a large window. That very solid lump of furniture was in my way.

I recalled being told that there was "one German teacher on the staff to avoid any hanky-panky," so if that was correct, providing he had no hidden alarm push or weapon on his side of the desk, I knew I had to have a go. My allies consisted of one Paul, hidden in the hay outside the main entrance, one French driver who played no part in even driving his cart, and one French horse that was so untalented that the Germans evidently did not consider him worth commandeering. Even to eat.

I asked if I could smoke, and in good English, was told I could. I produced the very packet I had acquired from Pascale, put a cigarette in my mouth, and noted my hand was not as still as I would have liked. But in the circumstances, it was still bloody steady. I'd known it to shake more on lesser occasions. Foreseeing that the action of holding a match would perhaps give matey the chance of noting my apprehension, I asked if he had a light.

"With pleasure," he assured me, and leaned toward me with the small flame. When his arm was fully extended, I saw *he was shaking!*

That did it. For Sally's sake, for Tom's sake, for Marie's sake, and for the sake of all the other people I knew of who had suffered the tricks and fancies of the enemy, I grabbed that arm.

My left hand around his right wrist, my right hand at his elbow, a sharp twist, and he was over the desk. I can tell you, my strength was inspired by the frustration bred in me by knowing those mentioned above and the dead and dying I saw in London, Birmingham, Coventry, Dunkirk and places I knew of but did not see with my own eyes, to say nothing of the bastards who shot RAF bomber crews as they descended by parachute. And pulled fingernails out of *dead Sallys*.

I felt that, if this crafty, smirking, arrogant bastard was a billiard ball, he would have been talcum powder.

Still with my hold on, I got him over the desk. On the way, some article hurt him, He yelled, but I got him over, and let him fall the three feet to the floor. With more luck than judgment, I managed to get his head to make contact first with the floor, even though it was carpeted.

I can't describe the attack in detail. But having the initiative, I kept it until the end.

He was a sorry looking sight as I sat in his chair, wet through and through, but feeling quite exhausted and ten feet tall. I felt the pack for a cigarette and took one out, only to find I already had one in my mouth. I had done all that without knowing. It was, I noted, a very steady hand that lit that well-earned smoke.

A la the training, I checked the drawers of the desk, even for concealed bits, but everything appeared to be genuinely educational, and of course, in French.

Then I needed a piddle. Well, I couldn't help it. I did, and what's more, had it in the principal's private latrine. I admit I had wandered in there by mistake, but I had entertained the idea of dumping the inert body in the office, if necessary. However, either cock-a-hoop or as conceited as the officer had once said I was, I made my way inwards along the corridors, hoping I would find the principal, for I knew that he was friendly with us and had the means of getting the news through that the position had changed drastically in the past few hours.

At last I found a student and asked in my best French, combined with a little Sussex English, if he would kindly escort me to the principal.

He roared with laughter. I told him it was not bloody funny, which made him laugh all the more. I thought he was likely to annoy me more than the previous character I had met, so I repeated my question. He seemed to sense my urgency and led me along the corridor, on the way suddenly saying, "I am top of my class in English."

Such was my mood that I found myself following along with a high degree of urgency, for it was a question of do or die, and I had done and had not died and I felt that my coup-de-gras would be to hear my request going over the air to London. In a short space of time, these thoughts raced through my mind. I wonder what Sue's reaction would be when she learned, not only of my position, but of the tragic deaths of Sally and Tom. She would not need to make quite so many cups of tea in the future.

Suddenly, my escort stopped at a door, opened it, and bade me enter. The room was a small study, and he invited me to sit at a table. I asked him again to either take me to the principal or bring the principal me. He explained that every day of this particular week the principal joined with other members of the Maquis to keep in touch with the latest developments in the fight against the Germans and tonight was such a night.

I reminded him that it was daylight, which could in no way be termed as tonight, so perhaps he would take me to the principal's quarters so that I could see for myself whether or not he had left the school for his rendezvous. The student led the way along what seemed endless corridors and changes of floors, but at last I knew we were there by the reverence he exercised with his knock.

He was more surprised than me, for the door opened and the principal held open a welcoming arm, nodded to the student, and I was in. I had no means of knowing who trusted who, but having seen this man greet the priest from the church and afterwards produce Father Martineaux, I felt reasonably certain I could divulge my information to him. I secretly made a note in my mind not to mention that soon he would discover a dead German in his study. Time was important, and not knowing the periods of contact with London, I felt I did not wish to miss the next contact time.

He invited me to sit, but I preferred standing. I felt I had to make haste slowly, and do nothing more I might later regret. He listened quietly to my account of events and was visibly shaken to learn of the fate of my two friends and the loyal Frenchmen, who were also killed. He at once grasped the urgency of notifying London, for Father Martineaux was his old friend, but said he could only be away for a short time to avoid questions being asked. I used this remark to try to get him on his feet and on the way to the wireless I had heard so much about. But did he move? No, he put his head in his hands and was either in deep thought or prayer. I waited a few moments and suggested he finish. He looked to me as though he had a few more birthdays, and it was a worried man who explained that it was not so easy as that.

Then a brainwave. "Do not forget the time, for you will be late for your weekly meeting."

This seemed to shatter him; his mouth opened and nothing came out.

I began to have a sinking feeling in my stomach; things were not going my way. He asked me what I knew about the meetings and I explained about the student telling me of this.

"My friend, I do not dare mix with anyone, even though my sympathies are sincere. That story is one put about by Wolfgang to discredit me and to exploit his Nazi tendencies, but it is true that I do meet someone later this evening, but for a very personal nature. A lady, in fact. But you are a little young to understand."

"If I am too bloody young to understand your purpose of seeing a lady," I responded, "then I am too bloody young to be out here scratching about like a hunted fox trying to make some sense of you more mature people. I suggest you get on that wireless *now*, and I will hear you do it and get the reply. I can't very well walk home, but I shall try if you don't get cracking soon. Anyway, who the hell is this Wolfgang that seems to have such a hold on you?"

"He is the German teacher." *Was*, I thought.

I must admit to thinking I would be led upwards to the top of the building, a sort of ingrained assumption that wireless signals would work better there than in the cellar where I found myself. But, at least and at last, there was the wireless. I watched as he prepared to make contact. I had seen our girls do this many times, but this man did not exude very much confidence; however, he bashed away with his Morse key and I detected he was sending a "call in" signal. He repeated this several times, removed his headphones and disconnected the apparatus, saying, "We will try later from another place."

This decision made me mad, for time was going fast; not only that, Paul was, or should be, outside. I was not too worried about the horse, as he could eat his load, assuming Paul had the sense and opportunity to give him some.

Back up to the principal's room we went and he changed into his going out garb. While he was so doing, I explained about Paul and how, after about two hours, I was concerned about him, but I was assured that he would have given no concern. I gathered the dumb looking driver was, in fact, not so silly.

It was dark as the principal and I left the school. Perhaps it was a little unfair to call it a school, for it was more a college, but whatever it was, it was a very big building in very large grounds. Once outside the boundary and in the streets, my old fears crept back, as from time to time I saw German troops in ones or twos. Fortunately, there were quite a lot of people about, which made it easier to progress.

At last, after a half mile or so, the principal walked up the steps of a very imposing building and rang the bell. We were admitted into a dark hallway, and after closing and bolting the door, a woman spoke in French to my companion. He answered with quite a long series of sentences. I tried to note how the hall was furnished. There were lots of lamps, but only one was lighted, and that not very bright. There were big bulky pieces of furniture down one side, a staircase going down at the end, and, as my eyes grew accustomed to the gloom, a very grand stairs going up.

And it was up those we went, the lady leaving us and going out of sight.

It was a very glamorous stairs, the type that went round in a curve to the left. It had a continuous handrail, about five inches wide, as smooth as glass. At the top was a long landing with lots of doors. I followed the principal past several, trying to note as many details as possible. Suddenly he stopped outside a white-painted door identical to all those we had passed. He knocked, opened it, and turning to me, asked me to wait. He closed the door behind him. I moved over to the hinged side to try to get a glimpse of the interior when it next opened. But it did not open, even after fifteen minutes. Being too "young" to understand, I allowed him a good half hour before I knocked. After a few more knocks, each time a little louder, I made up my mind that I would go in, but suddenly the door opened.

A girl of about my own age said, "Entre."

It was an enormous room, softly lit, white carpet and furniture, gold colored curtains, several full length mirrors, potted plants. The few seconds it took me to note this amount of detail was about equal to the time it took for the girl to close the door, and walk a few paces, and stand before me. She was a pretty girl, except that she wore far too much makeup and had upset her scent over herself.

I could not see the principal in the room, and knowing he had not left via the landing door, I assumed there was another exit at the other end of the room. I walked in the obvious direction and saw a door.

The girl overtook me and placed herself between the door and me. To me that meant that there was something she thought I should not see. I had to find the principal and get that report on the air, so I refused to let a juicy little mademoiselle stand in my way very long. I did not speak, but merely indicated that I wished her out of my way. She stood fast, so it was a question of forceful removal. I did not hurt her, but she screamed, anyway. The door opened quickly, for the scream had alerted a young man in the other room. It was Paul!

"What the bloody hell are you doing?" I asked.

His reply was in French, so I cannot repeat it.

He went at once to the girl, who apparently was exaggerating her bruise. She received no sympathy from Paul, who I could tell was putting her in her place, where ever that was. He joined me and together we went through the room, a bedroom, and along a smaller landing to a very narrow door.

Inside the room, against the wall, was a vertical ladder, which Paul climbed. I followed and found the principal and what turned out to be the lady who had let him in the anteroom. She sat at a small table in front of a very powerful wireless transmitter and was using a Morse key with great skill. From time to time, she would stop sending and would listen through her headphones and write on a pad. She had almost finished by the time I arrived. She closed down the equipment, removed her headphones, and handed the principal her pad. He looked up at me and said just one word, "Bon."

"Do they know?" I asked.

He nodded.

"What are the instructions for me?"

"You stay here with Madame for two days, then a plane will take you and my friend to London."

We were in an attic and the aerial for the wireless was along the apex of the roof. It was, as I thought, a very powerful instrument. The woman stood and came toward me. She wore a full length dress, all black, deep neckline, sleeveless, with a tight waist. The one lantern showed sufficient light to allow me to note a small brooch on her dress; other than that, she had her back to the light and I could not properly see her face. But she was having a jolly good look at me, and stepping closer, I detected a faint trace of a very pleasant perfume.

I could not imagine how she would negotiate that vertical ladder with that dress. It was the only thing odd about the whole setup. I kept her gaze until, suddenly, she gently kissed me on each cheek, turned to the two men, and spoke. She had a soft voice and a lovely, kind accent I could tell.

The principal guided me toward the wall and we joined Paul with our backs to the room. I faced the wall and, for a fleeting moment, I thought we were to be shot. The lantern was moving and so were the shadows. Beside me was the black shadow of a female tucking her dress up to the waist. The legs were as well proportioned as this very attractive lady's other female features.

I began to wish I knew in advance what was going to happen next, for this playing everything by ear was getting a bit wearing. I suppose the thing that prompted that thought was the fact that I would have been happy to have assisted the lady down from the ladder, but then, I couldn't be everywhere at once.

I worried needlessly, for having assembled in the large white room, the principal, Paul, and I were given a cooked meal and some delicious wine. This was served by the young girl who had barred my way out of the room. She did not fully accept me in the company of her mistress, much to the amusement of the two Frenchmen. The principal suggested that perhaps I did not have the accent or charm that was inherent in his country.

After the meal, they spoke in French, and seemed to become more relaxed as the conversation progressed. I relaxed, too, but was desperate to try to get one jump ahead now that I knew I would be on my way within forty eight hours.

I assessed the position that Sally had no papers on her when I checked her pockets. That meant that either she had for some reason taken them out before being injured, or they had been removed after she was on the floor. I made a mental note to ask about that. I did not check Tom's pockets at all, so I did not know about his documents. If I was to stay here until going to the strip for takeoff, I would not be able to ask, for Paul would be the only one to know. But blimey! What if one of the Germans had taken the papers! Surely at any minute we would have some visitors. I felt I should warn them, left my seat, and approached Paul.

I asked my question, but he did not fully understand. However, the principal overheard and soon assured me that the papers were in safe hands. I had to be content with that for the time being. The next problem was that, back at the school, there was a body on the floor of the office—not that he could do any harm, but no doubt his condition would be queried. But as far as I knew, there was little to connect me with his condition, so forget that one. Now, lastly, what was to be the fate of the two bodies?

I asked that question to the principal directly. With a hand laid on my arm, he assured me it would all be taken care of, and not to worry, as I had done my bit. Yes, I thought, done my bit. Blown a little hole in a track. The remainder was merely a game of hide and seek. I could see my report being so short that it would go on a postcard.

There was a standing up of Frenchmen, adieus and kisses on both cheeks between them and our hostess. The two men shook hands with me and the elder one told me to stay in the building until I received a message to leave for the airstrip, adding that Madame would look after me. They left the room and I made to sit in the armchair vacated by the school head. As I sat, I felt an object which evidently had fallen from his pocket. I showed to Madame, and without opening it, she suggested that quickly I should catch him before he left the house, but not go into the street.

I raced along the landing. I could not see the men, owing to the curve in the stairs. I mounted the handrail, and gripping the rail in front of me as best I could with both hands, I sizzled down, nearly falling on the curve, and broke all records to the large newel post at the bottom. I nearly broke something else, but at least I caught them before they had the street door open. My reward for that was a re-minder that perhaps now I would believe I had done my bit.

I took my time going back up the stairs. Not that I was tired—it was just a little painful raising alternate legs, having just had a "contretemps"' with the end of the banister. But I made it.

At the top of the stairs stood Madame. Her perfume was as good as three whiskies. She put her arm through mine and led me away from the white room into a room with full lighting and a small couch just large enough for two. We sat very close. I felt dirty now in her company, not having shaved for I didn't know how long. My old French clothing was coarse and I had sweated more than usual. In every way, I felt uncomfortable and did not know what to say. It was not embarrassment, but more a defense on my part, for I was none too sure who this attractive lady was and what she knew of the past few days.

I ventured that I was very tired and very dirty, adding that no doubt I would be a little more sociable in the morning. She simply said I could have a bath, a drink, and a comfortable bed and that I could say whatever I liked or remain silent. She bade me stay and went to the door, turned, and with a very open smile, added that some things do not require many words.

She returned with two large glasses of brandy, put them on a small table, and went through the room, leaving two wide doors open to reveal an enormous bathroom. I could see her working hard with some control valves, prompting a lot of noises from the water pipes. Leaving the light on, she returned to her seat. Handing me one of the drinks, she raised hers and murmured softly, "Vive Anglaise." '

I did not drink straight away, for I thought of Sally and her dopey stuff. She sensed my reluctance, took my glass, and exchanged it for hers. I know I should.have retained my suspicion of everyone, but something told me that this lady was trying to help. I enjoyed the drink. It restored me to normal. I felt confident. But dirty. I asked when the water would be hot. She said it was hot all the time and she would prepare. I finished my drink and could feel it doing the right things. For instance, it helped me ask if she was married, if could I have another drink, and what was her name?

She laughed and said I had my questions the wrong way round, but she was called Annette, she was not married, and yes, of course, I could have another drink. She returned to the bathroom, turned on taps that emitted such hot water and steam that I at once forgot all criticism of French plumbing, for it was such a gurgling, thumping, knocking affair that I could only laugh; the noises were most amusing.

I joined her at the bath and my amusement made her laugh. She said it was most unusual to be so noisy. She asked me to take off my clothes and empty my pockets, putting my effects into a drawer on the small table near the bath. That way, she explained, they could be within my sight all the time.

That settled it for me, as I thought she had now proved herself to be genuine. I started to strip off, and when she saw my French underwear she, too, had a laugh. She waited until I had emptied my pockets. My false papers and other odd items that would help support my story if I were caught went into that drawer in quick time. She scooped up my outer clothing and made for the door, looked back, and said she would be returning soon.

The water was just right, with a bath essence as good as an English flower garden after a shower, lots of foam, and none of the eight inches of water that was the rule in England.

I really relaxed. I found myself thinking of the past few days— Sally, the trips into the town, Sally, the environment in the crypt; Sally—I could not believe she was dead. What a hard word that word, *dead*. Passed away, gone, anything, but not that word. It was too final, that word. I closed my eyes.

The facts were that I was the survivor of a trio of highly trained people who had entered France. Two of the three were what? Not on earth?

The priest, whatever-his-name-was and his elder brother, Father Martineaux, were in the church. Why the Father had to have someone escort him to the church was a mystery to me, for the man in his religious robes could have made the journey by his own steam any day. Or night. So why have me do the rescue act?

Then there was Pascale. Nobody in London said anything about her. Surely they knew she existed. Then there was that German bloke in the school. Why? I understood why he was there, but why did he have the arrogant manner? Why had someone not knocked it out of him before? Yes, the German staff member. They would surely have found him by now. Very kaput. And why not? He had his sight set on me from the first, and I was playing "away," so got in first. Then this Madame, who had a good line on hot baths. What was she? She could rattle a fine tune on a Morse key as well, but why the hell did they not mention all these people, who were either very trustworthy or very otherwise? Just wait until I get into that office in London. I'll tell them what happens, not what they say will take place.

Up to my neck in lovely, hot, perfumed water, slightly hungry, with the cognac biting nicely, I found my thoughts interrupted by the Madame's entrance. She banked the door open and carried in a tray with two glasses and one nearly-full bottle of cognac. Not only that, she had changed her dress. This one was a waste of time, for it nearly did not exist.

She sat on the edge of the bath and dispensed the booze with a steady hand. This top-up of brandy in the warm environment was a heady experience, and a strong head was very much required to combat the way the lady's clothing behaved, for it was not all the time very efficient in regard to the purpose of its design.

I mentioned that Madame was very kind and she explained that Madame was known to her friends as Annette, and since I was English, no doubt I would comply with her wish and call her Anne. So Robin had an Anne. If he so desired.

Well, the brandy by had now had its effect and he did not desire an Anne, for his Sally was only a few hours gone away forever, and this Anne was no substitute. She was too easy. On a plate.

There for the taking. Eat, drink, and be merry, for tomorrow? Yes, well, if she had been the last woman on earth, or I was the last male, then perhaps it would be different, but this was just not on. I felt that if *this* was the relationship between male and female, then perhaps I should have been born a rabbit or a dog.

As I have mentioned before, a couple of drinks and I am "normal," and that confirms my earlier view that I was born a few tots below par. And so it was now, with this attractive lady, partly clothed, sitting on the edge of the bath in which I languished. It was like giving me a meal and not providing a knife and fork. Or nice shoes with no laces. She had provided the shelter, made all the right noises, but halfway imposed a condition by invitation via her manner and dress. I had to get out of this with dignity and not risk compromising myself. Two prude words would do it, but what of the consequences? I needed to be on that plane and back where I belonged. In England.

So I pretended to be drunk. Not too difficult, with the excellent brandy on an empty stomach. I made quite a mess of leaving the bath and being "sozzled," was not in the least bothered about drying myself in front of the lady. Sensing she had the message, I explained that I was too full of drink and too tired, to which she smiled, and reminded me that there was plenty of time tomorrow!

With a large towel around me, I followed my hostess, and slipped into a lovely, soft bed. It was a wonderful feeling and I was for once relaxed and pleased to think I had partaken of the wine and the French hot water. It was not many moments before sleep came.

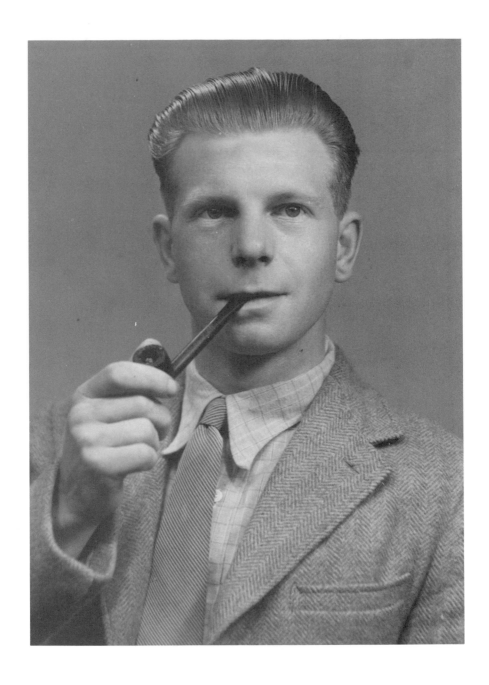

CHAPTER TWENTY-EIGHT

I recall being wakened next morning by a voice calling something like, "Monsieur Robeen." It was some time before I opened my eyes. I needed those moments to sort out where I was and why I was there. The first thing I was aware of was that I had no clothes on. The next was an urgent need to appease my bladder. The owner of the voice was easy to identify, for it was the young girl I had frog-marched along the landing the day before. She bore no grudge, evidently, for she placed a tray on my lap as I sat up. I had three fried eggs, lots of slices of soft bread, and a cup of hot coffee.

The girl sat on the edge of the bed as I made a start on the food and the thought crossed my mind that, perhaps, she was tarred with the same brush as her mistress. But no, she seemed content to sit and watch me enjoy my meal. When I had finished, I thought it a good idea to ask for more coffee, so that I could leave the bed and find the toilet, so I suggested that the coffee was so good that, please, could she bring another? She understood and went to the door with her tray.

As soon as she had gone, I was out of bed and making for another door. Before I was halfway across the room, the girl reappeared, saying something about bringing my clothes. Then, seeing me naked, she laughed, placed her hands together in some kind of approval, and exclaimed, "You have the fair hairs!"

Events moved swiftly from then on.

Clothed again, I joined Anne, as she insisted I call her, in the anteroom to listen to the BBC news. It was good to hear the voice of the announcer, Stuart Hibberd, even though the German High Command claimed to have destroyed half a dozen more planes that we possessed. What was distressing was a more feasible account of the losses at sea to the merchant shipping.

After the news, I noted Anne moved the tuner from the English wavelength to a French station before switching off. I said nothing, but felt she had been wisely trained in that respect. She also refrained from telling me anything about the setup that existed in her house. Her relationship with the priest and the powerful wireless upstairs were not likely to present a hazard from me if I was questioned.

It was during more coffee that the maid appeared and held open the door to admit Father Martineaux. He did his kissing bit with Madame, shook hands with me, sat down and launched into a long account about something that was meaningless to me until he mentioned the name Wolfgang. Like a good chap, I showed no reaction to this and stirred my coffee with great diligence, but being very aware that two pairs of eyes turned in my direction. I looked up and smiled at the both and related the story regarding the girl's opinion of my "fair hairs." It raised not a titter, but evoked a statement from Anne that apparently there had been an incident in the principal's office that day before and the Gestapo were making very serious enquiries, since the examination of the body showed that he was tackled in such a way as not to have been in a position to call for help or defend himself. The Gestapo were of the opinion that there was in the vicinity a person or persons acting against the German occupation. And so on.

They were still gazing at me. I smiled a little and said, "Oh! dear, does that mean I dare not get near the landing strip for my return?"

Consideration of this question required quite a lot of French words, and it was some time before I was addressed again, even though the inspiration for their thoughts were nurtured by the repeated glances in my direction. When at last they spoke to me directly, it was to the effect that, indeed, it would not be wise for me to risk being out of the building, and furthermore, the plans would now have to be postponed. The police, troops, even the Miliciens, were fairly easy to dodge, but once the Gestapo was interested, there were few chances of escape.

All this meant that further contact was to be made with London that day, which would mean I would have to wait until it was decided what best to do in the light of these new circumstances. But in any event, I could tell I would not be going home as soon as I had hoped, and that feeling was not a pleasant one.

After some more chat, the French priest made his farewells and left the room. Anne came to me and sitting on the edge of my armchair, suggested that the sudden end of Wolfgang would affect the entire school. Pupils would talk and elders would speculate, with the inevitable conclusion that the British were active in the district. Not a very healthy state of affairs, she ventured, and certainly not the easy, safe, and rewarding job she had enjoyed until this had occurred. She thought there was something very strange going on.

I tut-tutted in the right places and tried to change the subject by asking if there was any more of that nice cognac in the bottle. Apparently there was, for Anne summoned the girl, who brought in the bottle and two glasses on a tray. I poured one for Anne, but she waved it aside and paced the room. So I drank it and mine as well. I poured two more for me and thought I had a very good thing going for myself.

Anne finished her walkies up and down and having tired herself, sat in a chair facing me. In silence. After some deep thought, she announced that at least I could not be responsible for the present state of affairs, but it appeared I might have to suffer a long delay before I saw my home again. In the light of her new reasoning, it became apparent that I was not suspected of harming the Wolfgang chap, and a further couple of drinks enabled me to confirm to myself I had never seen or heard of the bloody man. Even so, I knew I had messed in my own nest and relied on others to get me out. Now, since Anne was my now most direct link with escape, I felt I would be wise to go along with her to achieve that end. Blimey! It was good stuff, this booze. Made a chap think straight, so I had a little doze.

When I awoke, it was just after five in the afternoon and I was alone in the room. I used this opportunity to walk around. The furnishings were of great taste, what I imagined were either antique or perhaps family possessions. I was intrigued by the photographs of large groups of people posed in an orderly manner, rather like a class of school children taken in a playground. It was while I was looking at one of these pictures that Anne entered the room and seeing me studying the group, joined me and asked if I understood who the people were.

I replied that I was merely admiring her room in general.

She slipped an arm through mine and said that the photo was taken just before the war and the persons were the last of her father's employees before he closed his largest factory. Now most of them were in the French forces and he, her father, was in Switzerland. She guided me to other photos and explained who and what they were, all the time keeping a firm grip on my arm. I accepted that, but the message came from the way her hip managed to grind against my body. On one occasion, during the survey, I found she was facing me and, as we were standing very close to my drink, I was able to pick up my glass without losing too much contact. I held the drink to her lips. Much to my surprise and delight, she drank the lot, and without much delay, it showed in her eyes.

I placed the empty glass on the table and this time used both my arms to hold her close. She offered her lips, but I asked for the truth regarding the message to London bit. She explained that she had made contact; they understood the position, and would be in touch as soon as they could provide an alternate date. In the meantime, I was to keep out of sight and place myself entirely in the hands of my hostess. She added that there was one further request. I was to be bloody careful!

So, for the time being, I appeared to have got away with my little conflict with the school teacher, and feeling now very much myself, I cemented my own frustrated idea of Anglo-French relations by holding the Madame Annette so close that not even a very thin German could get between us. She, being of the same mind, did not obstruct me in the slightest, and it was a mutual, unspoken plan that was interrupted by the young maid, who entered and received the rough edge of Anne's tongue for not knocking.

I thought it was a bit hard on the girl, since, even in the short time I had been in the house, I had not noticed her knock first before entering. I suppose Anne felt a little embarrassed. It certainly broke the spell, for she sat down and became rather petulant.

We sat in silence for a long time and I found myself with another worry. How did the girl fit in with this setup? Surely she was aware of all the comings and goings. She took it for granted that I was there, and this was no pension, hotel, or guest house. Even if it was, there were not many that had a powerful wireless among the appointments.

So I decided I would be a little more friendly toward the maid in future and not be so stern with her, for she was nice enough to look at, very nice in fact, and definitely nearer my age than Madame Anne. Yes, I would find out what I could from the maid. As I might have said before, I was often more at home with the maid than the mistress.

This decision seemed to settle me, and I concentrated all attention on Anne. She appeared to be going through some very bad and turbulent emotions, for her hands were constantly on the move— very disturbing for me, since she was my only hope of getting home. Not only that. I was in the soup for several reasons and felt it was time I had an ally, and somehow the lady Anne did not inspire great confidence. Especially now, having changed since the door had opened unexpectedly.

Anne was older than me, between thirty-five and forty, I guessed, and without any ring on her left hand to indicate any relationship with a male. Yet there was no doubt she was very attractive. But fickle. Yes, that was it. One minute she was all lovey-dovey; the next moment she was the opposite.

All this went through my mind as I watched her busy fingers agitate themselves consistent with her worried countenance. If only she would open up and speak of her fears and problems. I decided to ask her outright about them, and if she confided in me, so much the better. If not, then, in the light of my nature and my training, I would regard her with some suspicion and employ my idea to get what I could from the maid and fight for myself.

To this end, I left my chair, went to Anne, and kneeling down, held her hands. I asked if she would tell me of her concern, for if I stayed under cover and she had the wireless, then surely the only risk was the physical one of my getting from the house to the strip to meet the plane.

She looked at me as though I were not there, her eyes locked in a vacant stare. The thought hit me that she was well and truly scared and I suggested this to her. Her reaction was to admit I was right, that I was the danger, and that I should go, but the orders were that I was to stay.

CHAPTER TWENTY-NINE

So she was well and truly scared, and that did not give me very much confidence. I thought for just a few seconds and found myself getting big-headed, as some people would call it. But for me, it was another chance to grow up a fraction more and make a decision. Definite. I would find the young girl, extract from her as much as I could, then make my way back to the church, and to hell with the orders from London via French females who blew hot, then cold.

I helped myself to a generous amount of brandy, made for the door with my glass, and wandered along the passage or landing in the hope of finding the maid. I half expected Anne to call me back or follow me, but a backward glance confirmed that her door remained closed.

Not knowing which door or even which floor she had occupied, I settled down on the landing with my glass, knowing that she would need to pass that way when summoned by Anne.

I did not have long to wait, for she appeared from two doors further along, and on seeing me, seemed most alarmed. I stood and blocked her way, asking exactly how good her English was with regard to understanding me. She laughed and explained surprisingly well that anyone with the "fair hairs" was easy to comprez, and with a more subdued smile, added that she would be pleased to talk after she had seen Madame. So I sat again and, realizing I was influenced a little by the brandy, determined to control myself.

She soon reappeared and motioned me to follow. We did not enter the door through which she had appeared, but did a long route march along corridors and down several stairs, which became increasingly narrower and darker, until at last we reached what I imagined were the servants' quarters.

She stopped at a door, opened it, and let me in. She closed the door and operated some kind of catch with a complicated piece of wood, which she forced into a slot in the door frame. She turned and leaned against the closed door and I sensed that she thought that at last she had captured the mystery boy and he was well and truly caged.

There was no doubt about it. She was a very pretty girl. Dark, shoulder length hair, eyes that smiled without the lips moving, but when they both went to work, she was even more attractive than her mistress. The difference was that Anne knew it and this girl did not, and I felt that this was often the reason I preferred the maid to the mistress.

She leaned with her back to the door. I looked around the small room. There were two beds, small ones, a dressing table, a chest of drawers, and several curtains draped to disclose rails of female clothing.

I looked at all this and then at the girl who was still standing still. I went to her and started to put into action my idea of finding out all the things I wanted to know. I thought I should know how to play the big man. So I held out my hands. Hers had been behind her back all this time, but she readily moved them and joined mine. Once in contact, she took charge and swung me round so that we were sitting on one of the beds. In spite of everything, I was disappointed to hear her giggle. That cooled it, to some extent. It meant to me that she was not as mature as I thought. On the other hand, I had deplored the overconfidence of her Mistress on occasions. Ah! well, none of it was easy, it seemed.

As for the girl—I had rough handled twice since I met her. Now I wished to use to my advantage and I felt a rotter, but she seemed so thrilled to have me captive in her room. I felt that with the receding effects of the brandy, I could get the information I required. I put my arm around her shoulders and asked again just how much English she understood. She gave me the same treatment and quietly, but seriously, explained that she understood nearly all English, but was not too good with the saying.

I had heard that before and knew what was meant, so with our arms around each other, I asked her if she would explain what she thought of my being there. She giggled and moved a little closer as she said she "would share her leetle bed with Robeen."

For the first time in my life, I used the advantage of the sexes. If this girl was feeling broody, then she would have to tell me all I needed to know first. I thought. And with the craft that would have done me credit thirty years on, I laid her gently down on the bed and gave her every hope of a lot of loving. But I suggested that to be on the safe side, I ought to know all about Madame, the wireless, the principal, and anything else that goes on in the house, also in the church or anywhere else in the area.

Lying close by my side, she interrupted my long series of queries with kisses and little pecks on my cheek. I thought of Sally and how she never did that when we were talking, even though she would have been entitled to, if she wished. But she never did and now, in the circumstances, I wished she had.

I sat up and stretched myself and asked for a cigarette. The girl, eager to please, went to a drawer and found a pack. With fumbling fingers, she undid the end and gave me one, and after tapping my pockets and pretending not to have any means of lighting it, I asked for Lucifers. This was too much, for she stamped her foot and made for the door, undid the latch and made a hurried exit.

As soon as she had gone, I leapt to the drawers and had a quick look. There appeared to be nothing of interest, except lots of small pill bottles. I didn't know for sure what I expected to find, but being the big shot now with a girl, well, I had to do it, didn't I? Mind, if I had found my funny looking maps or documents, I had not the faintest idea what I would have done but, as there was nothing very obvious, and feeling not at all as confident as an older, more experienced person, I was pleased with a negative result to my search, even though it was not very professional.

By the time the girl returned, breathless, I was sitting on the bed that was not obviously hers. I was removing my boots and making a study of my laces when she did her latch on the door. I noted my secret knot was still in place. I also felt the outside of my pocket and found the outline of a cork. Our cork, Sally. The one thing I hope to keep for a very long time.

So I had a light for the French cigarette. I had my cough and removed my jacket, folding it and placing it beneath the pillow, the idea being that I wished to keep tabs on my papers and other items. The girl watched with approval and sat beside me. I noticed her chest had stopped heaving and deduced that she had, indeed, made a great effort to purloin matches from some source and had made good speed back to the room. For my part, the undressing stopped there, for there was something else I needed to know. What on earth was her name? I had not heard it mentioned. So I asked, and it turned out to be very simple.

She said it was Danielle Devereaux, to which I immediately said that I would call her Danny. This pleased her and she reduced the space between us a few inches. With my arm around her, I asked about her knowledge of who had fixed the wireless. It seemed that Father Martineaux was the man who had it installed. He was very good at getting to London but had not done so very much recently. Already, I thought this young lady knew too much and this opinion was endorsed even more when I learned that Wolfgang visited the house many times a week from the school, and Danny would take up breakfast for two.

At this she giggled a bit, as though savoring the thought. She also edged her way so that we were very close together. She laid her head on my shoulder and I felt her soft, dark hair against my cheek. I stroked her neck under the hair and she nearly purred. I asked quietly if they were lovers. She nodded, and I wondered if that was the reason for the change of attitude in Anne, for she knew now that Wolfgang was dead.

The way Danny was lapping up the gentle stroking meant that she was not likely to be very forthcoming with more news and information, so I stopped the movement of my fingers. Straight away she stiffened, and turning her face to mine, said simply, "Do again pleeze."

I whispered I must know more about everything so that we could be safe and that I would "do again," if she told me who else came to see the mistress. I was startled to hear her reply that some-times many German officers came to have a party and "it makes much work and they smack my derriere."

I rewarded her with a few more strokes and she relaxed again.

After a while, she got my idea: do a trick and you get a fish, and not before. Quite a pleasant way to get information, and as time went on, I found myself thinking that this young filly would go like hell with her harness off. I also found it increasingly more difficult to concentrate on working out the questions, but determined not to lose the initiative, I stopped stroking, and asked about Paul and the Fa-ther.

She said that Paul was her cousin and the reason the Father had to be rescued was because he was seen in this house by one of the German officers, who had him arrested. That was why I had to go through the town to get him back to the church and why he had not been to London so much recently. In the same breath, she added, "Would you take me to London soon, Robeen?"

I ignored the question about taking her anywhere, but contin-ued with the neck stroking. It seemed there was a missing link in the chain, for who sheltered Father Martineaux if then he had been ar-rested? I asked about this and relaxed my touch. She responded after a while and said that Pascale had got the Father away from the police cells and got him to the school. He was ill and very frightened. This much had been relayed to London and the message came for him to lay low and await help via the aid of three lively people who, be-tween them, would get him away and back to London to report and rest.

So, I was one of the three—the only one now.

Then a voluntary bombshell from the girl. She said she thought that every message that was telegraphed was given to Wolfgang. Her cousin Paul had told her and she had listened to conversations some-times and agreed that it was so.

"But what matter, Robeen? You are English and I have never been with the wonderful English before, only a few French boys at school and they were not much good. The Boche officers touch my derriere sometime at dinner and smile at me, so, but I am very busy with the plates and have no time. Madame say I should be nicer to them or she send me away and I am frightened till I hear you English come to the town, then I think it all is over, but you are all worry and get shoot some of you. I do not know, except that you are man to me when we meet and make me feel woman with your hands on me. I do not know anymore."

She left me and the bed and very quickly removed her black dress, and in her stockings, knickers, and bra—all black material— she turned her back, and holding a mirror, combed her hair and gave it the biggest belting with a brush I have ever known hair to receive. But I learned that a good rough, tough brushing did wonders for a lady's hair, for this lot shone and fell around the shoulders in a very appealing manner. She looked very attractive, there was no doubt, and I felt as though I had my dinner in front of me, ready to eat.

Danny no doubt thought the same, for her stockings were coming off, her bra was off, and she was making her way to the bed that had been my observation post until now, and I felt no good rea- son to refuse the girl. On the other hand, I felt no urgent desire to tangle with her; after all, if it had been intended for me to take advan- tage of every bit of female contact that came my way, then no doubt I would have been a rabbit.

A fraction of time before Danny joined me on the bed, there was a loud thumping on the door with the latch going crazy from the effort of someone trying to get in.

Danny veered toward the door, realized her state of undress, continued in an arc, picked up her dress from the bed, and shimmied her way into it.

She operated the latch, opened the door, and was nearly knocked down the entrance of the bust-heaving Pascale!

She took a firm hold of Danny's dress at the neck and did a quick downward snatch. The material gave way and Danny was ex- posed good and proper. Not satisfied with this, Pascale continued the disrobing until the dress was at the girl's ankles, which restored her to the state she was before the knock on the door. Before I could make much of a move, Danny ceased holding her arms to cover her bosom, and with a determined look on her face, secured a firm hold on Pascale's hair. This at once produced shrieks from Pascale and a lot of what I imagined to be very obscene French language.

I tried to part them and from time to time, made very close contact with one or the other and sometimes both of them. At the time, I did not fully appreciate the advantage I had, for since then I have often thought I could have enjoyed this wrestling more than I did. I might have done so even then, had not I seen Danny get a firm grip at the top of Pascale's shirt. I had to be quite rough to get the hand relaxed and away, the action continuing the movement so that Danny and I fell awkwardly onto the floor.

Still struggling, she was now fighting to get to her feet. So I kissed her and she ceased moving in anger. Her breathing was hard and the motion was very pleasant, even though I was fully dressed except my jacket. Pascale joined us in rather a rough fashion and grabbed my hair, pulling hard enough for me to lose contact with Danny.

I got to my feet, took my jacket from under my pillow, put it around Danny's shoulders, and sat her on the bed. Then pulling Pascale toward me, I managed to get them seated with me between them.

They were both slightly out of breath and glaring at each other. Placing an arm around them, I went into a patter that could only come from an N.S.C. or A.O. I put it to them that they were both French girls and lived in their own country, which was occupied and influenced by an enemy. They had little or no freedom, but there were many people doing their best to rid the France they loved of the nightmares that existed, and so on.

Further, as they calmed down—and I felt them relax—I continued, "One day, there will be many armed forces land in France quite openly, fully armed and trained, thousands of them will drive your fear away and you will be restored to the peace and life of a free France. But you'll get no bloody help from me or any other English if you fight among yourselves. What are you now fighting for? Yourselves or an Englishman that is here to help as best he can? If this is an example of how you behave, no wonder you have traitors at the top and at the bottom. You make a high wind with all the arms flapping.

"Now, Pascale, you came to this room for a reason, what was it? Is there a message for me?"

Pascale studied her feet for a long time and it was obvious that there was no official message because, even in the present circumstances, she would not have allowed any personal feelings to interfere with her job.

I repeated my question, turned her to face me, and kissed her. Her response was even more lively than the bare-busted Danny, and after a few seconds, I broke away to explain that I thought I was very lucky to be in the company of two of the nicest French girls I had ever met.

They seemed to think that was like meeting the president and getting the Crois de Guerre!

Bloody fools, for they did not know that, other than themselves, I had met only Annette. Well, a bit harsh really, but I was giving myself a pep talking, for it was time to exercise a little old-fashioned discipline with all these hot-panted females so near. It seemed to work, for Danny stood and removed my jacket, handing it to me and leaving her topmost charms quite bare and without any attempt to cover up nor any sign of shyness.

Pascale also stood and moved towards the door, but had some difficulty with the latch. I joined her and had equal results. It was left to Danny to operate the pieces of wood and let us out, Pascale not saying anything but looking very sullen.

I gave Danny a quick squeeze and left to follow the other girl. I was not sure where we were going, but she knew the way along the many passages and stairs. Halfway down one flight, it became very gloomy, for that part was in the shadow of even meager light. She stopped. It was so sudden that I bumped into her. Now a step lower than me, she held me at arm's length, one hand on each of my shoulders.

In the dim light, she looked straight at me, and I did a little chuckle—well, I couldn't help thinking back to the last time we were together. That was on the stairs as well, except that this time she was not obliged to show me a part of her anatomy.

But she was very serious, and took my hand to lead the way

along this maze of rooms and corridors, for it was really a very large building and it was not at all easy to learn the layout, especially in the circumstances.

When I found we were likely to leave the building, I had to stop her lively progress and explain that my orders were to not leave the building. To this she responded that the circumstances changed by the hour and it was important that we get to the church and see Father Martineaux.

I said I dared not risk being seen nor yet caught, for I had no story to tell as to where I was from or where I was going. I was too vulnerable and very much lacking confidence. No, I was sorry, I must stay in the house until I moved out shortly before the plane arrived.

Pascale would have none of it. She convinced me that I had to move today. She had it all worked out: I was to hand over all my papers to her, then adopt the dress of a priest, walk to the church, and remain there until the rescue plane arrived. That would make it easier, since both the Father and I would be picked up together.

I did not think much of that phrase "picked up," but I was in the hands of this very confident young woman and felt I had no option but to go along with her suggestion. I gave her full credit. She was not at all bossy and did not give the impression she was superior. She was—well, very logical—and her reasons were feasible.

So, deeper down in the basement of the house, I did my strip in front of her. When she had finished producing the necessary clothing, she placed a chain around my neck, clasped her hands together, and laughed until the tears streamed down her face!

"What's so bloody funny?" I asked.

She almost shrieked and when, after some composure, she was able to speak, she suggested that I had better note that my language was not quite right, even if I did look bloody chic!

At that, we both laughed and found support from one another, holding hands as she led me to a full length mirror. I saw, for the first time, Father Robin and oh! What a bloody bird he looked, for that lovely little cold-footed, red-breasted dicky was very much maligned by the reflection in the glass.

I could not help wondering what Sally would have thought. Or said. Or do.

CHAPTER THIRTY

I dare say the flying of kites was verboten during the occupation. Whether they were or not, it had not prevented a young French lad from trying to get his handmade kite in the air. It was a diamond shape with a long tail which seemed to comprise a series of tuffets of paper spaced at regular intervals along the tail-line. The lad had been trying to get the thing up for a long time and was busy rolling up his line in frustration when Pascale and I saw him. I had handed over my false papers and all evidence supplied by London to Pascale. Now, dressed in the robes of a priest, all I had on my person was a cork and a swollen bladder. I mentioned this to Pascale as we passed the field the kite lad was using. At the same moment the noise of a vehicle made us move to the side of the road, and turning to look behind, I was shocked to see the Germans faces, six of them.

They stopped, and with automatics at the ready, crossed the road and approached us. Pascale slipped a piece of paper into my hand and whispered that they would not search a priest.

Now the pockets of this wear were not in the traditional area of English suiting, and although I managed to get the paper inside the outer clothing, I did not think I would be wise in experimenting at that stage with the design of clerical garb. I came to this conclusion by force of circumstance more than anything, since one of the Jerries decided to level a vicious looking gun at me.

I am, by nature, rather poker-faced and that, plus my training, made it difficult to assimilate a divine providence over the girl and me. But with a smile that hid the urgent loosening of the bowels, in addition to the desire to relive the bladder, I managed to indicate that we were trying to assist the lad to get his kite airborne.

I did this with so many faked French phrases that poor Pascale bit her lip to keep from laughing. When at last she could control herself no longer and burst out laughing, she doubled up, or down, literally.

It was infectious, for slowly the Germans joined the laughing. They looked at the girl, then at one another, then to me.

I did a jolly good French shrug and laughed, too. That did the trick, for the sudden mirth in a lonely road attracted the young kite flyer. He stood and stared at us with a straight face, his eyes going from one to the other in turn. As he met each countenance, he prompted more mirth, and for my part, I only wished there was in existence some kind of transmission from there to London, for otherwise, how could a report or debriefing ever describe such an instance. All the same, I noted that more than one machine gun or carbine was aimed at our middles.

After a while, the Germans thought the joke was over and then all the guns were concentrated on our bodies. What was more, they indicated that the three of us were to get into the vehicle.

Pascale threw me a look that warned me of the danger with regard to the message. I did some more fake French and indicated that we should help get the kite up. Taking the thing from the lad, I made my way slowly toward the field, jabbering away as I went. I turned and beckoned the others to follow.

There was a subdued conference in German, and much to my surprise, all but one of the enemy returned to their truck, the sixth one following, with his weapon slung on his shoulder, the French lad, Pascale, and me.

I gave the kite line to the German, motioned the boy and the girl to follow me, and with the kite in my hand, led the way back into the field.

Afraid the line would be too short to allow me to work out my plan, I stopped and handed the kite to its young owner, extended the tail, and placed it in Pascale's hand, explaining at the same time that the reason the kite dived and swooped was because the tail was too light to stabilize the kite. Turning my back to the German, I folded the message into a long slip and attached it to the lower part of the tail. Then, making a signal to the German to get over and upwind, raised the kite, and after a short run, had the satisfaction of seeing and feeling it rise. Slowly and with frequent tugs on the line, the kite gained height until I let go the line to give the German complete control.

He seemed overjoyed to be in command, and as the tail snaked in the breeze, I too enjoyed some kind of satisfaction, for I knew that the bottom piece of paper would have put us all in the hands of the Gestapo. I had managed to get the gist of it as I folded it and it was like music for me. Father Martineaux and I would be leaving at 00.15 that day. Or just a quarter of an hour into tomorrow.

After a while, the novelty of kite flying and watching wore off and the truck started. In German, the occupants called to Fritz, and he, with obvious reluctance, handed the kite line to its owner.

I beamed as best as I could within the scope of a Royal Engineer sergeant as the soldier made his way to his companions, climbed aboard, and moved off. Pascale sighed with relief. The lad smiled. The sergeant piddled. The need for bowel relief diminished with the withdrawal of the German patrol.

Pascale overcame the problem of getting back the message that was now flicking the air on the end of the kite tail. She did this by asking the lad if he would like to go with us to the church and have a cup of coffee.

He readily agreed and pulled in his kite line. On the way to the church, Pascale removed the message. He seemed to be unaware of her action, for she cleverly chatted away during the fumble with the line.

Inside the church, it was a very worried pair of priests that greeted us. Understandably, for the German patrol had called, making enquiries regarding the priest and his friends flying a kite.

Father Martineaux was well aware of my disguise but, of course, had no knowledge of the kite, nor the young French lad. The patrol had left only seconds before our arrival. While sorting this out, Pascale had found some coffee, which the young French boy eagerly accepted. She also produced a piece of bright red paper, which she tied to the line of the kite tail. I watched her do this with a great deal of admiration, for she had understood the reason for the extra weight and appreciated my action in using the message as a very artful substitute; more importantly, she realized the lad would not be able to get his kite flying without the aid of a couple of subversive operators. She did this without a glance in my direction and thus did not show a deliberate desire to impress me.

She was a very cool and efficient lady, that one. When the young man had finished his coffee, she motioned me to join them as she escorted him to the door, saying softly to me as we hit the light outside, "Pat him on the head, Father!"

On our return to join the priests, she organized some lovely cognac which went down well during the exchange of events since we had last met. I felt excited at the prospect of getting into that rescue plane in a few hours time and felt I had now come to terms with myself over the loss of my two colleagues.

I dare say the cognac helped, but if I had been able to see it at the time, the fact was that I was still growing into a mature and experienced person. What bothered me was that Pascale seemed to be so much more mature than I felt. I seemed to be a few years behind in self-confidence. I couldn't explain it, but that is how I felt.

The status of those of us that occupied was quite clear in my mind, I thought. The Father was evidently a trusted person in the organization, a kind of administrator, his mate, also a priest, was in on the "goings on," the girl, Pascale, was a genuine French Resister. Of these, I was the visitor. I was the one flown in to do whatever it was, but I was the only Englishman among them and sergeant or no, I was the one that could only operate a la instructions from my boss in London. In the circumstances, there was only one sensible course to take. Get back to the Museum, have a cup of Sue's tea, receive a fine old wigging from the boss, a bit of leave.

Then it hit me again. *A bit of leave without Sally.*

I fought it—and won, for the lovely Pascale appeared. I discovered that the more cognac I drank the more beautiful the females became, later to encompass the phrase "any port in a storm."

I had to admit she was not the girl in field clothing. She was not the girl in a sawn-off dress. She was someone ready for a dinner at the Mayfair. She looked lovely.

My eyes went to her bust-line. It was there, no doubt, but very small. Even so, it was enough to discriminate the sex. That, if nothing else, confirmed she was a female, and a very attractive and seductive one at that. She seemed to have the ability to forget her sex when involved with her job, only switching on her charm when she needed either to boost ego or impress her authority.

I learned she had more to admire as my glass of brandy frequently emptied, for she freshened it and told me that there would be no more drink tonight. I replied that I needed only to stagger into that plane and all would be well. During this exchange, I was sitting on a type of hassock about three feet long. Pascale sat beside me and took my glass. She drank a little and returned the glass, remarking that she did not think I would be in a fit state to make-love-goodbye if I had any more.

She emphasized her point by sliding her hip hard against mine, adding, "And pull your shoulders back, sit up straight."

We were alone, the priests having gone off to another part of the church.

"This make-love-goodbye thing, Pascale, what do you mean?"

She relaxed into her female role and somehow pressed her hip closer. She spoke softly now.

"Soon we make glorious, exciting love, Robin. I want to remember you forever, for you are kind to me when I show you how I feel with no breast, you do not laugh like the French and say bad things to me. Not only that, I like the way you work. I like the way you lose the Sally and not try and be the big man about it. You care for her and us in France. I care, too, for you and your friends come and help us against the Boche."

Feeling a little humbled at this and not at all in the mood for affection from anyone, I ventured that I had not had a good wash or bath for quite a time. Not only that, I was still dressed in the unlikely garb of a priest. I asked about my own clothes. I was told I would have them after we had eaten in the house of Madame Vernier.

CHAPTER THIRTY-ONE

After dark, Pascale led me through the church yard, into the village, past the house where the priests and I had refreshed previously, down a cutting, and into a small garden that fronted a cottage. Pascale knocked and I felt there was a trace of coding in the taps she applied to the door. A middle-aged lady answered. She did not seem to realize there was any danger in having an English person in her house. Indeed, she was so jolly that I doubted if she appreciated there was a war in her country, for she kissed and hugged us, bade us sit at her kitchen table, and generally made us feel at home. The lighting was poor, but the cooker was good, for she produced coffee and croissants as if we had booked.

More to eat, with coffee followed by more cognac. It was all a party, with the food preventing the booze from being too potent. All the same, with a grand sense of well-being, I contemplated the steaming hot bath, and as I sank down up to my neck, I though of my last hot wash with Annette administering the ablutions. I wondered if Pascale would also appear and supervise. What with the brandy and the relaxing effect of the water, I was in no doubt that I didn't care what they did, for I was not at all an English warrior at war. I didn't think I could punch my way out of a paper bag. I felt so wonderfully weak that I really did not care what happened. After all, I had done my bit. I couldn't help it if the two companions of mine had been killed. I was not present when it happened. There was nothing I could do to put it right; I couldn't get them back to life. Heavy-eyed, I came to accept the terms of our little trio now being forever reduced to one, and dopey as I felt, I knew that I could still call upon my own reserves to act should the occasion arise. Little did I know then that I was shortly to put those reserves into practice.

A sudden commotion in the house ended my revelry. It appeared to my fuzzled state that there were men about; I could detect heavy footsteps. There were also agitated female voices which, added to the stompings, tended to alert me. I sat up, changed my position in the bath to a kneeling position. I was ready to leap out if necessary, although what I was going to do in those circumstances, I had no idea. After a while, all noises seemed to subside, which made me uneasy, for it crossed my mind that perhaps I was alone in the house. I listened intently, became fully awake, and dried myself.

Wrapped in a large towel, I left the bathroom and made my way down to the lower floor. In the kitchen, I found Pascale with her arm around the owner of the house. The older woman was bleeding slightly from a gash on her forehead and a rapidly closing eye.

I moved closer to give some comfort. As I did, Pascale snatched a corner of my towel to apply it to the injured face, and the whole towel left me. The swabbing didn't seem to help, but when the wounded party focused her one good eye on me, she laughed herself back to health very quickly. It was like a Whitehall farce. No West End playwright would ever dream of writing such things as happened to me.

To hell with it all, I thought, for naked or not, there was still a nasty wound in Madame Vernier's head, and without being told, I knew the Germans had been in the house, indeed in this very room. What if they returned?

I asked for my clothes and was surprised to find them almost cleaned and pressed. Whatever had been done to them gave me a much nicer feeling than the clerical garb I had been wearing. That, plus the recent hot bath, gave me the confidence of a visiting doctor as I rejoined the two ladies.

I did my best to apply first aid to the damaged forehead, but could do nothing to help the now completely closed eye. The thought crossed my mind that those who helped me often seemed be doing it because they like me, as opposed to doing it in the line of duty. This lady, for instance, in spite of a frightening experience with the German patrol, still maintained her friendly welcome toward me. All that knowing, as Pascale and I did, that the enemy was rightly suspicious that subversive elements were active in the area. Finding nothing positive, they would no doubt return and perhaps not be quite so gentle next time. There was no doubt in my mind. The French people in the main ran grave risks to shelter those of us engaged in our work.

Now that Madame Vernier had composed herself, she too felt the need for cognac and would not hear of drinking for only medicinal reasons. I had to have more. She insisted.

I accepted the brandy and enjoyed its effect, for it increased my confidence to such an extent that I convinced the two ladies that there were no Germans for miles. Then I had another drink and convinced myself. Before leaving, I mentioned that I would like to see the Fathers at the church. Pascale sensed that our time was now very short before my plane rescue. She spoke in French to the older woman. There were many references to amour. They each treated the subject with great seriousness, and even a bloody fool like me could not doubt that they were deciding where best Pascale and "Robeen" should "make-love-goodbye."

It was fixed, apparently. We were to go upstairs and use the bedroom of Madame. Pascale led the way; Madame sloshed more booze into my glass, hugged me tight, upended the bottle into her own glass, muttered away about the wonderful love, and followed up the stairs. I noted that Pascale knew which room was the boudoir. I also was aware that Madame made herself at ease in a small armchair beside the bed.

I discovered that, for me, these French-planned seductions failed to rouse the desired enthusiasm. It did not help to see Pascale remove most of her clothes; in fact, it made it worse. For one thing, I had a single thought in mind—to get on that plane.

Not the circumstances for rational moralizing perhaps, but I recall my thoughts quite clearly, including the old cliché that all is fair in love and war. Yes, well, if killing Sally in war was fair, then I couldn't see how making love to a French girl would even things out. It did not make sense and I wished something would inspire me to act in such a way to avoid offending these high-spirited, free-loving French females. After all, Sally and I had a code of conduct. And so on.

All the same, I wished the gods had not been so violent when they answered my wishes, for down below there was a stamping, banging, and bumping, which got the Madame to her feet. She made good time to the door and on the way had time to say, "Boche!"

I don't recall what Pascale did, but I know I was out of the small bedroom window without regard to what was below. I remember thinking that I might well fall into the enemy's arms or break something when I hit the ground. Worse still, I might even catch my knickers on a French roofing spike. But I did none of that at all.

I slithered down a steep roof and came to rest beside a chimney, where I clung on for dear life, not knowing how far I was above the ground. It was dark and raining. I looked upward as the noise of the window closing attracted my attention, the dim light of the room just making a silhouette of Pascale. Then darkness as the light went out. My escape then was downwards, into the unknown darkness.

I recalled the voice of an officer during training. He warned to be alert at all times and to never enter a room without first noting the best way of escape, also never allow yourself to be in a position which left you in any doubt as to which was the next move.

Yes, well, he did not mention anything about the Pascales, nor about being wedged against a wet chimney on a French roof with the Germans below. For the third time in a week, I vowed to myself that if I ever got out of this in one piece, I would not let anyone push me about. I meant it then, and for those who died in the Services, I say the same now on their behalf.

I decided that if I could slowly edge my way downwards, I might get to some kind of guttering. Did the French have gutters? I did not find out, for my intention to edge slowly was frustrated by a buildup of speed to the extent that I sizzled down, out of control. It did not take long for me to reach the ground. I made a kind of "grumpf!' sound.

I panted a bit and tested myself, counted my legs and arms, finding the correct number, I then nearly fainted with fright as a hand helped me to my feet. Assuming it was a German, I lashed out in the gloom and though very unsteady, proceeded to have a go. Fortunately, a wild swing to where I imagined a face to be missed. Just as well, for it turned out to be Father Martineaux, who apparently looked at his watch and announced that I was right on time to get to the landing strip.

I whispered that the Germans were inside. It seemed he was aware of that and led me away through the rear of the property, one hand holding my wrist, the other clutching his long robe upwards to allow freedom of movement.

No doubt he was fine as a priest, but as a subversive operator he had a lot to learn, for he crashed and stumbled along, in my opinion making far too much noise, and my fears were justified when suddenly we were confronted with two shadowy figures, who in German language asked us to stop crashing about.

My religious colleague replied in German and while doing so tightened his grip on my wrist, preventing me from exercising a plan to try to make a dash. Somewhere.

The same action also prevented me from producing my automatic. My eyes had now grown accustomed to the dark and I judged the Jerries to be about my own height. It mattered not, for whatever Errol Flynn might have done in the circumstances, the Germans had other ideas. That was why I found myself in a prison.

CHAPTER THIRTY-TWO

Well, they called it a prison. Actually, it was a latrine, for the stuff flowed in a gully underneath my bed. It stank so much it tended to cut the saliva in the throat. And if it wasn't stinking, then it was stench, and if that is still not the correct word, then it was bloody horrible.

Besides me, there were three other men in the cell. Frenchmen. One of them tried me with different languages, including English. I did not know any of them and was not sure how best to play this game. All I knew for sure was that I had been relieved of all my papers, my gun, and my watch. Two other items had left on my person: an innocent looking cork and a small pill, which I now felt might quite soon be put to use, for it would end it all very quickly. So I was told.

In the early hours of the morning a disturbance caused me to go to the grill of the door and peer out into the passage that led to the dreaded inspector's office. There seemed to be some kind of unofficial commotion with shouting and general chain-clanking. It was impossible to make out exactly what was going on, but there was no doubt that something was up. I soon found out, for my cell door was opened, not with a key, but with a long piece of metal. Whoever he was, he had a diploma in getting thick cell doors open.

Once outside, I was swiftly forced down the stinking pavement, into an office that was crowded with men holding carbines and adopting a very threatening attitude toward one French police inspector, one German officer, and three fierce-looking men in civilian clothes wearing large wide-brimmed hats, light colored macs, and mean expressions. They looked as though none of them had never known a mother and certainly not a father.

One of my rescuers used his weapon as an extension to his arms and motioned me to a position behind the desk. He nodded downwards, indicating a drawer. I opened it and saw work permits, identity documents, and many items that had nothing to do with the war effort: pictures of females without uniforms, one of Hitler with uniform, and another of a lot of medals with Goering protruding here and there. My action was speeded up by a vicious jab in the ribs. I reclaimed my own documents, stood aside, and in turn, those of us under arrest did the same.

One of the civilians made a dive for the phone. As his hand touched the receiver, a carbine smashed down, resulting in severe damage to the hand and the telephone. Two of the Resisters motioned for my three cell-mates and I toward the door. Out in the street, we were hustled in a Citroen and driven very fast into the country.

Sitting in the back of the car, I checked my gun and found I had made yet again another mistake. It was empty. Of course, the inspector had cleared it. No doubt, had I concentrated more on the contents of that drawer, I would have found my ammunition. But then, I was not in the habit of being in a cell, nor was I trained to know that, before being prodded in the back, I should check my gun. I made a mental note to do so in future.

The Citroen was near to flat-out. I could sense the high speed by hearing the door handles scrape the road when we cornered. Not only that, from time to time I had someone on my lap. Fair to say, I sat on my companions from time to time, for indeed it was a very fast ride. The speed, combined with at least a twenty minute journey, gave the impression that I was miles away from that landing strip. Imagine my surprise when, at last, the car stopped outside the church administered by the two friendly priests. As a further bonus, Pascale was there to open the car door. With an air of urgency and she led me back at the double towards the now familiar outskirts of the village. We hurried through gardens, upset some dozing chickens, fell into a ditch, and helped each other out. When at last we slowed down, we were in the company of the priest who was due to return to England.

It was chilly, with what turned out to be my last French rain settling on my eyebrows. My clothes were wet from the fall in that blasted ditch. In silence, the small group stumbled into a grassy area, and guided by hands on arms, I found myself on the edge of a clearing with my colleagues, augmented by dark, silent forms who smelled of wine, brandy, and farmyards, to say nothing of burning French tobacco.

Pascale made her presence felt by standing very close to me. She whispered her repeated appeal to get her to London. I quietly explained I could promise nothing, but would try to arrange it, if I could. That was not good enough for an answer, for she now spoke louder and reminded me of the many ways she had saved my life, either directly or indirectly, in circumstances that I knew nothing about, and many other ways she did not know about.

Louder now, she added the reminder of the many times she had offered herself and how I had always arranged to be busy and even on one occasion arranged for the Germans to appear. Attempting to calm down this amorous young lady, I made a mistake, for I turned her to face me and she, sensing at last some action, closed with me in a hug that would have done justice to a grizzly bear. It was a sincere enough gesture on her part, and she did feel my leaving with considerable sorrow. She seemed content to be close and remained quite still until that lovely noise of a light aircraft invaded the silence. There was action from the party around us as, one by one, the torches lit. The plane was now low and did not seem to be in the correct approach line. I paid little heed to the girl's mutterings.

The priest parted us and led the way across the soggy grass. Pascale ran behind. At last that wonderful little Lysander was still. The door opened, out came what looked like bundles and suitcases, followed by a man in the garb of the complete subversive operator, for he wore what seemed to be a large leather overcoat. It had to be large in order to conceal the entire stock of all the arms and weapons in the Allied Forces. What was more, the saucy blighter had a revolver in his hand!

There was much more to this incident than the above, but it was a once-only experience and details are obscure now in retrospect. I tried to shake hands with as many hands as I could find in the semi-dark. I probably shook the same ones twice and hope that one of them was Pascale's hand. I was not sure because the priest pushed me through the door and I turned to take one of the two small seats facing the tail of the plane. After some heaving and puffing, I had my friend beside me and the door closed.

Does it matter where we landed? It could have been Biggin Hill, Croyden, Stansted, or Tangmere. I don't bloody well know. But if anyone wishes to check, there are, no doubt, official records to peruse. Like a wedding, when one is the bridegroom, it is all very much a hazy memory. The details, I mean. I don't remember much about the flight home. All I know is that we made it all in one piece and bumped our way along some English grass, in daylight no doubt green, but as I say, *English*. And the officer who met the plane was English, too, but his manner was not at all one that said, "Welcome, well done," or even "Sorry." Indeed, my companion, the priest, looked at me with some disdain.

True, I did not envisage a red carpet, but at least I assumed we would be greeted with much the same welcome as on previous occasions. None of that at all and I got the impression that the brave pilot was likewise ignored. What a reward, I thought. In London it was much worse. None of the original staff was there and nobody seemed to know or care where they were, or even how they were. A full and proper statement of the events were called for by people who evidently had no idea of what went on the other side of the Channel.

The fate of Tom and Sally, the why, the lack of this and that, seemed to be the theme.

"Did you realize we could ill afford to lose such people? Did you not realize that it takes a long time to train such operators? Do you have the idea that the point of this training is so they can risk their necks for the likes of people like you?"

I listened to this for some time. I did not think much of it. I thought of Tom and Sally, with her guts shattered and with no finger-nails. I had the cork in my hand, concealed in my pocket. I aimed at the man's chin. He ducked slightly, and so got it full blast on his nose.

I walked out, and for the first time, did not salute. Balls to this lot, knickers, and even District Nurse, for what a way to administer a subversive organization.

Of course, it was necessary to be debriefed, to make a full report on events as they happened. But this new. lot were new, all right. All they were after was to glean a little glory from the exploits and type out reports as though they had been active themselves. This was especially true of the captain who sported the MC for something or other. I found out later he had, indeed, been out of the country on Active Service. All the way to the Isle of Wight, he went. Poor chap. No doubt with a balloon on a stick.

Fortunately, there were seniors later who were much more understanding. Therefore, to that extent, it all finished as a round peg in a round hole—but that initial welcome was, to say the least, very disappointing.

We wish that my brother Ray could have continued sharing the activities that he experienced in Ceylon, India, etc. where he had some contact with the Japanese, some of which, were not that pleasant either.

As mentioned earlier in the story, the officer hoped that there would be some sort of "old comrade" association formed to keep in touch, as there would be difficult times in readjusting to civilian life. I have thought, too, it would have been good and helpful to have had some sort of counseling available for the men surviving this type of work. Indeed, he endured much hardship in civilian life, especially in the later years.

He did marry and they adopted two children, but the marriage did not last. Ray had a small electrical business for awhile, but that failed eventually. He worked at various jobs and cared for our mother, as time permitted, until her death in 1978.

He developed prostate cancer. After spending time in a comfortable, private rest home where he received excellent care, Ray passed away on September 10, 2000.

Jean Zetocha

To order additional copies of
THE SOE ON ENEMY SOIL
please complete the following.

$16.95 EACH
(plus $3.95 shipping & handling for first book,
add $2.00 for each additional book ordered.

Shipping and Handling costs for larger quantites
available upon request.

Please send me _____ additional books at $16.95 + shipping &
handling

Bill my: ❑ VISA   ❑ MasterCard   Expires _____

Card # _____

Signature _____

Daytime Phone Number _____

For credit card orders call 1-888-568-6329
TO ORDER ON-LINE VISIT: www.jmcompanies.com
OR SEND THIS ORDER FORM TO:
McCleery & Sons Publishing
PO Box 248
Gwinner, ND 58040-0248

I am enclosing $_____   ❑ Check ❑ Money Order
Payable in US funds. No cash accepted.

SHIP TO:
Name_____

Mailing Address _____

City _____

State/Zip _____

Orders by check allow longer delivery time.
Money order and credit card orders will be shipped within 48 hours.
This offer is subject to change without notice.

NEW RELEASES

Grandmother Alice
Memoirs from the Home Front Before Civil War into 1930's
Alice Crain Hawkins could be called the 'Grandma Moses of Literature'. Her stories, published for the first time, were written while an invalid during the last years of her life. These journal entries from the late 1920's and early 30's gives us a fresh, novel and unique understanding of the lives of those who lived in the upper part of South Carolina during the state's growing years. Alice and her ancestors experiences are filled with understanding - they are provacative and profound. Written by Reese Hawkins (178 pgs.)
$16.95 each in a 6x9" paperback.

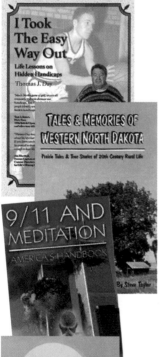

I Took The Easy Way Out
Life Lessons on Hidden Handicaps
Twenty-five years ago, Tom Day was managing a growing business - holding his own on the golf course and tennis court. He was living in the fast lane. For the past 25 years, Tom has spent his days in a wheelchair with a spinal cord injury. Attendants serve his every need. What happened to Tom? We get an honest account of the choices Tom made in his life. It's a courageous story of reckoning, redemption and peace. Written by Thomas J. Day. (200 pgs.)
$19.95 each in a 6x9" paperback.

Tales & Memories of Western North Dakota
Prairie Tales & True Stories of 20th Century Rural Life
This manuscript has been inspired with Steve's antidotes, bits of wisdom and jokes (sometimes ethnic, to reflect the melting pot that was and is North Dakota; and from most unknown sources). A story about how to live life with humor, courage and grace along with personal hardships, tragedies and triumphs.
Written by Steve Taylor. (174 pgs.)
$14.95 each in a 6x9" paperback.

9/11 and Meditation
America's Handbook
All Americans have been deeply affected by the terrorist events of and following 9-11-01 in our country. David Thorson submits that meditation is a potentially powerful intervention to ameliorate the frightening effects of such divisive and devastating acts of terror. This book features a lifetime of harrowing life events amidst intense pychological and social polarization, calamity and chaos; overcome in part by practicing the age-old art of meditation.
Written by David Thorson. (110 pgs.)
$9.95 each in a 4-1/8 x 7-1/4" paperback.

Eat, Drink & Remarry
The poetry in this book is taken from different experiences in Lynne's life and from different geographical and different emotional places. Every poem is an inspiration from someone or a direct event from their life...or from hers. Every victory and every mistake - young or old. They slowly shape and mold you into the unique person you are. Celebrate them as rough times that you were strong enough to endure. By sharing them with others, there will always be one person who will learn from them.
Written by Lynne D. Richard Larson (86 pgs.)
$12.95 each in a 5x8" paperback.

Phil Lempert's Healthy, Wealthy, & Wise
The Shoppers Guide for Today's Supermarket
This is the must-have tool for getting the most for your money in every aisle. With this valuable advice you will never see (or shop) the supermarket the same way again. You will learn how to: save at least $1,000 a year on your groceries, guarantee satisfaction on every shopping trip, get the most out of coupons or rebates, avoid marketing gimmicks, create the ultimate shopping list, read and understand the new food labels, choose the best supermarkets for you and your family. Written by Phil Lempert. (198 pgs.)
$9.95 each in a 6x9" paperback.

Miracles of COURAGE
The Larry W. Marsh Story
This story is for anyone looking for simple formulas for overcoming insurmountable obstacles. At age 18, Larry lost both legs in a traffic accident and learned to walk again on untested prothesis. No obstacle was too big for him - putting himself through college - to teaching a group of children that frustrated the whole educational system - to developing a nationally recognized educational program to help these children succeed. Written by Linda Marsh. (134 pgs.)
$12.95 each in a 6x9" paperback.

The Garlic Cure
Learn about natural breakthroughs to outwit: Allergies, Arthritis, Cancer, Candida Albicans, Colds, Flu and Sore Throat, Environmental and Body Toxins, Fatigue, High Cholesterol, High Blood Pressure and Homocysteine and Sinus Headaches. The most comprehensive, factual and brightly written health book on garlic of all times. INCLUDES: 139 GOURMET GARLIC RECIPES!
Written by James F. Scheer, Lynn Allison and Charlie Fox. (240 pgs.)
$14.95 each in a 6x9" paperback.

For Your Love
Janelle, a spoiled socialite, has beauty and breeding to attract any mate she desires. She falls for Jared, an accomplished man who has had many lovers, but no real love. Their hesitant romance follows Jared and Janelle across the ocean to exciting and wild locations. Join in a romance and adventure set in the mid-1800's in America's grand and proud Southland.
Written by Gunta Stegura. (358 pgs.)
$16.95 each in a 6x9" paperback.

From Graystone to Tombstone
Memories of My Father Engolf Snortland 1908-1976
This haunting memoir will keep you riveted with true accounts of a brutal penitentiary to a manhunt in the unlikely little town of Tolna, North Dakota. At the same time the reader will emerge from the book with a towering respect for the author, a man who endured pain, grief and needless guilt -- but who learned the art of forgiving and writes in the spirit of hope.
Written by Roger Snortland. (178 pgs.)
$16.95 each in a 6x9" paperback.

Blessed Are The Peacemakers
A rousing tale that traces the heroic Rit Gatlin from his enlistment in the Confederate Army in Little Rock to his tragic loss of a leg in a Kentucky battle, to his return in the Ozarks. He becomes engaged in guerilla warfare with raiders who follow no flag but their own. Rit finds himself involved with a Cherokee warrior, slaves and romance in a land ravaged by war.
Written by Joe W. Smith (444 pgs.)
$19.95 each in a 6 x 9 paperback

Seasons With Our Lord
Original seasonal and special event poems written from the heart. Feel the mood with the tranquil color photos facing each poem. A great coffee table book or gift idea. Written by Cheryl Lebahn Hegvik. (68 pgs.)
$24.95 each in a 11x8-1/2 paperback.

Pycnogenol®
Pycnogenol® for Superior Health presents exciting new evidence about nature's most powerful antioxidant. Pycnogenol® improves your total health, reduces risk of many diseases, safeguards your arteries, veins and entire circulation system. It protects your skin - giving it a healthier, smoother younger glow. Pycnogenol® also boosts your immune system. Read about it's many other beneficial effects.
Written by Richard A. Passwater, Ph.D. (122 pgs.)
$5.95 each in a 4-1/8 x 6-7/8" paperback.

Remembering Louis L'Amour
Reese Hawkins was a close friend of Louis L'Amour, one of the fastest selling writers of all time. Now Hawkins shares this friendship with L'Amour's legion of fans. Sit with Reese in L'Amour's study where characters were born and stories came to life. Travel with Louis and Reese in the 16 photo pages in this memoir. Learn about L'Amour's lifelong quest for knowledge and his philosophy of life. Written by Reese Hawkins and his daughter Meredith Hawkins Wallin. (178 pgs.)
$16.95 each in a 5-1/2x8" paperback.

Bonanza Belle
In 1908, Carrie Amundson left her home to become employed on a bonanza farm. One tragedy after the other befell her and altered her life considerably and she found herself back on the farm.
Written by Elaine Ulness Swenson. (344 pgs.)
$15.95 each in a 6x8-1/4" paperback.

Home Front
Read the continuing story of Carrie Amundson, whose life in North Dakota began in *Bonanza Belle*. This is the story of her family, faced with the challenges, sacrifices and hardships of World War II. Everything changed after the Pearl Harbor attack, and ordinary folk all across America, on the home front, pitched in to help in the war effort. Even years after the war's end, the effects of it are still evident in many of the men and women who were called to serve their country. Written by Elaine Ulness Swenson. (304 pgs.)
$15.95 each in a 6x8-1/4" paperback.

Outward Anxiety - Inner Calm
Steve Crociata is known to many as the Optician to the Stars. He was diagnosed with a baffling form of cancer. The author has processed experiences in ways which uniquely benefit today's readers. We learn valuable lessons on how to cope with distress, how to marvel at God, and how to win at the game of life.
Written by Steve Crociata
(334 pgs.)
$19.95 each in a 6 x 9 paperback

First The Dream
This story spans ninety years of Anna's life. She finds love, loses it, and finds it once again. A secret that Anna has kept is fully revealed at the end of her life. Written by Elaine Ulness Swenson. (326 pgs.)
$15.95 each in a 6x8-1/4" paperback

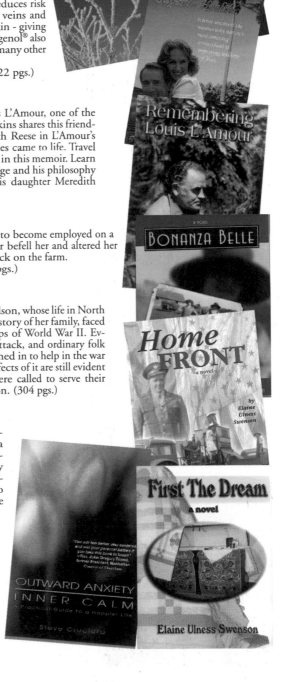

Pay Dirt
An absorbing story reveals how a man with the courage to follow his dream found both gold and unexpected adventure and adversity in Interior Alaska, while learning that human nature can be the most unpredictable of all.
Written by Otis Hahn & Alice Vollmar. (168 pgs.)
$15.95 each in a 6x9" paperback.

Spirits of Canyon Creek *Sequel to "Pay Dirt"*
Hahn has a rich stash of true stories about his gold mining experiences. This is a continued successful collaboration of battles on floodwaters, facing bears and the discovery of gold in the Yukon.
Written by Otis Hahn & Alice Vollmar. (138 pgs.)
$15.95 each in a 6x9" paperback.

Whispers in the Darkness
In this fast paced, well thought out mystery with a twist of romance, Betty Pearson comes to a slow paced, small town. Little did she know she was following a missing link - what the dilapidated former Beardsley Manor she was drawn to, held for her. With twists and turns, the Manor's secrets are unraveled.
Written by Shirlee Taylor. (88 pgs.)
$14.95 each in a 6x9" paperback.

Dr. Val Farmer's Honey, I Shrunk The Farm
The first volume in a three part series of Rural Stress Survival Guides discusses the following in seven chapters: Farm Economics; Understanding The Farm Crisis; How To Cope With Hard Times; Families Going Through It Together; Dealing With Debt; Going For Help, Helping Others and Transitions Out of Farming.
Written by Val Farmer. (208 pgs.)
$16.95 each in a 6x9" paperback.

Country-fied
Stories with a sense of humor and love for country and small town people who, like the author, grew up country-fied . . . Country-fied people grow up with a unique awareness of their dependence on the land. They live their lives with dignity, hard work, determination and the ability to laugh at themselves.
Written by Elaine Babcock. (184 pgs.)
$14.95 each in a 6x9" paperback.

Charlie's Gold and Other Frontier Tales
Kamron's first collection of short stories gives you adventure tales about men and women of the west, made up of cowboys, Indians, and settlers.
Written by Kent Kamron. (174 pgs.)
$15.95 each in a 6x9" paperback.

A Time For Justice
This second collection of Kamron's short stories takes off where the first volume left off, satisfying the reader's hunger for more tales of the wide prairie.
Written by Kent Kamron. (182 pgs.)
$16.95 each in a 6x9" paperback.

It Really Happened Here!
Relive the days of farm-to-farm salesmen and hucksters, of ghost ships and locust plagues when you read Ethelyn Pearson's collection of strange but true tales. It captures the spirit of our ancestors in short, easy to read, colorful accounts that will have you yearning for more.
Written by Ethelyn Pearson. (168 pgs.)
$24.95 each in an 8-1/2x11" paperback.

(Add $3.95 shipping & handling for first book, add $2.00 for each additional book ordered.)